The New Politics ·itis

By the same author

The CBI (with W. Grant)
Abortion Politics (with J. Chambers)
Private Members' Bills (with M. Read)

The New Politics of British Trade Unionism

Union Power and the Thatcher Legacy

David Marsh

Department of Politics
University of Strathclyde

MACMILLAN

First published 1992 by
THE MACMILLAN PRESS LTD
Houndmills, Basingstoke, Hampshire RG21 2XS
and London
Companies and representatives
throughout the world

ISBN 0-333-49300-1 hardcover
ISBN 0-333-49301-X paperback

A catalogue record for this book is available
from the British Library.

Printed in Hong Kong

Reprinted 1993

To Holly, who, I'm sure, will do better

Contents

List of Tables

Acknowledgements

George Taylor, Andrew Taylor and Gerry Taylor all provided helpful comments on chapters of this book – in fact you might say it was 'taylor-made'. I'd like to thank Jenny Mortimer, Linda Day and, especially, Hazel Burke for turning a handwritten manuscript into a legible text – I promise to learn to use my word processor for the next one.

DAVID MARSH

Abbreviations

ABP	Associated British Ports
ACAS	Advisory Conciliation and Arbitration Service
ACTT	Association of Cinematograph, Television and Allied Technicians
AEU	Amalgamated Engineering Union
(Formerly AUEW)	(Amalgamated Union of Engineering Workers)
AJ	After Japan
APEX	Association of Professional, Executive, Clerical and Computer Staff
ASLEF	Associated Society of Locomotive Engineers and Firemen
ASTMS	Association of Scientific, Technical and Managerial Staff
BG	British Gas
BIFU	Banking, Insurance and Finance Union
BR	British Rail
BT	British Telecommunications
CBI	Confederation of British Industry
CLP	Constituency Labour Party
CLPD	Campaign for Labour Party Democracy
CLV	Campaign for a Labour Victory
COHSE	Confederation of Health Service Employees
CPSA	Civil and Public Services Association
CTU	Conservative Trade Unionists
DEmp	Department of Employment
DHSS	Department of Health and Social Security
EC	European Community
EEF	Engineering Employer's Federation

EETPU	Electrical, Electronic, Telecommunication and Plumbing Union
ESC	Economic and Social Council (of the European Community)
ET	Employment Training
FBU	Fire Brigade Union
GMBATU	General, Municipal, Boilermakers and Allied Trades Union
HSC	Health and Safety Commission
ICCUS	Inns of Court Conservative and Unionist Society
IDS	Income Data Services
IPCS	Institution of Professional Civil Servants
ITB	Industrial Training Board
JIC	Just-in-case
JIT	Just-in-time
LACSAB	Local Authorities Conditions of Service Advisory Board
MDHCS	Mersey Docks and Harbour Corporation
MSC	Manpower Services Commission
MSF	Manufacturing, Science and Finance Union
NALGO	National Association of Local Government Officers
NAPE	National Association of Port Employers
NCB	National Coal Board
NDLS	National Dock Labour Scheme
NEC	National Executive Committee
NEDC	National Economic Development Council
NEDO	National Economic Development Office
NGA	National Graphical Association
NHS	National Health Service
NIRC	National Industrial Relations Court
NJC	National Joint Council
NRC	National Reporting Centre
NTA	New Technology Agreement
NUJ	National Union of Journalists
NUM	National Union of Mineworkers
NUPE	National Union of Public Employees
NUR	National Union of Railwaymen
NUT	National Union of Teachers
PLA	Port of London Authority
PLP	Parliamentary Labour Party
POEU	Post Office Engineering Union

PRG	Policy Review Group
PSBR	Public Sector Borrowing Requirement
PSI	Policy Studies Institute
SDP	Social Democratic Party
SOGAT (82)	Society of Graphical and Allied Trades
SUA	Single Union Agreement
TA	Training Agency
TASS	Technical Administrative and Supervisory Section of the AUEW
TC	Training Council
TEC	Training Enterprise Council
TGWU	Transport and General Workers Union
TUC	Trades Union Congress
TUCC	Trade Union Coordinating Committee
TUFL	Trade Unions for Labour
TULV	Trade Unions for a Labour Victory
TULRA	Trade Union and Labour Relations Act
UCATT	Union of Combustion, Allied Trades and Technicians
UCW	Union of Communication Workers
USDAW	Union of Shop, Distributive and Allied Workers
WIRS	Workplace Industrial Relations Survey
YOP	Youth Opportunities Programme
YT	Youth Training
YTS	Youth Training Scheme

Introduction

Without exception, journalistic assessments of Mrs Thatcher's achievements in office, following her departure as Prime Minister in November 1990, highlighted her industrial relations policy or, more graphically; her 'defeat' of the trade unions, as a major, perhaps the major, achievement of Thatcherism.

The *Guardian's* analysis was typical:

> The overdue reform of the trade unions will stand among the most positive legacies of the Thatcher era.
> (Keith Harper, *Guardian*, 23 November 1990)

Of course it is not only journalists who have emphasised Mrs Thatcher's success in this field. Some of the most well-known British political scientists have stressed the curbing of union power. So, Kavanagh argues:

> The government's legislation on industrial relations and trade unions has taken hold. Here is an area where the balance of advantage has changed since 1979, from union to employers and managers and from the consultative role granted to the unions to one in which they are virtually ignored by the government.
> (Kavanagh, 1987, p. 243; see also King, 1988, p. 62 and Gamble, 1988, pp. 126–7)

This view has also been shared by sociologists (Crouch, 1986, p. 131), economists (Minford, 1988, p.99), historians (Holmes, 1985, p. 214) and even some students of industrial relations (Roberts, 1989, p. 78).

The argument of Kavanagh and others is fairly straightforward. In 1979 the Conservative Government had a limited number of aims. It wished to: remove the unions' role in the policy-making process; assert its authority, and therefore its image of governing competence, by standing up to the unions; change the attitudes and strategies of unions instilling a New Realism; and alter the balance on the shop floor in favour of management. Overall, the government wanted to weaken the unions' position in relation to both government and employers; to restrict what many observers saw as their excessive power.

Political scientists, like Kavanagh, argue that the Conservative Government has achieved these aims but, in so far as they present empirical evidence to support such a conclusion, they concentrate upon the changes in the relations between the unions and government. Their argument emphasises three changes. First, unions are no longer involved in policy-making and have had no influence on legislation. Second, the government has been able to transform the legislative framework within which unions have operated and has had limited problems of compliance from unions. This 'success' is contrasted with the fate of the 1971 Industrial Relations Act which union non-compliance turned into a virtual dead letter by the time it was repealed. Third, the government successfully resisted a number of public sector strikes, notably of course, the 1984–5 miners' strike. This reinforced its image of governing competence and helped confirm the triumph of New Realism in the trade union movement. The political scientists pay little or no attention to changes in shop-floor industrial relations.

Of course, not everyone accepts the Kavanagh view. The industrial relations literature, particularly, is critical of the notion that the Thatcher Government has transformed industrial relations. This literature concentrates upon relations between employers and unions and is mainly concerned with the role of government in so far as it sets the framework within which shop-floor industrial relations operate. Two clear points emerge from the majority of this literature. First it is argued that less has changed than Kavanagh and others claim; in particular little has altered on the shop floor (Kelly, 1987, pp. 8, 12, 14, 16–17; McIlroy, 1988, p. 233; McInnes, 1987, p. 6). Second, it is suggested that, in so far as these changes have occurred, they result more from the transformation of the occupational structure and the macroeconomy than from government policy and legislation (Kelly, 1987, p. 17; McIlroy, 1988; McInnes, 1987; Wedderburn, 1985, p. 33).

These two positions are significantly different and result, at least in part, from the particular interests of social scientists as compared with industrial relations specialists. Each discipline pays insufficient attention to the other's literature. The aim of this book is to present a broader and more thorough analysis dealing with the unions' relations with both government and employers by drawing on the literature from a number of disciplines. To this end I will focus upon three key questions: How much has changed in the position of unions in relation to both government and employers? Why have these changes occurred? What is likely to happen in the future?

In order to address these questions the book contains ten substantive chapters. The first chapter looks at the development of labour law throughout this century, paying most attention to the Labour Government's 1969 White Paper, *In Place of Strife* and the Conservative Government's 1971 Industrial Relations Act. This is crucial, as it is impossible to understand fully the particularities of the Thatcher Government's legislation, or the strategy the government adopted, without such a historical perspective. The second chapter assesses the extent of trade union power before 1979, paying particular attention to their role in the 1974–9 Labour Government. Without such an analysis it is impossible to comment on the putative decline in their power.

Having established this background, the third chapter analyses the evolution and content of the five major pieces of legislation passed by the Conservative Government; the 1980, 1982, 1988 and 1990 Employment Acts and the 1984 Trade Union Act. Of course, legislation can easily be passed by a government with a large majority. However, the legislation may not be used by employers or unions. Indeed, that is what happened, to a large extent, in the case of the 1971 Industrial Relations Act. For this reason, Chapter 4 examines the use of the Conservative legislation by employers.

Many authors emphasise that the Conservative Government has ended the cosy process of consultation and excluded the trade unions from policy-making. Chapter 5 looks at the extent to which relations between unions and government have changed since 1979. At the same time, the relationship between the trade unions and the Labour Party is crucial for any understanding of the position of unions. In Chapter 2, I look at this relationship during the key period of the

Social Contract. Chapter 6 concentrates upon the changes in that relationship since 1979, changes which it is necessary to understand if we are to attempt any assessment of the likely future of unions.

In Chapter 7 I examine the economic changes which have contributed to the decline in the unions' position. Subsequently, Chapters 8 and 9 deal with the most important question, as far as industrial relation specialists are concerned: how far have things changed on the shop floor? Chapter 8 looks at changes in the private sector, while Chapter 9 considers the public sector.

The final chapter initially presents a summary of the conclusions of the book. Subsequently, however, I raise the broader question of what this case study of one area of policy-making reveals more generally about the influence of Thatcherism on British politics.

1

The Historical Background

The evolution and shape of the trade union legislation of the Thatcher Governments can only be fully and properly understood in the context of the historical development of labour law in Britain, the system of immunities, and the principle of voluntarism and the role of the judiciary to which it has given rise.

There are two main branches of labour law: individual labour law, that is, law regulating the relationship between the individual employee and his or her employer; and collective labour law, that is, law regulating the collective relationship between management and trade unions. In the nineteenth century individual labour law was based upon legally-enforceable contracts of employment. This suited employers, given that the law assumed that it was a contract between equals; a legal fiction which legitimised the dominance of employers and their ability to dictate terms to employees. As Lewis and Simpson point out:

> This situation was, however, modified by the gradual enactment of statutory protections from a few of the grossest forms of exploitation. The state intervened to control the notorious practice of 'truck' by stipulating the payment of wages in cash rather than kind for manual workers. It also attempted to regulate industrial safety and, mainly in respect of women and young persons, health and welfare at work. What is remarkable is that until the 1960s, with the exceptions of truck and industrial safety, protective legislation was largely conspicuous by its absence. This bare minimum of state intervention in the individual employment relation gave all the more scope to the development of voluntary institutions and collective bargaining.
>
> (Lewis and Simpson, 1981, pp.7–8).

1

If there was little individual labour law, the history of collective labour law is altogether more conflictual. Even in the 1860s the position of unions and workers was fairly desperate: the Master and Servant Act made it a criminal offence for a worker to leave her employment in breach of contract; strikes were virtually illegal given that participants were liable to be charged with criminal conspiracy; in common law, unions were regarded as 'societies in restraint of trade' and, as such, had few legal rights; and a series of judicial decisions had established picketing as illegal.

In the 1870s, however, a number of legislative initiatives changed the situation significantly; in effect, the Conservative Government responded to the rapid growth of unionisation which occurred in the early 1870s, and the political activity of the newly-formed Trades Union Congress (TUC), in the context of the extended franchise. The two 1875 Acts, the Conspiracy and Protection of Property Act and the Employers and Workmen Act, settled the legal status of the trade unions for a generation. This legislation repealed the Master and Servants Act; abolished imprisonment for breach of contract; specifically excluded trade disputes from the law of conspiracy; and established the legality of peaceful picketing. The key point was that the criminal law no longer applied in relation to trade disputes, except in so far as picketing was involved. Instead, it was the civil law, and in most cases the common law, which was crucial. More specifically, the majority of industrial relations legal cases involved the law of tort. A tort is the breach of a duty imposed by law, and when the breach occurs some person (usually in industrial relations cases, the employer) acquires the right of action for damages. In this field a tort committed by a union or unionist will often involve a breach of contract.

Obviously unions and workers benefited when the threat of criminal action was, in most circumstances, removed. However, the law of tort, and common law in general, is judge-made law; law created by judges, not by Parliament. This was to prove a recurring problem, as after 1875 judges developed new civil liabilities for trade unions for torts. Certainly, the turn of the century proved a golden period of judicial creativity. In this period judges defined important new torts: unionists were held to be liable for claims for damages by employers for the torts of simple conspiracy – given that the 1875 legislation had merely removed liability for criminal conspiracy and inducing a breach of an employment contract. In addition, in the Taff Vale Judgement (1901), the House of Lords held that trade unions could be sued for losses sustained by an employer as a result of a strike. These decisions severely weakened the growing union movement and caused great political upheaval, given that the Liberals, in particular, were very conscious of the need to attract the newly-enfranchised working-class males.

It was the 1906 Trade Disputes Act that re-established the structure of legal immunities which had first emerged in 1875. In essence, unions and unionists were given immunity from liability for actions in tort. Specifically, the Trade Disputes Act established: a blanket immunity for unions as distinct from unionists; immunity for individual unionists from liability for the torts of simple conspiracy, inducing breach of the employment contract, and interference with a person's freedom to use his/her capital or labour; and some legal protection for peaceful picketing.

The alternative to a system of immunities would have involved the establishment of a series of positive rights for unions, for example, a right to strike, such as exists in most other countries. In contrast, the British system gave unions and unionists a different status in law, not in fact a privileged status (see Lewis and Simpson, 1981, pp.3–7). They enjoyed immunities providing they were within what Wedderburn has called the 'golden formula' (Wedderburn, 1965, p.222), that is, that their action was undertaken in furtherance or contemplation of a trade dispute.

It is quite clear that the unions preferred a system of immunities rather than a system of positive rights because they wanted the law, lawyers and judges kept out of industrial relations. They had learnt by experience to rely for the protection of their interest on their collective strength rather than the law, which had proved expensive and antagonistic. The unions believed in 'collective *laissez-faire*'; in the operation of the market and free collective bargaining where the workers were represented by strong, well-organised, trade unions.

It is equally clear that the Trade Disputes Act reinforced the voluntarism which was already a growing feature of British industrial relations. In fact, this voluntarism, which characterised industrial relations until the 1960s, had two elements. In the first place, both individual and collective labour law were at a minimum. As Lewis and Simpson emphasise:

Generally the law played only a minor role in the shaping of
British industrial relations. The historic emphasis was not on legal
regulation but on voluntary self-regulation by employers' and
workers' organisations. The characteristic was reflected not only
in the immunities but in the overall framework of labour law.

(Lewis and Simpson, 1981, p.7)

At the same time, voluntarism was also enshrined in the collective
bargaining system. Indeed, collective bargaining developed in
Britain in the absence of state regulation or support. The little
collective bargaining law which existed was not underpinned by
direct legal sanctions. As Lewis and Simpson emphasise:

the collective agreement itself came to be regarded as a 'gentle-
man's agreement' which, unless the negotiating parties specified
otherwise, was not intended to be a legally enforceable contract.
On the contrary collective agreements in Britain were enforced
not by legal but by social sanctions.

(Lewis and Simpson, 1981, p.8)

In the absence of such legal sanctions, a particular style of collective
bargaining developed which was the second distinctive feature of
voluntarism. Each industry, and indeed often each factory, developed
its own customs and practices. As such, the pattern of industrial
relations, and the shape and outcomes of collective bargaining,
depended not on the law but on the informal institutions and
processes within the factory and, of course, the economic position of
the employer.

Except during the 1926 General Strike, the judiciary played only a
minor role in the inter-war period (Griffiths, 1985, pp.58–60).
Growing unemployment, falling union membership and the union's
'defeat' in the General Strike, which was enshrined in the Trade
Disputes and Trade Union Act of 1927, weakened the unions'
challenge to employers. For this reason, employers had little recourse
to the law and so the judiciary had correspondingly few opportunities for creating new torts. After the Second World War the
unions became more involved with government as part of the post-
war settlement; indeed to many observers voluntarism was a
key element of the post-war consensus. During this period relative
prosperity and harmony convinced all partners, government, unions
and employers, that they were involved in a positive-sum game.

There was little need to use the law in industrial relations; instead the informal system of industrial relations flourished and the judiciary were for the most part inactive in this field. However, the days of voluntarism were numbered. The pillars of voluntarism began to crumble in the 1960s, although the process wasn't continuous. The acceleration of Britain's relative economic decline increasingly brought into question the utility of Keynesian demand management. As such, governments, notably the Labour governments of 1964–70 and 1974–9, turned to supply-side management and to a neo-corporatist solution. Integral to the success of such a strategy was a developed framework of both individual and collective labour law. The Labour governments believed that changes in individual labour law were needed to give workers employment rights in return for their co-operation in the modernisation of British industry necessary to restore competitiveness and profitability. Similarly, changes in collective labour law were seen as an essential complement to the government's increasingly interventionist economic strategy ensuring that agreements reached between both employers and unions and unions and the State, were honoured.

In fact, an entire framework of individual labour law was developed to protect workers' rights as part of an attempt to establish a new neo-corporatist settlement. The majority of these statutes, although not all, were passed during the two periods of Labour Government. They included: the Contracts of Employment Act 1963, which required minimum notice periods for employees; the Redundancy Payments Act 1967, which entitled workers to minimum redundancy payments; the Industrial Relations Act 1971, which gave employees the right not to be unfairly dismissed; the Employment Protection Act 1975 and the Employment Protection (Consolidation) Act 1978 which extended the statutory rights of workers; the Health and Safety at Work Act 1974 which provided increased protection for employees in the case of accident; and the Equal Pay Act 1970, the Sex Discrimination Act 1975 and the Race Relations Act 1976, which attempted to reduce discrimination in employment.

In addition, a new system of 'labour courts', the industrial tribunals, mushroomed after 1965. By the end of the 1970s, 40,000 cases per year were registered with the tribunals which dealt with complaints by employees about breaches of their rights in relation to: unfair dismissal; redundancy pay; equal pay; trade union membership and activities; industrial safety; maternity leave; and protection from dismissal on the grounds of race, sex or marital status.

Whereas, in the field of individual labour law, changes proved beneficial to employees, changes in collective labour law aimed to reduce the power of the unions. At the same time, while from 1963 until 1979 there was an almost continual expansion of the rights of employees, the conflict over collective labour law ebbed and flowed. At first, the 1964–70 Labour Government acted to re-establish the immunities, threatened by a new wave of restrictive judgements and the creation of new torts by the court, in the Trade Disputes Act 1965. However, in 1965 the Labour Government established the Donovan Commission to investigate trade unions and employers' organisations. As Coates emphasises, its terms of reference implied that legal restrictions on unions would redress the balance of bargaining power in the labour market, so increasing the efficiency and profitability of industry (Coates, 1989, Chap.3).

In contrast, the Commission concluded that industrial relations were now characterised by informal plant-level bargaining which produced market-led anarchy and inflationary pressures. It recommended that management should formalise these changes and develop, jointly with the unions, procedures to regulate industrial relations at the company level. In addition, collective bargaining should be extended to include questions of work organisation. It argued that the law should be kept out of industrial relations and that the state should play a limited role while the reformed procedural relationships led to voluntary co-operation between capital and labour.

Despite the Commission's recommendations, the memory of the damaging strikes by the seamen in 1967 led the Labour Government to break with the past, to go beyond Donovan and move firmly into the area of industrial relations legislation. The proposals in the Government's White Paper *In Place of Strife* are outlined in Table 1.1. It was certainly a radical break with voluntarism in that it envisaged a series of criminal restraints upon management, unions and individual employees. In fact, the major proposals included: a compulsory cooling-off period, with the sanction that workers could be legally ordered to return to work; a compulsory strike ballot; and a statutory recognition procedure covering demarcation disputes between unions with defaulters being liable for fines.

Crouch sees these proposals as a compromise between the

managerial liberal collectivism of Donovan and the state corporatist proposals favoured by industry and the Conservative Opposition. Certainly, the proposal marked a nail in the coffin of voluntarism and, as Crouch argues, the corporatist elements were designed as a 'means of coopting labour's own organisations to assist the State and the employer in the control of labour' (Crouch, 1977, pp.161–2). The proposals met with major opposition from within the trade union movement, the Parliamentary Labour Party and sections of the Cabinet led by James Callaghan. After a protracted struggle, the government was forced to withdraw its proposal and to accept TUC assurances that it would deal with some of the problems voluntarily (see Jenkins, 1970).

When the Conservatives came to power in 1970, they were committed to trade union reform. The importance of the 1971 Industrial Relations Act is such that it warrants a more detailed study later. However, as even a brief consideration of Table 1.1 indicates, its contents closely paralleled the proposals contained in *In Place of Strife* and returned the law to centre stage in industrial relations. In fact, there can be no doubt that the Act, together with the Code of Industrial Relations Practice which accompanied it, severely restricted the autonomy of trade unions and trade unionists. As Crouch argues:

In theory the Act marked a distinct increase in the monism of power in industrial relations by considerably reducing the circumstances in which workers would take industrial action and thereby exercise countervailing power. Certain constraints were also imposed on employers' powers in industrial conflict ... But it is clear ... that the overall weight of the changes was to reduce workers' power to put pressure on employers.

(Crouch, 1977, p.165)

As we shall see below, the Industrial Relations Act had been rendered ineffective by the time the Conservatives lost the February 1974 General Election. At this stage, the time appeared right for a reassertion of voluntarism. During the period of confrontation between the Conservative Government and the unions, relations between the Labour Party and the unions improved. The structural manifestation of this improvement was a Trade Union–Labour Party Liaison Committee formed in January 1972. It was in this Committee that the Social Contract was developed. Not surprisingly, a major element in the Social Contract was the repeal of the Industrial Relations Act. This commitment was fulfilled by the incoming Labour Government in two pieces of legislation, the Trade Union and Labour Relations Act 1974 and the Trade Union and Labour Relations (Amendment) Act 1976 (henceforth jointly TULRA). Two Acts were necessary because the Conservative majority in the House of Lords significantly altered the initial legislation against the background of the imminent, second, election in 1974.

In fact, TULRA removed the restrictive provisions of the Industrial Relations Act and restored the immunities which two judicial decisions in the 1960s had removed. Indeed, as Lord Scarman put it in 1979 referring to TULRA:

> Briefly put, the law now is back to what Parliament had intended when it enacted the Act of 1906 – but stronger and clearer than it was then.
>
> (Scarman, quoted in Lewis and Simpson, 1981, p.5).

Even then, however, judicial creativity was not totally stifled and in the late 1970s Lord Denning, in the Court of Appeal, gave a series of judgements which drastically restricted the scope of the immunities. All these decisions were subsequently overturned by the House of Lords, but Denning's decision confirmed once again the un-certainties of the law of tort and the antipathy of the judiciary towards trade unions.

From the beginning of the 1960s, governments also began to intervene more directly in collective bargaining in an attempt to slow down the rate of growth of earnings, particularly given the view of many observers that wage-push inflation was the key problem. Incomes policy in the 1960s was initially voluntary, but from 1966 there were statutory targets.

At the same time, the Labour Government created the National Board for Prices and Incomes (NBPI) to police its incomes policies. The NBPI emphasised the need to link pay increases with improved productivity. As Coates emphasises:

> When the National Board for Prices and Incomes looked for productivity bargains to analyse in 1966, it could only find seven major ones; but by 1969 productivity agreements had been signed

on behalf of over six million workers in a vast range of privately-owned industries, productivity agreements that involved the buying out of control of aspects of the job by management from shop stewards and organised work groups.

(Coates, 1989, p.52)

When the Conservative Party came to power in 1970 it was committed to a reduction of government intervention in the economy and, as such, opposed to incomes policy; certainly to statutory policies. However, despite the introduction of tripartite and later multipartite talks on a voluntary policy, the government continued to listen to the Treasury which instituted a system of statutory controls. A statutory policy was thus introduced in 1972 and lasted, with modifications, to the February 1974 election. In essence, the Labour Government between 1974 and 1979 followed a similar pattern. Initially it allowed a wages explosion, but from mid-1975 the Social Contract became, in most senses, an incomes policy (Dorfman, 1979, pp. 120–32). Agreement was reached in 1975, 1976 and 1977 on three phases of a voluntary, but tight, policy which effectively restricted wage levels until the policy collapsed in 1978.

The shape of incomes policy changed over the two decades. Incomes policies were usually voluntary, rather than statutory, and most often agreed with the unions. However, there is no doubt that the government's role was interventionist for almost the entire period; successive governments were no longer willing to leave wage negotiations to the market and free collective bargaining.

How does a brief history of the development of British labour law enhance our understanding of the evolution and shape of the Thatcherite legislation? Two points stand out. First, well before the election of the Conservatives in 1979, it was no longer accurate to view British labour law as being characterised by voluntarism. The overall tradition of non-intervention was abandoned in the field of individual labour law in the 1960s. As far as collective labour law is concerned the pattern is more complex. *In Place of Strife* marked the first post-war legislative attempt to move the law to centre stage. Although both this attempt and the 1971 Industrial Relations Act failed, they restored trade union reform to the political agenda. At the same time, from the beginning of the 1960s the state consistently intervened in the system of collective bargaining, either establishing a statutory incomes policy or attempting to negotiate, and often impose, a voluntary policy. Clearly then, the Conservative Government elected in 1979 was not faced with a tradition of voluntarism which it had to confront; voluntarism was already a thing of the past.

Second, the history of labour law is marked by an antipathy between the judiciary, the legislature and the trade unions. In earlier times the legislature often came to the unions' rescue to restore immunities removed by judicial decisions. However, faced with a government which threatened its immunities and rights, it was clear that the unions could not rely on the courts for protection. Indeed the Law Lords were far from happy with the labour law and the 'golden formula', even when they ruled to sustain the immunities. In this vein Lord Diplock, in passing a judgement in 1980 overturning one of Lord Denning's decisions, described TULRA as:

> intrinsically repugnant to anyone who has spent his life in the practice of law or the administration of justice. Sharing these instincts it was a conclusion that I myself reached with considerable reluctance, for given the existence of a trade dispute it involves granting to trade unions a power, which has no other limits than their own self-restraint, to inflict by means which are contrary to the general law untold harm..... Recent experience has shown that almost any major strike in one of the larger manufacturing or service industries, if it is sufficiently prolonged, may have the effect (figuratively) of bringing the nation to its knees. It is the ability in the last resort to carry out a threat to do this without involving any breach of the civil or criminal law as it now stands that gives to trade unions, individually and collectively, their 'industrial muscle'.
>
> (Diplock quoted in Lewis and Simpson, 1981, p.6)

Clearly such views, particularly when they were so publically expressed, must have sustained the new Conservative Government in its commitment to trade union reform.

The Industrial Relations Act 1971

The Industrial Relations Act 1971 deserves separate consideration because its fate clearly affected the political and legislative judgements of Mrs Thatcher and her supporters. Indeed, almost all commentaries on the Thatcher Government's policy towards trade unions emphasise that, in one way or another, the government had learnt from the experience of the Industrial Relations Act. We shall consider such assessments later. However, any such consideration presupposes a brief examination of the evolution, shape and fate of the Industrial Relations Act.

It is important to emphasise that a section of the Conservative Party had been committed to the use of the law to resolve industrial relations problems for a considerable time. In 1958 the Inns of Court Conservative and Unionist Society (ICCUS) published *A Giant's Strength* which criticised what they saw as the privileged legal position of trade unions. However, as Moran points out, there is hardly an idea in *A Giant's Strength* which did not feature in previous Conservative thinking. Indeed, as Moran emphasises:

> The pamphlet did not shape the final Act (the Industrial Relations Act 1971); rather it reflected Conservative concerns – over strikes, the closed shop and the constitutional position of unions which were also found in the 1971 legislation. Nevertheless, the pamphlet was a good indicator of one important strand of Conservative thinking.
>
> (Moran, 1977, p.56)

ICCUS argued that the trade union immunities prevented efficient and effective management and this power was being ruthlessly used in an era of full employment; it also severely restricted the freedom of the individual. The pamphlet also proposed that any strike could be unilaterally referred, by either of the parties, to an independent tribunal. The tribunal's report would be binding; the immunities would be removed from action called in breach of the operation or report of the tribunal. In addition, unions should be registered and the immunities would only protect registered unions. As such, unofficial strikes, which were seen as the main problem, would be subject to criminal and civil proceedings.

As Strinati argues:

> What, in effect, the ICCUS did was to set the ball rolling on the need to reform the trade unions and to set it rolling in the direction of a legalised corporatism which relied on increased state intervention in the affairs and rules of trade unions, through the

Registrar and independent tribunals, providing for strong, responsible, official trade union organisation.

(Strinati, 1982, p.144)

In the period leading up to the 1964 election, Conservative publications consistently criticised trade unions, paying particular attention to the closed shop, the political levy and restrictive practices. However, it was the election defeat which brought about a root-and-branch re-examination of policy. Indeed, Edward Heath, as head of the party's Advisory Committee on Policy, established 19 study groups to examine the major policy areas. One dealt with industrial relations and it produced the initial proposals which were revised and finally published as *Fair Deal At Work* in 1968, before the publication of the Donovan Report. *Fair Deal at Work* suggested: the establishment of a Registrar; the narrowing of immunities; legally binding collective agreements; a legal right to join or refuse to join a union; and the creation of an Industrial Court.

The Conservatives fought the 1970 General Election with trade union reform as an important plank in their platform. After they were elected, a consultative document on labour law was produced. The aim was to facilitate many of the reforms proposed by Donovan, while introducing new legal sanctions. The TUC was sent a copy of the Green Paper on 5 October 1970 and told that no consultation would be possible after 13 November. Indeed, at a meeting between the TUC and Mr Carr, the Employment Secretary, on 13 October, the minister outlined the eight 'basic pillars' of the new Bill and declared them non-negotiable. The government subsequently forced through its legislation, despite strong opposition from the Labour Party inside Parliament and the trade unions outside.

As a number of authors have pointed out, the Industrial Relations Act enshrined a major contradiction. It aimed at one and the same time to reform industrial relations and restrict trade unions. The reform strategy was explicitly set out in the Industrial Relations Code of Practice (1972) which accompanied the Act. It assumed the importance and legitimacy of trade unions but, unlike the Donovan Report, it saw the law as the main instrument for achieving reform. As such, it reflected a collectivist ethic and was corporatist in essence. In contrast, the strategy of restriction was based upon the view that trade unions were a crucial constraint on the operation of the market. This necessitated the use of law to reduce the strength of unions, in particular by curtailing their ability to take collective industrial action. Wedderburn summed up the contradition well when he suggested that the Act seemed to be the work of two distinct draftsmen:

> The first may be though of as a civil servant or 'organisationman' concerned mainly to bring 'order' and a tidy structure into collective British industrial relations. The second is quite different, a Conservative lawyer involved above all else with doctrines or individual rights, often without regard to the shop-floor problems of collective bargaining.
>
> (Wedderburn, 1972, p.282)

This contradiction was to prove a key, perhaps the key, cause of the Act's failure.

The strategy of reform was reflected in: the requirement that unions register with a Registrar of Trade Unions, only registered trade unions were to have legal rights and to enjoy certain legal immunities; the provision to make collective agreements between employers and unions legally enforceable, unless a disclaimer clause was inserted; the creation of a National Industrial Relations Court (NIRC) to consider complaints by unions and companies about unfair industrial practices; and the granting of power to the Secretary of State to apply, at his discretion, to the NIRC to defer strike action – the cooling-off period – or to require a ballot before strike action. In contrast, the strategy of restriction was promoted in: the removal of the blanket immunity which trade unions had enjoyed since 1906; the granting to the individual employees of the right to join, or not to join, trade unions; and the restrictions on secondary action.

It is clear that the Act was a very broad one. It was similar to, but more radical than, the *In Place of Strife* proposals (see Table 1.1). In particular, it sought to restrict further the immunities enjoyed by unions and to place collective agreements within a legally-binding framework. Perhaps most importantly, a new institution, the NIRC, was created specifically to deal with collective labour law cases.

The Industrial Relations Act proved to be a major failure for the Conservative Government and, as such, had a significant effect on future Conservative thinking. It had very little influence on industrial relations and was little short of a political disaster. Weekes *et al.*, in their thorough study of the operation of the Act, argue: 'Our

Table 1.1 *Changing industrial relations proposals/legislation, 1969–90: the major features*

1969 'In Place of Strife' proposals	1971 Industrial Relations Act	The 1980s legislation
1. Registration – trade unions required to register with Registrar of Trade Unions	1. Registration – unions required to register with Registrar of Trade Unions	1. Initial restrictions then abolition of closed shop
2. Collective agreements legally binding *if* specified	2. Collective agreements legally binding *unless* specified	2. Removed blanket immunity for trade unions
3. Discretionary power to allow Secretary of State to defer strike action (the cooling-off period) or to require ballot before strike taken	3. Removed blanket immunity for trade unions	3. Removed series of immunities enjoyed by unionists but restricting definition of legitimate trade dispute – removed immunity if (a) secondary action involved; (b) ballot held prior to strike; (c) secondary picketing involved; (d) action taken to protect closed shop
4. Creation of industrial board to impose fine for breach of Secretary of State's orders and to hear complaints by members against their union	4. Secretary of State could *apply* to National Industrial Relations Court (NIRC) to defer strike action (the cooling-off period) or to require ballot before strike taken	4. Outlawed union labour only clauses in contracts and tenders
5. Establishment of statutory rights to safeguard employees against unfair dismissal and to guarantee the right to belong to a trade union	5. Creation of NIRC with status of High Court to consider complaints by unions and companies (but not individuals) about unfair industrial practices	5. Required secret (postal) ballots for election of union officers every 5 years
	6. Improvement in employee protection and the requirement	6. Required unions which operate political funds to conduct ballots every 10 years

6. Establishment of a Commission on Industrial Relations with powers to examine inter-union disputes and questions of union recognition if those not resolved

that companies disclose information to trade unions

7. Major restrictions on closed shop – pre-entry closed shop virtually illegal; post-entry closed shop compulsory if approved in ballot; employee had right to join *and refuse to join* union

8. Restrictions on secondary action

7. Established rights for union members *vis-à-vis* unions

8. Provided public funds for union ballots

9. Established Commissioner for rights of trade union members to help trade union members to pursue legal action

10. Secondary picketing unlawful

11. Restrictions on unofficial strikes

evidence is that the Act had little influence on the general practice of industrial relations' (Weekes *et al.*, 1975, p.232). In particular, their evidence indicates that: the closed shop provisions in the legislation were little used and 'in the end the law had to bend to the inevitable. The main reason was that the employers defended it almost as tenaciously as did workers' (Weekes *et al.*, 1975, p.63); 'there was little evidence of change either in union rules or policy generally as a result of the IR Acts or the Courts' doctrine of union responsibility (ibid., p.110); and 'the employers with multi-union problems whom the IR Act was designed to help were not keen to use the procedure to obtain a solution' (ibid, p.151).

Two of the conclusions drawn by Weekes *et al.* concerning the laws' influence on industrial relations deserve more comment. First, as already suggested, employers were reluctant to use the legislation. As Table 1.2a, which is adapted from figures given in the Weekes text, indicates, only 31 applications were made to the NIRC and these were heavily concentrated in three industries with poor industrial relations; transport, engineering and printing. In addition, as Table 1.2b shows, large employers were involved in only 18 per cent of the cases for which Weekes *et al.*provides data. The legislation was mainly used by smaller employers in inases for which Weekes provides data. The legislation was mainly used by smaller employers in industries with a history of bad industrial relations.

The second point is a related one. The Act had little effect in highly-organised companies and workplaces, yet it was precisely in such companies it was supposed to remove what management saw as ineffective procedures. As Weekes *et al.* argue:

> The Act's provisions and remedies and the Code of Industrial Relations Practice appear to have been entirely ineffective in workplaces of this kind. The conclusions that emerge are that the law is only one influence among many on the conduct of industrial relations, and that where workers possess industrial strength management can only, unless the balance of power is altered, introduce effective changes by negotiations.
>
> (Weekes *et al.*, 1975, pp.184–5).

The Act was also a clear political failure. In introducing the Act the government had hoped to bypass functional representation (Moran, 1977, p.157); as such it had declared the main pillars of the bill non-

Table 1.2   *Applications to the National Industrial Relations Court for relief from unfair industrial practices*

(a)   **By sector**

Sector	% of cases (number in brackets)	
Transport	48	(15)
Engineering	26	(8)
Printing	13	(4)
Television	6	(2)
Others	6	(2)
Total	100	(31)

Source: Adapted from Weekes *et al.*, 1975, pp.201–2.

(b)   **By size**

Size	% of cases (number in brackets)	
Small (less than 100 employees)	46	(13)
Medium	36	(10)
Very large	18	(5)
Total	100	(28)

Source: Adapted from Weekes *et al.*, 1975, pp.201–2.

negotiable and, in response, the TUC had withdrawn from all consultation. The government apparently believed that after initial opposition the trade unions would co-operate (see Moran, 1977, p.122). In fact, the unions' reaction was remarkably united and successful. Certainly Weekes *et al.* argue:

> TUC union opposition to the Act was widespread, immediate and thoroughgoing. While sections of most unions saw some advantages in certain provisions and difficulties in carrying out a policy of total de-registration and non-cooperation with the Act

and its institutions ... to the majority of unions the new legal remedies for dismissal and recognition seemed inadequate or defective, and in no way compensated for the Act's restrictions on industrial action and the real threat of internal friction if the law's view about 'union responsbility' was acted upon.

(Weekes *et al.*, 1975, p. 229)

This perhaps overestimates the unity involved because, as Moran shows, although there was no doubt that the TUC would oppose the bill, or that non-registration under the Act would be the main element in their strategy of resistance, there were significant splits and indecisions as to what instructions would be given to member unions as regards registration. As Moran argues:

The opposition of the TUC to registration was complicated by three matters: differences between the varying shades of constitutionalism; fear of the extension of TUC authority, especially among the smaller unions; and, above all, the threats posed by non-registration to the institutional interests of unions.

(Moran, 1977, p.128)

At the March 1971 special TUC Congress, the most the TUC could achieve was a motion which meant that affiliates were 'strongly advised' not to register (Moran, 1977, p.128). Even when, after the September Congress, the General Council wrote to affiliates instructing them to come off the provisional register, the results were not encouraging (Moran, 1977, pp.135–7). Indeed, Moran suggests that, if it hadn't been for three sets of events in the spring and summer of 1972, the TUC's policy of non-registration might have collapsed (ibid., p.136). First, the miners' strike in 1972, and the subsequent recommendations of the Wilberforce Tribunal, was a major setback for the government's anti-inflation policy based upon restricting wage increases in the public sector. As Moran puts it:

defeat at the hands of the miners was the catalyst which produced a change in Government strategy. During the summer and autumn of 1972 the Government conducted the so-called 'tri-partite' talks with the TUC and the CBI. This was indicative of an important shift in thinking: wage inflation was no longer to be fought by introducing greater market discipline into wage negotiations, and by curbing the organisational power of the unions, but by the operation of a compact with the trade union movement involving wage restraint in return for economic expansion, welfare measures and some price control.

(Moran, 1977, p.138)

Second, the IR Act failed to produce the outcome the government wanted in relation to a pay claim from the railwaymen. The government used the emergency procedures which the Act provided and applied to the NIRC for a conciliation pause. The Act worked in a simple legal sense: the unions reluctantly co-operated; the conciliation pause was operated; and the ballot produced a large majority. Unfortunately for the government, there was a majority for strike action. Once again, Moran makes the point very well:

the Government had suffered an important defeat: the final settlement was well above what it had hoped, and its first attempt to use the Act had been a humiliating failure. It established an impression that the Act was accident prone, an impression that was to be strongly reinforced by the episodes involving the dockers.

(Moran, 1977, p.139)

As Moran suggests, it was the cases involving the dockers and the courts which proved crucial in rallying union support for the deregistration policy. The cases essentially involved the blacking of lorries which were delivering goods from a number of container firms, given that the move towards containerisation meant a significant decline in the work available for dockers. The series of cases were quite complicated and are well dealt with by Moran (Moran, 1977, pp.139–43). However, the major point for our purposes is that the law, the NIRC, and the government were discredited. Indeed, the courts were seen, almost throughout the operation of the Act, as interpreting the legislation in a partial way. As Weekes *et al.* argue:

[The courts] conveniently discovered that there was an Official Solicitor who could act for some of those who refused to seek to put a case before them. The NIRC freed unrepentant contemnors when their continued imprisonment threatened to cause industrial chaos. It accepted money from an unnamed third party in payment of a union's damages and costs. It deliberately and self-

consciously adopted a new procedure to avoid making orders
against workers and unions when employers brought apparently
good legal cases before it. And it recognized its own powerless-
ness to upset illegal closed shops.

(Weekes *et al.*, 1975, p.229)

Two other points are important if we are fully to understand the
reasons for the political failure of the Act. First, not only were
individual employers reluctant to use the legislation but the employers representative organisations gave it limited support. As
Moran points out:

> In addition to advising employers against any speedy use of the
> new measures, the CBI also began – almost as soon as the Act was
> on the statute book – to negotiate a conciliation procedure with the
> TUC which would by-pass its provisions.
>
> (Moran, 1977 p.153)

What is more, before the 1974 election the CBI was very anxious for
the IR Act's repeal; a view which was well reported in a well-
quoted, off-the-record remark by Campbell Adamson, then the
CBI's Director-General, just before the February election (Grant
and Marsh, 1977, p.39.)

Second, the government itself didn't rush to use its own legislation. As Weekes *et al.* argue:

> If employers, unions and even individual workers only rarely used
> the Act, at least the government which introduced it might have
> been expected to operate those parts of its own legislation which
> gave it the initiative, and to have encouraged others, particularly
> employers in the public sector, to apply the Act. For a short time
> the government showed some enthusiasm for its own legislation:
> senior Department of Employment officials gave lectures on the
> new law, and conciliation officers, when disputes were notified to
> them, advised employers of their new legal rights; Commissioners
> strongly in favour of the wider role of the law in industrial
> relations were appointed to the CIR. ... The failure of the railway
> ballot, from the Government's point of view, and the events of
> summer 1972 further weakened its confidence in its own legis-
> lation. The Government was forced to draw a number of un-

palatable conclusions about the possible consequences of using the Act. Trade unionists would not automatically obey the law, organized workers had a sanction against legal judgements, the law could make disputes harder to settle, and the operation of the IR Act could bring the law into disrepute.

(Weekes *et al.*, 1975, p.227)

Overall then, the legislation was a failure. The government had wanted to introduce the law into industrial relations and keep the unions at arm's length. By 1972, the government had discovered that, now it was converted to the view that an incomes policy was essential, it needed to resurrect functional representation in the form of tripartite talks with the TUC and the CBI. As such, the Industrial Relations Act, strongly opposed by the TUC and having little positive affect on industrial relations, was an embarrassment. Once again Moran makes the key point: by the autumn of 1972 the unions had won the key battle with the government: the jailing of the London dockers and the success of the TUC's non-registration campaign combined to ensure that the Act would no longer be an important part of the government's strategy. By then the government – spurred on by the miners' victory in their 1972 strike – had turned to tripartite talks with the CBI and the TUC in an effort to secure acceptable economic policies; the confrontation associated with the Act was now simply an embarrassment. The spectacular cases involving the Amalgamated Union of Engineering Workers (AUEW) served not to cause the Act's failure – that was already assured – but to remind the government of the legislative millstone which hung round its neck (Moran, 1977, p.125).

Conclusion

Two major conclusions are clear from this chapter:

1. The Conservative Government elected in 1979 was not faced with a tradition of voluntarism which it had to confront; voluntarism was already a thing of the past.
2. The 1971 Industrial Relations Act was a failure. It failed to have any real effect on industrial relations and in political terms it was a major disaster. In particular, its operation revealed that

compliance was the key problem. Governments can pass legislation but implementation is not always easy. In this case most
employers didn't use the legislation and the unions refused to
comply with it. The government was left with an image of
governing incompetence.

2

Union Power before 1979

This chapter has two aims. First, it examines relations between the unions and the Labour Government of 1974–9. Second, and more importantly, it attempts to assess the power of the unions before the Conservatives won the 1979 election. This is crucial because any assessment of the extent to which Mrs Thatcher and the Conservatives have curbed union power, or changed the balance between capital and labour, must first establish what the position was prior to 1979. The Conservatives were in no doubt about the extent of union power in 1979. Indeed, their election manifesto asserted:

The crippling industrial disruption which hit Britain last winter had several causes: years with no growth in production; rigid pay control; high marginal rates of taxation; and the extension of trade union power and privileges. Between 1974 and 1976, Labour enacted a 'militants' charter' of trade union legislation. It tilted the balance of power in bargaining throughout industry away from responsible management and towards unions, and sometimes towards unofficial groups of workers acting in defiance of their official union leadership.
(Quoted in *Times Guide to House of Commons*, 1979, p.284)

Many academics shared a similar view. Keith Middlemas's *Politics in Industrial Society* presents perhaps the most sophisticated expression of this position. He is most concerned to examine the development and collapse of what he calls 'corporate bias' in Britain. However, he concludes that:

in the 1970s the political potential of the trade union movement has transcended the relationships of the system characterised by corporate bias. Whatever may be true in the sphere of wage bargaining and specifically industrial activity, it overshadows the potential of employers, owners and management to influence the organisation of the state, and however negatively the General Council may transmit the inchoate political will of its membership trade union hegemony has broadened out further than any comparable Western nation, profoundly to alter the nature of the state.

(Middlemas, 1979, pp.451–2)

The main aim of this chapter is to examine this view that before 1979, and particularly in the 1970s, the unions were the most important constraint upon the autonomy of government. For this reason the chapter is divided into four sections: the first section deals briefly with the changes which occurred in British trade unions in the 1960s and 1970s and which affected the unions' relations with government; the second part is concerned with the pattern of the relationship between unions and government in the period; the third section deals with their access to government; finally, I shall look at the influence of unions on government policy-making during the decade before the Conservative victory in 1979.

The changes in British unionism in the 1960s and 1970s and their consequences for patterns of representation

In their excellent review of the changes which occurred in British trade union structure and activity after 1960, Undy, Ellis, McCarthy and Halmos emphasise how little ministers, civil servants and employers knew about unions (Undy *et al.*, 1981, pp.344–6). They might well have added journalists and academics to their list. British unions were characterised by many observers as unchanging monoliths. Undy *et al.* indicate both how false a view this was and how the two major changes which occurred during this period had significant consequences for the unions' relationships with both government and employers. In this section I shall identify the changes while in the following one I will be concerned, among other things, with the consequences these changes had for the strategies and tactics of the unions.

The growth and concentration of unions

Trade union membership grew until the end of the 1970s, as Undy *et al.*, 1981, indicate (see Tables 2.1 and 2.2). At the same time, after the 1964 Amalgamation Act removed obstacles to union mergers there, were a considerable number of mergers. So by 1979 there were fewer, larger unions than in the past. The pattern of growth however, was uneven. The general unions grew fairly rapidly: the Transport and General Workers Union (TGWU) by 26 per cent between 1970 and 1978 and the General and Municipal Union (GMU) by 13 per cent. The white-collar unions grew even more significantly: Association of Scientific, Technical, and Managerial Staffs (ASTMS) by 113 per cent, Technical Administrative and Supervisery Section of AEU (TASS) by 90 per cent and Bankers, Insurance and Finance Union (BIFU) by 42 per cent. However, it was in the public sector where the Labour Government encouraged union membership that the growth was most spectacular: National and Local Government Officers' Association (NALGO) grew by 66 per cent, National Union of Public Employees (NUPE) by 91 per cent, Confederation of Health Service Employees (COHSE) by 139 per cent and the Civil and Public Services Association (CPSA) by 22 per cent. In contrast, even in a period when union membership grew by 21 per cent overall, some unions failed to grow while others contracted: the Union of Communication Workers (UCW) membership fell by 6 per cent, the National Union of Railwaymen (NUR) by 9 per cent and the National Union of Teachers (NUT) by 6 per cent, while the Amalgamated Union of Engineering Workers (AUEW) and Electrical, Electronic, Telecommunication and Plumbing Union (EETPU) experienced little change (see Table 2.1).

Obviously these changes gave the unions greater legitimacy; so by 1978 Trades Union Congress (TUC)-affiliated unions could claim to represent 54.5 per cent of the work-force (Table 2.2). In addition, this growth also strengthened the bargaining position of the large unions, particularly unions in the public sector, in relation to both government and employers.

Table 2.1 Changes in the membership of TUC affiliated unions, 1970–89

Union	M'mship 1970 (000s)	M'mship 1978 (000s)	% Change 1970–78	M'mship 1979 (000s)	M'mship 1989 (000s)	% Change 1979–89
Transport & General Workers Union (TGWU)	1639	2073	+26	2086	1271	−39
Amalgamated Engineering Union (AEU)	1202	1199	n.c.	1218	741	−39
General, Municipal, Boilermakers, and Allied Trades Union (GMBATU)	853	965	+13	967	823	−15
National Association of Local Government Officers (NALGO)	440	729	+66	753	750	n.c.
National Union of Public Employees (NUPE)	373	712	+91	692	605	−13
Association of Scientific, Technical & Managerial Staffs (ASTMS)	221	471	+113	491	390*	−21
Union of Shop, Distributive & Allied Workers (USDAW)	330	462	+40	470	376	−21
Electrical, Electronic, Telecommunication & Plumbing Union (EETPU)	421	420	n.c.	420	370**	−12

Union					
Union of Construction, Allied Trades & Technicians (UCATT)	260 (1971)	321	+23	348	258	−26
National Union of Mineworkers (NUM)	279	291	+4	253	172	−31
National Union of Teachers (NUT)	311	291	−6	249	128	−43
Civil & Public Services Association (CPSA)	185	225	+22	224	176	−14
Society of Graphical & Allied Trades (SOGAT)	193	203	+5	205	203	n.c.
Union of Communication Workers (UCW)	210	197	−6	203		
Amalgamated Engineering Union – Technical Administrative & Supervisory Section (AUEW-TASS)	106	201	+90	201	251*	+25
Confederation of Health Service Employees (COHSE)	90	215	+139	212	209	−1
National Union of Railwaymen (NUR)	198	180	−9	180	103	−43
Banking, Insurance & Finance Union (BIFU)	89	126	+42	132	170	+29
Total	10002	12128	+21	12175	8405***	−31

*   Figures. ASTMS & TASS amalgamated to form MSF in 1988. MSF had 653000 members in 1989. ** 1988 Figures.
*** Excluded EETPU which was expelled from the TUC in 1988. Including EETPU the total membership would be 8775000 and the change between 1979 and 1989 would be 29%.

Table 2.2 *Union membership, 1974–89*

Year	All union membership[1] (number 000s)	(% annual change)	Membership of unions affiliated to TUC[2] (number 000s)	(% annual change)	Potential union membership[3] (number 000s)	(% annual change)	Density all unions (%)	(% annual change)	Density TUC unions (%)	(% annual change)
1974	11764	+ 2.7	10364	–	22297	+0.4	52.8	+2.2	46.5	–
1975	12026	+ 2.3	11036	+ 6.5	22313	– 0.4	54.1	+ 1.3	49.7	+ 3.2
1976	12386	+ 2.7	11516	+ 4.3	22048	– 0.7	56.2	+ 2.1	52.2	+ 2.5
1977	12846	+ 3.7	11865	+ 2.9	22172	+ 0.6	57.9	+ 1.7	53.5	+ 1.3
1978	13112	+ 2.1	12128	+ 2.2	22273	+ 0.5	58.9	+ 1.0	54.5	+ 1.0
1979	13289	+ 1.3	12173	+ 0.4	22592	+ 1.4	58.9	0	53.9	– 0.6
1980	12947	– 2.5	11601	– 4.7	22357	– 1.0	57.9	– 1.0	51.9	– 2.0
1981	12106	– 6.5	11006	– 5.1	21148	– 5.4	57.2	– 0.5	52.0	+ 0.1
1982	11593	– 4.2	10510	– 4.5	20614	– 2.5	56.2	– 1.0	51.0	– 1.0
1983	11335	– 2.2	10082	– 4.1	20744	+ 0.6	54.6	– 1.6	48.6	– 2.4
1984	11086	– 2.2	9855	– 2.3	20913	+ 0.8	53.0	– 1.6	47.1	– 1.5
1985	10716	– 3.3	9586	– 2.7	21115	+ 0.9	50.8	– 2.2	45.4	– 1.7
1986	10539	– 1.7	9243	– 3.6	21273	+ 0.7	49.5	– 1.3	43.4	– 2.0
1987	10475	– 0.6	8797	– 4.8	21555	+ 1.3	48.6	– 0.9	40.8	– 2.6
1988	10387	– 0.8	8652	– 1.6	22330	+ 3.5	46.5	– 2.1	38.7	– 2.1

Notes: 1. Certification Officer's figures.
2. TUC Annual Congress Report figures.
3. *Employment Gazette* figures

Decentralisation and diffusion

In the 1960s in the trade unions there was a general move towards decentralisation and diffusion in both the unions' bargaining structures and their processes of internal decision-making. In the bargaining area there was a move away from national agreements towards shop-floor bargaining. In many industries, the bargaining process in the 1970s involved the establishment of minimum wage levels at national level linked with plant or company-level bargaining. At the same time there was a steady decentralisation of decision-making with more ballots and greater control by members over the policy and administration of union leadership. As Undy *et al.* (1981) show, these changes did not occur everywhere, nor did they proceed at the same pace in all unions. The process was taken furthest in the TGWU and in NUPE, while in the NUM, for example, there was a move towards more centralised wage bargaining, at least until 1976–7.

Despite the variations, the general pattern appears clear; by 1979 the leadership of unions had less direct control over their memberships than previously. Inevitably, if union leaders entered into agreements or indeed disputes, with employees or with the government, they could no longer guarantee that their membership would accept their decisions. Perhaps surprisingly, Undy *et al.* indicate that this process of change owed more to the initiative of union leaders themselves than to pressure from members or outside agencies.

Union/government relations before 1979

How far were trade unions involved in politics in the UK before 1979? How far and in what ways did the internal divisions within the union movement influence their position? In this section I shall examine both of these questions.

Trade union involvement in politics

Middlemas's analysis is, intriguingly, at odds with most analyses of the role of the unions in the post-war period up to 1979. He shows that the TUC and, indeed, employers organisations, had been involved with government since the First World War. He argues that, a 'corporatist bias' developed in which informal functional representation replaced parliamentary representation as the main feature of British democracy (Middlemas, 1979, pp.371–4). However, he suggests that after the Second World War the power of the unions grew so that, by the 1964 General Election, the increase in the trade unions' political power, however negative, had become pre-eminent. Middlemas argues they enjoyed power because of their position in the economy. The commitment to full employment strengthened their position, weighting the balance between capital and labour in their favour (ibid., p.397). All governments were conscious of their power and their capacity to restrict economic growth and thus affect the government's re-election chances. As such, 'post-war cabinets worried more about production and the balance of payments, and pressed for settlements rather than strikes' (ibid., p.400). For this reason the TUC had privileged access to government:

> Whatever the case employers put up, as a matter of practical politics it became clear that even a Conservative Government would listen to the TUC, when talking of the national interest, rather than to its erstwhile mentors, the British Employers Confederation.
>
> (Middlemas, 1979, p.400)

As far as Middlemas is concerned, by the middle of the 1960s the employers organisations had recognised 'that the TUC had become so powerful that, as in 1919, they had to readjust, or abandon all pretensions to a share in political power'. (ibid., p.402).

Overall then, Middlemas stresses the key political role of unions; their structural position in the economy constrained the policy options open to government, while their political representations, mainly through the TUC, ensured that they prevented certain policies which would damage their interests being introduced, and, in the 1970s, positively shaped policy outcomes (see, especially ibid., pp.443–58).

In addition, Middlemas pays considerable attention to the key link between the Labour Party and the TUC, arguing that the unions act as a key constraint on Labour Party policy-making because of their dominance of the Party Conference, their key role as the financiers of the party and the presence of a significant number of

TU-sponsored MPs in the Parliamentary Labour Party (see Middlemas, 1979, especially pp 394–5, pp 448–2 and pp 440–4).

Much of Middlemas's analysis, at least of the period since 1945, is problematic. He fails to cite a number of the books which throw considerable doubt on his analysis, although they were published before his work. This chapter will take issue with Middlemas's conclusion that the unions were overwhelmingly powerful in the period before 1979. In this section, however, my aim is more modest. First, I wish to establish that the level of union political involvement grew significantly after 1964, less because of pressure from the unions than because of increased government involvement in union affairs. Second, I shall argue that Middlemas oversimplifies the relationship between the unions and the Labour Party.

After a thorough analysis of the activities of two large unions in the period between 1945 and 1970, Irving Richter concluded in 1973 that British unions had, as far as possible, avoided direct political involvement (Richter, 1973). Their overwhelming concern had been to improve the pay and conditions of their members. Of course, by the time Richter was writing, the situation had changed. The overt opposition by the trade union movement to the Labour Government's attempt at trade union reform in 1969 was the most definite move by the TUC into the political sphere, but, in fact, it is best understood as an outstanding example of a general trend. From 1966 until 1979 the trade unions were involved in politics to an extent to which they hadn't been previously.

The politicisation of British trade unions had two aspects with contradictory consequences. First, the unions were increasingly being incorporated by the government into decision-making. As Middlemas shows, this process had begun during the First World War, but there is no doubt that it underwent a major extension after the Second World War, and particularly in the 1960s and early 1970s under both Labour and Conservative Governments. In many ways this process of incorporation reflected the failure of successive British governments to solve basic economic problems and the related disillusionment with Keynesian demand management as a basis for economic policy. Governments believed that both the national interest and their own electoral success rested upon the achievement of a renewed economic prosperity. As such, they increasingly turned to economic planning and supply-side management as a solution to the economic crisis. This inevitably ensured the involvement of the trade unions more directly in consultations about policy-making. The National Economic Development Council (NEDC), and the little 'Neddies' which operated in certain industries, were the most obvious institutional manifestation of this trend in the 1960s. These were government advisory bodies – subsequently called quangos – with equal representation from the TUC, the Confederation of British Industry (CBI) and government. A number of similar tripartite agencies on which the TUC was represented were created in the 1960s and 1970s.

Unions were increasingly incorporated into the policy-making process. Hence government was, albeit in a more limited way than Middlemas suggests, asking the trade unions to co-operate in solving economic problems. At the same time, and in almost direct contradiction, government's concern with growing economic problems led them to intervene more in matters which affected trade unions. In effect, both Labour and Conservative Governments argued that in order to make industry more efficient and productive they needed to become increasingly involved in supply management in a way which threatened to restrict the autonomy of the unions; this move was reflected, as we saw in the last chapter, in *In Place of Strife* in 1969 and the Industrial Relations Act in 1971. Such intervention inevitably led to antagonism between unions and government which in turn politicised the unions.

The situation was compounded because it was a Labour Government which first introduced proposals to curtail the unions' autonomy. As we saw, the Labour Government's decision to reject the Donovan Committee's recommendations and legislate on industrial relations greatly disturbed the unions and changed the nature of the relationship between the two branches of the labour movement. The unions were no longer willing to rely upon the Labour Party to promote their political interests. The subsequent challenges to the unions' legal position inevitably brought the unions directly into the political arena, involving a series of strikes against each piece of legislation and non-cooperation with the administration of the 1971 Industrial Relations Act.

Governments also began to intervene consistently in collective bargaining. Obviously this development had two aspects. The extension of the public sector meant that the government was increasingly – directly or indirectly – an employer. Much more importantly, from the 1960s governments turned to prices and incomes policy as a means of controlling inflation. The main purpose of trade unions has been wage bargaining, and as such they reacted to incomes policy with, at best, reluctant acceptance or, most often, opposition. This opposition took two forms, both of which increased the politicisation of unions. First, the trade unions, through the TUC and their position within the Labour Party, attempted to change the policy. Second, strikes by individual unions in both the private or the public sector had obvious political repercussions.

There can be little doubt then, that trade unions became increasingly involved in politics from the end of the 1960s, or that they were more militant in support of their political ends. The inevitable consequence of this increased politicisation, as a number of authors have pointed out, was to strengthen the position of the TUC. There were a number of related reasons for this change. The unions' increased involvement in the policy-making process was co-ordinated by the TUC who selected the nominees to serve on the various committees. As the trade unions became more politically involved, and thus more reported, the media almost inevitably chose the General Secretary of the TUC as the spokesman for the union cause, a fact which increased the importance of the TUC generally and the position of the General Secretary specifically. Perhaps the major cause of the growing importance of the TUC, however, was the individual unions' perceptions both that organised and concerted action was necessary in defence of their position, and that the TUC General Council was the obvious forum for the development of strategy. Thus it was in the General Council that the effective strategy against the 1971 Industrial Relations Act was developed and the success of this strategy itself did much to strengthen the position of the TUC.

The organisational weaknesses of the British trade unions

By the mid-1970s the growth in importance of the position of the TUC, together with the unions' effective action against both the Labour and Conservative Governments' attempts to restrict their autonomy, gave the British union movement a growing belief that unity meant strength. However, although there were 12 million trade union members affiliated to the TUC in 1979, the resources of the individual unions and the TUC were not great. Indeed, the combined capital of the top 25 British unions was and is considerably less than that of the 26th largest British company. More importantly, the TUC's resources were and are limited in comparison with its smaller European counterparts; in 1979 only 100 staff were employed at Transport House with 30 officials in its regional offices. This meant that the staff of the TUC was not large enough to perform the range of tasks with which they were involved. Thus, one TUC official might be involved in discussions with Whitehall in an area with which 10 or 20 senior civil servants were concerned. Inevitably, the civil servants were almost always better prepared.

At the same time there were, and still are, many divisions within the union movement which affected its strategy and weakened its influence. First, different unions often had different interests which they advocated to government or within the Labour Party. Thus, low pay unions tended to favour, or at least be willing to accept, flat-rate incomes policies, while unions with a high percentage of skilled workers and greater economic leverage continued to press for free collective bargaining. Such dissension obviously made it difficult for the TUC to agree a policy and weakened its position in negotiations with government. Second, the TUC had, and has, little power to enforce its decisions, or ensure unity. This is particularly important because, while the TUC was involved in negotiations with government, the individual unions controlled the sanctions – the strike and non-cooperation with the administration of legislation – which could be used against government. It is true that, under Rules 11, 12 and 13 of the TUC's constitution, the General Council can expel member unions. Indeed, in the case of the Industrial Relations Act, 20 unions were expelled when they refused to deregister under the Act. However, in reality the TUC is only in a position to take such an action in dealing with a small union, or in a case where an individual union or group of unions is opposed by the combined weight of other unions, as was the case more recently with the EETPU. All this meant that when the TUC entered into an agreement with the government or, indeed, opposed government policy, it couldn't, and cannot, be sure that individual unions will support it. In other words, the TUC is effective only when the trade union movement is united. It is not often united.

As we saw earlier, Undy *et al.*, 1981, show that in many unions power has been devolved from the centre. In the field of collective bargaining, there was a growth in plant bargaining and therefore a considerable expansion in the role and power of the shop stewards. This diffusion of power meant that individual union leaders couldn't necessarily ensure that their shop stewards, or indeed their rank and file members, would accept any agreement they had negotiated although, of course, there are formal sanctions and informal pressures which leaders can exercise in an attempt to assert their authority.

Finally, national union leaders or shop stewards may be out of step with their members. Certainly Moran's study of the Post Office Workers Union indicated that its leadership was more concerned about politics and legislation than its membership (Moran, 1974). Similarly Fosh, in a study of the Iron and Steel and Kindred Trades Association, indicated that union activists had significantly different levels of knowledge of, and views about, politics from the ordinary members (Fosh, 1981). This doesn't necessarily mean, as some commentators might have us believe, that all union leaders were radicals. Indeed Fosh's study shows that the activists she studied had fairly modest reformist aims. However, it does mean both that union leaders must be wary of adopting too radical policies for fear of alienating their more conservative members, and that union leaders cannot be sure that their members will accept their recommendation to strike, or indeed to settle.

Certainly Undy *et al.* demonstrate that unions were not all hierarchically structured with leaderships which could dragoon their members into accepting policies they opposed. Some unions were less democratic and their leaderships more radical, but they were by no means the norm. At the same time, and more importantly here, the divisions between unions and within unions inevitably weakened their position and bargaining power.

The trade unions' access to the political sphere

There is no doubt that the trade unions became more politically involved in the 1970s, but what form did this involvement take? How did trade unions attempt to influence political decisions? It is common in the literature to identify three channels of access used by interest groups: Westminster, Whitehall and political parties. In the case of the trade unions almost all contacts with Parliament are with Labour MPs; the TUC has no contact with the Conservative Party. In this section, therefore, we shall concentrate upon the trade unions' contact with the Labour Party both inside and outside Parliament, and on union contacts with Whitehall which existed regardless of the party in power.

Trade unions and the Labour Party

Timothy May's book, *Trade Unions and Pressure Group Politics*, deals exclusively with the political strategy and tactics of unions until 1974 (May, 1975). May sees the close historical ties between unions and the Labour Party as crucial to trade union political strategy. In fact, the TUC, and indeed individual unions, attempted, and still attempt, to influence Labour Party and Labour Government policy in five distinct arenas: the Parliamentary Labour Party (PLP); the Labour Party Conference; the National Executive Committee (NEC); the Trade Union – Labour Party Liaison Committee; and in the constituency parties.

Table 2.3 presents data on the number of trade-union-sponsored MPs in Parliament between 1955 and 1987. In the post-war period the percentage of sponsored MPs fluctuated between 31 per cent (after 1945) and 42 per cent (after February 1974). So the proportion of union-sponsored MPs in the Labour Party remained relatively stable, although the numbers sponsored by each union changed; in particular, the number sponsored by the larger unions, the TGWU, the GMBATU and the AUEW increased, while the number sponsored by the NUM declined. However, these MPs hardly represent a radical force in the Labour Party, although by 1979 they were a little more radical than the average members of the PLP. While there were 54 Tribune Group members in the PLP after the 1979 election, representing 20 per cent of PLP membership, 23 per cent of the sponsored MPs resigned the whip to join the SDP after the 1979 election.

It would be misleading to suggest that relations between the trade unions and the PLP were close. The individual unions tended to ignore their sponsored MPs and approach ministers through the TUC. So when the trade unions opposed the Labour Government's trade union reforms in 1968–9, many trade-union-sponsored MPs complained that they were not consulted or briefed at all by their unions. Indeed, after a review of this period, Ellis and Johnson claim: 'At no stage did any union leader or conference attempt to

Table 2.3 *Trade-union-sponsored MPs, 1955–87*

Trade Unions	1955	1959	1964	1966	1970	1974	1974	1979	1983	1987
Total trade-union-sponsored MPs	95	92	120	127	112	127	126	134	115	104
Total Labour MPs	277	258	317	363	287	301	319	269	209	229
% Trade-union-sponsored MPs	34	36	38	35	39	42	39	50	55	45
National Union Mineworkers (NUM)	34	31	28	26	20	18	18	16	14	8
Transport and General Workers Union (TGWU)	14	14	21	25	19	23	22	22	25	24
General and Municipal Workers Union (GMWU)	4	4	9	11	12	13	13	14	11	10
National Union of Railwaymen (NUR)	8	5	6	7	5	6	6	12	10	8
Union of Shop Distributive and Allied Workers (USDAW)	9	9	10	8	7	6	5	5	2	5
Amalgamated Engineering Union (AEU)	6	8	18	18	16	22	21	21	17	11
Electrical, Electronic, Telecommunication & Plumbing Union (EETPU)	–	–	1	1	3	3	3	4	3	2
Association of Scientific, Technical and Managerial Staff (ASTMS)	–	–	–	1	2	6	10	8	10	4
Clerical and Administrative Workers (APEX)	2	2	3	4	3	6	6	5	3	5
National Union of Public Employees (NUPE)	2	1	2	5	6	6	6	7	4	6
Conservative Party sponsored MPs	18	16	20	18	17	16	16	17	8	2

Sources: Adapted from *British Political Facts and Times Guide to House of Commons,* 1987.

instruct its sponsored MPs how to behave or vote, and trade union MPs had themselves to solicit their sponsors' views' (Ellis and Johnson, 1970, p.25).

This pattern persisted because most unions agreed with politicians that an MP's first allegiance should be to the party. Certain union leaders, for example, Arthur Scargill (President of the National Union of Mineworkers), have consistently argued that unions should be able to mandate their sponsored MPs, but this view has found little support.

The conviction that trade-union-sponsored MPs should have autonomy was inevitably reinforced by the fact that these MPs, when subjected to cross-pressures, tended to disagree with their unions while supporting the leadership of the PLP. Indeed, after an analysis of trade-union-sponsored MPs in the previous 100 years Muller concludes: 'It is clear that expectations of party loyalty take precedence over union loyalty for all but a few MPs' (Muller, 1977, p.189). As Norton has shown, the MPs who defied the Labour whip most in the 1974–9 Parliament were almost without exception Tribune Group MPs (Norton, 1980, pp.431–6). Similarly, Longstreet's analysis indicates that the group of trade-union-sponsored MPs were slightly less likely to dissent in that Parliament than the Parliamentary Labour Party as a whole (Longstreet, 1984, Chap.5). Certainly, all the evidence indicates that these MPs tend to be supportive of, rather than antagonistic to, the PLP leadership.

May tends to oversimplify the position of the unions within the Labour Party Conference, a deficiency remedied by Minkin, who deals with the period between 1956 and 1970, although in a short appendix to the second edition he also considers the changing role of the trade unions between 1970 and 1977 (Minkin, 1978). He shows that it was only in the late 1960s that the trade unions began consistently to oppose the platform; so at both the 1966 and 1967 Conferences the Labour Party leadership sustained three defeats and in 1968 five. The pattern changed again when the Labour Party went into opposition and the party reconsidered its relationship with the unions. However, after the first flush of Labour's return to power in 1974, the pattern reasserted itself so that in both 1975 and 1976 the platform suffered seven reverses.

In fact, Conference regularly asserted its independence from the parliamentary leadership and in doing so was often led from the mid-1960s by a section of the trade unions, particularly when the revolt concerned industrial relations or prices and incomes policy. However, this assertion of independence by the Conference had little effect on the parliamentary leadership. Indeed, Minkin concludes decisively:

Thus by the time of the [1970] General Election, the Labour Party Conference appeared to have moved into irreversible decline as a political institution. Its authority over a Labour Government was openly defied. Its immediate decisions and even the response of the NEC was to some extent selective.

(Minkin, 1978, p.314)

Certainly trade unions usually supported the Labour leadership except on the industrial relations and incomes policy issues. What is more, the Conference led by the unions consistently rejected any efforts by the constituency parties to make the NEC, rather than the PLP leadership, ultimately responsible for the drafting of the manifestos. It is this change which would do most to restrict the autonomy of the PLP and it is not one that most unions have been willing to support. In theory, then, unions had, and have, enormous power at Conference. In practice, they most often exercised it when Labour governments proposed legislation to restrict the unions' autonomy or to impose a prices and incomes policy. Even then, the PLP leadership normally ignored their pressure. In addition, as Minkin indicates, the trade unions saw the Conference as their major channel of influence over a Labour Government.

In theory, the NEC of the Labour Party could be dominated by the trade unions as, with their voting supremacy at Conference, they could elect 19 of its 29 members. In theory also, it is the NEC which makes Labour Party policy between Annual Conferences. In practice, however, the pattern is rather different. Although the PLP need only have two representatives on the NEC, the leader and deputy leader who are ex-officio members, both numerically and in terms of influence the PLP has controlled it. In 1975 only 12 of the 29 members were trade unionists, while by 1979 that number had dropped to 10.

The preponderance of parliamentarians is easily explained. The seven members elected by and from the constituency parties and the five women elected by the whole Conference are almost inevitably MPs; other candidates are unlikely to be well enough known to ensure victory. In addition, a sizeable proportion of the 12 NEC members elected by and from the unions are always trade-union-sponsored MPs. One other point concerning the NEC membership is also important. The Standing Orders of the Labour Party make TUC General Council members ineligible for membership of the NEC. This means that the leaders of the large unions, who inevitably sit upon the General Council, are not NEC members – which obviously considerably weakens the credibility and the influence of the trade union representation on the NEC.

Until the 1970s the PLP leadership had little trouble controlling the NEC which was not a major source of radical pressure. The pattern began to change, however, when the Labour Party lost the 1970 election. In opposition the Home Policy Committee of the NEC produced a series of radical policies which were enshrined in the Labour Party Programme in 1973. There were serious divisions in the Labour Party leadership on this programme, particularly in relation to the plans for extensive intervention by government into industry. However, the programme was approved at Conference and measures to implement it were contained in the manifestos on which the Labour Party fought the 1974 elections. Subsequently, the legislation enacted by the government was a pale reflection of the original proposals. In particular, the plan to take equity holdings in profitable private enterprises through a powerful state holding company, and to require large companies to reach planning agreements with government about their plans for investment, employment, marketing, and so on, was almost totally emasculated as it went through the policy-making process. In fact, the 1975 Industry Act made planning agreements voluntary and created a National Enterprise Board which differed little from its predecessor, the Industrial Reorganisation Corporation.

One might speculate that such changes occurred because of the Labour Government's minority position and its increasing need to gain the support of the Liberal Party, which was opposed to such radical change. However, it must be borne in mind that much of the PLP leadership itself opposed these policies. Whatever the explanation, this case indicates a number of facts about the role of the NEC which are important for any analysis of the trade union position prior to 1979. First, the radical proposals came not from the trade union element but from the left of the Parliamentary Party and their supporters. The radical industrial policy was the brainchild of Stuart

Holland, then a university lecturer, later a back-bench Labour MP, but it was strongly supported by Tony Benn and Eric Heffer, prominent members of the PLP left wing. Second, the case makes it clear that even if the NEC develops radical policies, the PLP leadership is likely to, and able to, ignore them.

It is surprising that there has been no major study of the Trade Union–Labour Party Liaison Committee, despite the fact that for a period after its formation in January 1972 the Committee played a crucial role in the development of Labour Government policy. It was composed initially of six leading representatives each from the PLP, the NEC and the General Council of the TUC. The original initiative in the Committee, particularly in the field of industrial relations, was taken by the TUC, with Jack Jones, then General Secretary of the Transport and General Workers Union, playing a key role. By mid-1973 the Liaison Committee had approved in outline three Bills suggested by the General Council. The Social Contract, which was the basis of the Labour Party's manifestos in February and October 1974, assured trade unions that these three Bills would be enacted. The first Bill, which became law as the 1974 Trade Union and Labour Relations Act, repealed the 1971 Industrial Relations Act. The second Bill, which became law as the 1975 Employment Protection Act, extended trade union and individual worker's rights. The third proposed Bill, which was to deal with industrial democracy, was never introduced.

By 1976, however, the role of the Liaison Committee was less important. This decline was probably accelerated by the retirement of the leaders of the two largest unions, Hugh Scanlon, President of the Amalgamated Union of Engineering Workers (AUEW), and Jack Jones. They had been long-established and respected figures in both the union movement and Labour Party circles and although their replacements were heads of powerful unions they were unable to exercise the same influence. Moreover, Terry Duffy, who replaced Hugh Scanlon, was to the right of the AUEW. The importance of the Liaison Committee was further diminished as Labour's move into a minority position amidst an economic crisis ensured that both the International Monetary Fund and the Liberal Party had an increasing influence on policy.

Of course, it might be argued that the trade unions' influence was through their role in the constituencies, influencing candidate selection and policy formation. Unfortunately we have little evidence to draw on here although, as we have already seen, the grassroots policy preferences, even if successful at Conference, are frequently rejected by the PLP.

Barnes and Reid in an analysis of government-union relations, particularly in the 1964–74 period, feel able to claim:

> The relationship [between the Unions and the Labour Party] is at times that of patron and dependent. Ministers are free to form their own view of the public good and act on it on issues where the unions have little or no interest.
>
> (Barnes and Reid, 1980, p.222)

The material we have examined makes this statement appear extreme. This evidence suggests that it was, and indeed is, the PLP which determined Labour Government policy and that the PLP leadership was only influenced by the trade union when it so chose. As such, the unions influence on Labour policy was greatest during the 1974–5 period when the PLP leadership felt it needed TUC support, first to win the election, and then to operate the Social Contract. As we shall see, union influence on policy declined as the Labour Government lost its majority and became dependent on minority party support. This analysis also indicates that, while the trade unions used a number of channels of access to the Labour Party, particularly during the 1972–6 period, the most important channel was probably the least well known; the Trade Union-Labour Party Liaison Committee.

Trade unions and the government

Most economic interest groups are primarily concerned with establishing good relations with government. The trade unions are atypical in that their links with the Labour Party have been most important, but even they have been concerned to improve their links with government. Indeed, as May points out, trade unions have many formal and informal contacts with government (May, 1975). He suggests that in 1974 the unions had members on about 60 advisory bodies, a number which probably increased during the period of Labour Government. Such bodies varied widely in importance, with the most publicised being the NEDC, but the vast majority were merely advisory with no executive function. The TUC, like other economic interest groups, preferred bipartite discussions with ministers and civil servants where it felt its case could be put, and responded to, more directly.

In fact, the TUC had a wide range of informal contacts with Whitehall departments, most particularly with the Department of Employment (DEmp), and met fairly regularly with the Prime Minister. However, contacts between the TUC and the government are subject to frequent change, probably more frequent than is the case with other groups. In particular, during both the Heath and Thatcher Governments, relations deteriorated rapidly.

What is more, it is sometimes claimed that trade unions did not, and do not, have as good contacts with government as do the CBI, although this is clearly not a view shared by Middlemas. It is evident that civil servants and ministers share common social and educational backgrounds with industrial leaders which are very different from the backgrounds of trade union leaders. This does not mean that the CBI and Whitehall necessarily share common attitudes and policy objectives, but it may explain why industry had better informal contacts with the departments than has the TUC.

The tactics of the trade unions

We have already seen that the trade unions became more politically involved after the end of the 1960s – but what tactics did they use? As the last section indicated, in the 1970s the trade unions concentrated primarily upon influencing the Labour Party. In this respect, the Trade Union–Labour Party Liaison Committee was particularly important. However, this strategy was effective only because the Labour Party was in power for the second half of the decade. At the same time, the unions increasingly used direct action to strengthen their bargaining position.

In fact, the trade unions had, and still have, two main sanctions; non-cooperation with the administration of legislation and the strike weapon. The cost of administering legislation is high and becomes even higher if there is no co-operation from the people or organisations to whom the legislation is to be applied. It is not common for trade unions to use this sanction, but if they do so in a consistent way the effects can be dramatic. This was demonstrated between 1971 and 1974 when, as we saw in the last chapter, the 1971 Industrial Relations Act was rendered almost totally ineffective by the non-cooperation of the vast majority of unions.

When most people talk of the sanctions at the disposal of the unions, they are thinking first and foremost of the strike. Before the 1970s it was common to distinguish between a political strike and an economic strike; between a strike against the government and its policy and a strike against an employer. However, this distinction became less easy to sustain as governments intervened consistently in wage bargaining through prices and incomes policies; a strike against an employer could quickly assume political significance. Similarly, the combination of the growth of the public sector and increasing union militancy often entailed confrontation between the unions and the government.

In most literature, the use of the strike as a political weapon is played down. In an advanced industrialised society, however, organised workers in certain strategic industries can, by striking, cause a general dislocation of the economy. In the UK, most strategic industries are within the public sector: coal-mining, gas, electricity, water, railways, road transport, sea transport and health. Strikes in these areas have both direct and indirect influence on government action and policy as government reacts both as decision-maker and as employer. A number of extended strikes in these industries took place in the 1970s and had political and economic consequences – perhaps the most significant being the miners' strikes in 1972 and 1974 and the lorry drivers' and public sector workers' strikes in 1978–9.

Nevertheless, it is easy to overestimate the importance of the strike weapon, politically and economically. There can be little doubt that unions were willing to use it to forward their ends. At the same time, the lack of growth and the existence of an almost permanent incomes policy forced trade unions into conflict with government in order to forward their members' immediate economic interest. Furthermore, it is clear that the level of unemployment represents an important additional factor. The 1960s and early 1970s saw *relatively* low levels of unemployment. As unemployment increased rapidly at the end of the 1970s, so the trade unions' position weakened . Certainly, the threat of unemployment is an important weapon used by the employer in wage bargaining and by the government, both in pay negotiations in the public sector and in discussions with the TUC. Despite all this, however, the crux of the matter was the outcome. Interest groups possess resources and use tactics to forward an end. How successful were the unions in achieving their political and economic ends before 1979? This question will form the basis of the next section.

Trade union power in Britain before 1979

It is very difficult to assess the influence or power of interest groups given the plethora of conceptual, methodological and empirical problems involved. Nevertheless, sweeping assessments of the power of British trade unions prior to 1979 are often made with scant attention to these problems. In effect such assessments, which always seem to conclude that the unions had excessive power, emphasise either their economic or their political power.

I have examined in some detail the literature on the economic power of the unions elsewhere (Marsh and Locksley, 1983). Here we need only concern ourselves with the conclusions of that analysis. The evidence suggests that there is a union/non-union differential in wages; that is, unions increase wages above the level they would otherwise be, although there is little agreement as to the extent of this differential. In addition, there is evidence that unions reduce productivity because of restrictive practices and, of course, a number of observers have argued that union's wage demands were, and are, a major cause of inflation (ibid., pp.68–72).

It is interesting to note that most economists locate union power at the political rather than the economic level, although they present no evidence to support this conclusion (see, for example, Burton, 1979). Any detailed analysis of the literature on the political role of unions supports a different conclusion: unions enjoyed significant but limited political power. It is important to establish this point because any assessment of what has happened since 1979 must be based on an accurate judgement of the unions' role in the 1970s.

In the 1970s there was a resurgence of interest in the political role of unions which was accompanied by an increased emphasis upon their power. Finer's work is typical of those who view the dominance of the trade unions as axiomatic:

This trade union power which has brought successive governments to a standstill in recent years ... is manifestly a political power ... The government is no longer a neutral keeping the ring clear for contending interests. On the contrary, it is the prize for which the interests contend [sic]. The unions are not alone in seeking the prize. But for a number of reasons they are perhaps the most powerful of all contenders.

(Finer, 1974, pp.391, 398)

Similarly, Barnes and Reid boldly assert that '[the trade unions are] the most powerful interest group in the country' (Barnes and Reid, 1980, p.222).

Both these contributions, and similar ones by Milligan (1976) and Wigham (1976), point to a similar range of examples of union power: the successful action against the Labour Government's White Paper *In Place of Strife* in 1968–9; the success in defusing the effects of the 1971 Industrial Relations Act; the miners' action against the Heath Government pay policy in 1973–4; and the legislative concessions made to the unions under the Social Contract. There are already two excellent critical reviews of the material on the unions' political power in this period and there is no point in replicating them (Coates, 1983; Marsh and Locksley, 1983). However, three points require emphasis as they are important for the argument being developed here. First, the trade unions did enjoy significant negative power in the industrial relations field. Second, individual unions in strategic industries did exert considerable direct or indirect influence over government policy in the wages sphere. Third, during the period of the Social Contract the TUC, almost for the first time, had positive influence over policy. I shall deal at more length with each of these points looking at the four examples of the exercise of union power cited earlier. Even in these areas, however, there are important qualifications to any picture of overwhelming union power.

It is in the field of industrial relations policy where there was most evidence of the trade union's ability to restrict the autonomy of government in the late 1960s and early 1970s. As we saw in the last chapter, the Labour Government's legislative proposals, contained in *In Place of Strife*, and the Conservative Government's Industrial Relations Act both failed to change permanently the legal position of unions. However, two points are crucial. First, in both instances union opposition to the legislative proposals was only part of the reason for its failure. In 1969 the legislation based upon *In Place of Strife* was withdrawn, in large part because it was opposed by a significant section of the PLP led by James Callaghan (see Jenkins, 1970; Dorfman, 1979, pp.8–49). Similarly, the 1971 Industrial Relations Act was rendered a dead letter by the time the Conservatives were defeated in 1974, partly because large employers showed little interest in its provision. Second, although in both instances the unions had considerable power, it was a negative power. The legislation introduced by the Labour Government in 1974 and 1976 in most part merely returned the situation to that which existed before 1971.

Many authors also emphasise the crucial economic constraint which some unions held over government. As Dorfman says in the first paragraph of his second book on the subject:

> The disruptive power of unions in Britain has been painfully obvious in recent years. Strikes have had an impact throughout the society, stopping trains, darkening whole cities and even bringing down governments in dramatic political confrontations. The union movement has seemed at times an impregnable fortress of pressure group power, immune to the legal and political counter-force which Britain's elected leaders have attempted to bring against it.
>
> (Dorfman, 1983, p.1)

The stress here is on the individual unions' capacity to disrupt the government's incomes policy, and thus to effect detrimentally economic performance, indirectly reducing the government's re-election chances. In most cases, when this argument about the power of the unions in the 1970s is advanced, particular attention is paid to the position of the NUM which, with the print unions and the power workers, was generally viewed as a very powerful union. More specifically, the miners were seen as responsible for breaking the Heath Conservative Government's incomes policy in 1973–4 and, more colourfully, as 'bringing the Government down'.

There is no doubt that the miners did break Stage III of the Heath incomes policy, nor that when Heath called a General Election on the issue of union power, he lost. However, few things are simple, and the glib assertion that the miners brought the Heath Government down is just that: glib and simplistic. As the previous quotation indicates, Dorfman himself on occasions falls into the trap of oversimplification, but his book amply illustrates the fact that the picture is far more complex. Certainly it is true that the miners demanded to be treated as a special case under Stage III, and that any peaceful settlement would have involved them being considered as a special case. We might conclude that this is prima-facie evidence of the miners' privileged position, of their power, although it should be added that the Pay Board Relativities Report in 1974 suggested that they deserved to be treated as a special case. However, more important for the argument presented here is the conclusion Dorfman draws about Heath's inept political judgements:

> At nearly every point in dealing with the miners' dispute the Prime Minister – ironically, the leading politician in Britain – failed to understand and deal perceptively with the political choices he faced.
>
> (Dorfman, 1983, p.93)

Indeed, in early January 1974 the TUC offered the government a lifeline by promising that, if the government were prepared to give an assurance that it would make possible a settlement between the miners and the National Coal Board, other unions would not use this as an argument in negotiations for their own settlements. However, relations between the government and the TUC were still not good after the débâcle over the Industrial Relations Act. In this atmosphere, as Dorfman argues:

> The Government continued to reject the TUC offer, completely missing the opportunity for settling the dispute. The terms provided in effect for the counter-inflation policy that Heath himself had sought in bargaining sessions over many months. The TUC wanted and needed to restore its members to full-time work (at this time factories were working a three-day week); it was willing to pay the price necessary to win a settlement. The Prime Minister turned his back in anger.
>
> (Dorfman, 1983, p.100)

While in one sense the miners won, and this provides a good example of the leverage strategic unions can enjoy, this again is hardly a picture of overwhelming trade union power.

Despite all this, it is the period of Labour Government between

1974 and 1979 which is the most significant one for any judgement of union power prior to 1979. After all, some authors suggest that during this period the Labour Government was a creature of the trade unions. (See Barnes and Reid, 1980, especially p.222). The period of the Social Contract is important because it was during this time that the unions played a major role in the evolution of policy rather than merely affecting, often substantially, its implementation. My argument here is fourfold. First, unions, through the Liaison Committee, did have considerable positive influence on government policy in 1974 and 1975. Second, that the TUC's positive influence largely disappeared after 1976. Third, even in those areas where the unions achieved policy concessions, the administration of the legislation, once passed, was less favourable to them. Fourth, and most importantly, many analyses forget that the Social Contract between 1975 and 1978 *was first and foremost an incomes policy.*

During the period of conflict between the unions and the Conservative Government over the Industrial Relations Act, relations between the trade unions and the Labour Party substantially improved. After the dispute over *In Place of Strife* and the 1970 election defeat, the Labour Party wanted, and needed, to improve its relations with the unions. As we saw earlier, the structural manifestation of this new relationship was the Trade Union-Labour Party Liaison Committee. Dorfman presents a thorough analysis of the Social Contract period and the role of the Liaison Committee. As he says, the period was marked by remarkable co-operation between the unions and the Labour Government:

> It was co-operative primarily to the unions advantage between February 1974 and June 1975. After that [until] the middle of 1978 [the time when Dorfman was writing] it was co-operative primarily to the advantage of the [Government].
>
> (Dorfman, 1983, pp.131–2)

In the first few months the Labour Government made changes which can be regarded, at least in part, as concessions to the unions. In this way the government: ended the constraints on collective bargaining, while continuing and strengthening the system of price controls; increased pensions and raised taxes on the rich; repealed the Industrial Relations Act; and created an independent Arbitration and Conciliation Service.

After its re-election in October 1974, the government again made initial concessions to the unions. It honoured its commitments under the Social Contract, passing the Employment Protection Act (1975) and the Health and Safety at Work Act (1975) and amending the Trade Union and Labour Relations Act (1976). Despite this, however, change was in the air. In 1975 the government introduced a voluntary incomes policy, admittedly after extensive consultations with the TUC. Dorfman accepts the importance of this change:

> There was no mistaking the significance of the policy that the White Paper announced. The Labour Government had broken through the taboo against incomes policy which had stood as a cornerstone of union-Labour relations ever since the defeat of *In Place of Strife*. The growing fears at Congress House about the economy withered TUC resistance. Events sapped union strength and the Government took advantage, however much its buffering measures 'sweetened' the bitter medicine.
>
> (Dorfman, 1983, pp.120–21)

A year later in June 1976 the TUC Special Congress agreed a second year of restraint. Once again Dorfman emphasises the point:

> The delegates were unusually docile. Even Hugh Scanlon dropped his opposition, openly admitting and urging the delegates to accept that the TUC could do no better in this period when living standards were likely to fall even more.
>
> (Dorfman, 1983, p.124)

However, it wasn't only an incomes policy which the unions were forced to accept. In July 1976 the government, after minimal consultation with the TUC, announced large cuts in public expenditure. The Chancellor, Dennis Healey, told the TUC that public sector deficits could not continue at their high levels because spending would destroy government economic policy, increasing inflation by driving up interest rates and increasing the money supply. The government, led by the Treasury, and under pressure from national and international capital, was being converted to monetarism. Corporatist strategies based on supply-side management and inevitably involving the incorporation and, given it was a Labour Government, influence of unions, were moving out of fashion, largely as a result of pressure from other economic interests. As a result, not only was the public expenditure programme cut by £1 billion, but there was a relaxation of the price code, increased charges for prescriptions and school meals and cuts in food subsidies and spending on education. The TUC opposed all these changes with no success.

In October the Chancellor introduced more deflationary measures to prevent the export of capital and announced that the government would seek a loan from the International Monetary Fund (IMF). As a condition of the loan, further cuts in public expenditure were accepted by the government. When the TUC General Council met the government next in early 1977 Dorfman describes their strategy as one of 'acquiescence' (Dorfman, 1983, pp.129–31). They refused to agree formally to a third year of wage restraint but accepted its implementation. At this stage the government, in a minority situation, committed to the stimulation of the private sector as a way to growth, and increasingly steeped in monetarist doctrines, was more concerned with other interests than those of the TUC. It needed the unions' co-operation or acquiescence in wages policy, but no more. As Coates, in his excellent review of the whole tenure of the Labour Government says:

> The Governments concern was always to reassure industry about its commitment to a healthy private sector and about its willingness to subordinate its social programme to the gaining of greater industrial production.
>
> (Coates, 1980, p.57)

This strategy necessitated wage control and public expenditure cuts and, as Coates argues:

> The industrial struggles of 1978–9, and the subsequent election defeat, should not distract our attention from the remarkable degree of working-class industrial restraint that Ministers managed to orchestrate prior [to the 'Winter of Discontent'].
>
> (Coates, 1980, p.260)

In the Social Contract period the unions did make a number of legislative gains, but for most of its life the Social Contract was mainly an incomes policy. It was an incomes policy based at first on the active co-operation and, subsequently, on the acquiescence of the unions. In the end it collapsed in the 'Winter of Discontent' of 1978–9 as the TUC could no longer deliver the support of its member unions and union leaders could no longer deliver the support of their members. This latter period showed again the negative power of certain unions and is well documented in Dorfman's second book. However, the major reason for the collapse of the incomes policy was that the Social Contract had collapsed. The government from June 1975 onwards took little notice of the TUC's advice or interests. In so far as the Labour Government had adopted a corporatist strategy – in fact it would be better to say they had developed a corporatist relationship with the unions – by late 1975 that strategy was abandoned. The government, under economic pressure perhaps, adopted a limited form of monetarism as the basis of its economic strategy. Such a strategy, with its stress on public expenditure cuts and monetary control and with unemployment as the inevitable consequence, was bound to undermine the relationship between the unions and government.

Obviously individual unions still exercised economic muscle after 1975. However, if unions are to enjoy political influence, they almost inevitably need governments to be willing to talk to the TUC. In fact, they probably need governments to advocate and operate a corporatist economic strategy. At the same time, their political position is likely to be stronger under a Labour Government. By late 1975, whilst they still had a Labour Government in power, it was a government which was preoccupied with the needs, and therefore the demands, of national and international capital. It was a government which was moving away from a corporatist strategy and embracing a monetarist position. As such, the TUC's role faded and the decline of their influence clearly dates from 1975.

Conclusion

This review of the political power of the unions prior to 1979 suggests a number of conclusions:

1. Heroic assertions concerning the overwhelming power unions enjoyed before 1979, and particularly in the period between 1974 and 1979, are clearly misguided. Union power was limited even at its height.

2. In fact, the limited nature of union power prior to 1979 is well reflected in its decline since. Middlemas, writing in the late 1970s, expected union power to grow further. Indeed, it is worth quoting him at length:

> It is hard to see trade unions' economic political power confined to the old, negative formulation. Even if trade union leaders remain diffident about claiming the full political potential of their movement, for fear of public recrimination, the movement's representative function has increased, over a wider area of state policy, as a result of the 'social contract' and the powers granted by legislation after 1974; and it is unlikely that a future government will make the mistake of treating the TUC as a mere agent.
>
> (Middlemas, 1979, pp.450–54)

Of course, any social scientist who makes predictions can be wrong; it is a hazardous business. However, Middlemas' poor prediction stems less from his failure to foresee the future, or from Mrs Thatcher's subsequent transformation of the whole pattern of industrial relations in Britain, and more from his failure to read the past, and in particular, his inflated view of the unions' political role and political power prior to 1979.

3. The unions' position was already weakened politically before 1979. When the Thatcher Government was elected in that year, it was Conservative, monetarist and elected, at least in part, because of the unpopularity of the unions as a result of the 'Winter of Discontent'. Things could not get better, but they were already bad.

3

The Origins, Development and Content of the Conservative Legislation

Most observers agree that the industrial relations legislation introduced by the Conservatives in the 1980s has significantly affected the power of the unions. In this chapter I will examine the origins, development and content of that legislation. As such, the chapter is divided into four sections. The first section looks at the development of Conservative industrial relations policy in opposition between 1974 and 1979. Here I suggest that even in 1978 Conservative policy on the issue was uncertain and argue that the Winter of Discontent in 1978–9 gave a focus to that policy; for this reason the second section deals with the Winter of Discontent. The third section examines the evolution of policy when the Conservatives came to power. I pay particular attention to the change in ideology and pace which occurred in 1981, when Norman Tebbit replaced James Prior as Secretary of State for Employment, and to the importance of the muted trade union reaction to the legislative proposals, which meant that the key problem of compliance receded. The final section then outlines the scope and content of the legislation.

The development of Conservative industrial relations policy in opposition, 1974–9

It is far too easy with hindsight to characterise Conservative industrial relations policy as a developed, coherent one which was evolved in opposition and carried out in government. Hindsight is a dangerous tool of analysis. In fact, far from being consistent and coherent, Conservative industrial relations policy in opposition was imprecise, reflecting the tensions which existed in the party. One strand of

Conservative thinking was most directly reflected in a strategy document called *Stepping Stones* prepared by John Hoskyn and Norman Strauss for Mrs Thatcher. They argued that 'the one precondition for [economic] success will be a complete change in the role of the trade union movement' (quoted in Young, 1989, p.115). In contrast, Jim Prior personified another strand of Conservative thinking; he was committed to change with the trade unions and gradual and limited change in their legal position. In late 1978 it was impossible to predict what future policy would be because the Conservatives were faced with such contradictory views and pressures.

There were a significant number of factors which suggested that the Conservatives might move towards a policy inspired by individualism after 1974. The defeat of Mr Heath in February 1974 left an indelible mark on the Conservative Party to put the unions in their place. As Dorfman pointed out, the importance of Heath's mauling by the unions in general, and the NUM in particular:

lies in the legacies which the experience produces for union–Conservative Government relations in future. The prospect is that the union movement will suffer from this relationship, and probably suffer more than will future Conservative Governments.
(Dorfman, 1983, p.103)

This antipathy to the unions was increased with the election of Mrs Thatcher as leader in 1975. She had no love for the unions and was anxious to distance herself from Mr Heath's style of leadership. In particular, she attacked his 'U' turn which embraced collectivism, and his failure to curb union power. This inevitably meant that she stood to gain by taking a strong stand on trade union reform. She was particularly impressed with Hoskyn and Strauss's strategy document (Young, 1989, pp.115–17).

In addition, the Conservatives' emerging commitment to monetarism provided another justification for tough action against the unions. As Moran points out:

For ideological monetarists there is a logical solution: even the operation of free market mechanisms by linking free wage bargaining and tight control of the money supply with legislation designed to curb the power of unions to distort market forces.
(Moran, 1979, p.48)

However, there were strong pressures mitigating against an individualist or monetarist policy on unions. In particular, there were the four related yet separate problems involving: consent; compliance; electoral credibility; and party management.

There was never a problem of consent as far as public opinion was concerned. As Table 3.1 indicates, the public have supported union reform of the sort developed by Mrs Thatcher, ever since the Labour Government's *In Place of Strife* proposals in 1968–9. Nevertheless, the 1971 Industrial Relations Act fell in part because it was not broadly acceptable to large employers, let alone to the unions who had hardly been consulted by Robert Carr as the legislation was pushed through. It was for this reason that *Stepping Stones* paid such attention to the problem of gaining public and élite support for policies to curb union power (Young, 1989, pp.116–17).

The problem of consent, however, was dwarfed by the problem of compliance. The main reason for the failure of the earlier legislation was that the unions didn't comply with it. This not only ensured continued and extensive confrontation, but was also a major reason why large employers felt, at best, ambivalent towards the legislation. In addition, after Mr Heath's defeat, the public clearly viewed the Labour Party as more likely to be able to deal with the unions; they felt that unions were too powerful and favoured reform, but viewed the Conservatives as unlikely to deal effectively with them given Mr Heath's defeat. As such, the Conservatives needed to establish their capacity to deal with the unions in order to restore electoral credibility. It was not surprising then, that the Conservatives in opposition became crucially concerned with the problems of consent, credibility and compliance. However, they were also conscious of the divisions which existed within the Party which meant party management continued to be a problem.

In opposition the Conservatives remained anxious to retain electoral support for their proposals. As Jim Prior, then Employment spokesman, said as late as February 1979, it was important to recognise 'that the law has a part to play in industrial relations, but there is a need to ensure widespread public support for such legislation' (Prior, quoted in Riddell, 1983, p.36).

They were also aware that it was crucial that any legislation passed could be effectively enforced. The Conservatives didn't expect to agree with the unions on the shape of any legislation but Prior continually stressed, and Mrs Thatcher accepted, the need to

Table 3.1 *Public opinion on government proposals/legislation on trade unions, 1969–84 (% approving)*

| | Year and month | | | | | | | | | |
| | 'In place of strife' | | Industrial Relations Act | | Thatcher legislation | | | | | |
Issue	Jun '69	Aug. '69	June '70	Dec.'70	1979	1980	1981	1982	1983	1984
Secret ballots before strikes	63	65	68	69	84	82	81	83	83	NA
Closed shops should be ended/severely restricted	NA	53	55	NA	67	67	65	69	69	NA
Compulsory cooling-off period before a strike	61	64	69	73	NA	NA	NA	NA	NA	NA
Ban on secondary picketing	NA	NA	NA	NA	73	68	66	67	NA	NA
Union leaders should be elected by secret ballot	NA	NA	NA	NA	NA	NA	NA	NA	88	NA
Are political strikes justified?	NA	NA	NA	NA	NA	NA	NA	67	75	78

Source: Gallup data reported in D. Marsh (1990)

discuss proposed legislation with the unions in opposition, and subsequently in power (see Moran, 1979, p.51). More importantly, if Mrs Thatcher was to establish her credibility as a Prime Minister, and later her governing competence in office, she needed the policies to be accepted by union leaders and members. The problems of consent and compliance thus strongly mitigated against any quick, large-scale, change in industrial relations.

It is hardly surprising that, faced by a choice between ideology and pragmatism, pragmatism triumphed. Certainly in this field as in many others, Mrs Thatcher indicated that in so far as she is an ideologue, such commitments are tempered by a large amount of electoral pragmatism (see Young and Sloman, 1986, pp.73–4). In addition, there was a significant gap between the rhetoric and the substance of policy, largely because of the problems of party management. Moran, writing in 1978, made the point very well:

> It is perhaps a measure of the difficulty of managing a Con-
> servative Party increasingly characterised by internal dissent and
> factional division that Mrs Thatcher has adopted a strategy more
> common to Labour Party leaders: using the rhetoric of one
> tradition while supporting the substance of another.
>
> (Moran, 1979, pp.52–3)

Clearly, in opposition Mrs Thatcher preferred a solution based upon ideological individualism which would severely reduce union power; this fitted with her antipathy toward unions and her growing commitment to monetarism and was reflected in the fact that while she backed the Prior line in public, she supported the Hoskyn's position in private (Young, 1989, p.117).

However, her Shadow Cabinet was divided (see Moran, 1979, p.47), the electorate were unsure of the Conservatives' ability to deal with the unions and it was no good proposing, or introducing, legislation which wouldn't stick. For this reason, it was the voluntary collectivist approach to industrial relations policy-making which continued to dominate, even after the 'Winter of Discontent' where the emphasis was upon gradual change and frequent consultation with the interested parties, particularly the unions. In this vein, at the 1976 Party Conference Prior emphasised that there would be no ban on the closed shop (see Moran, 1979, p.46). In 1977 he went even further: 'If Mrs Thatcher is ever unwise enough to make me

Secretary of State for Employment there will be an absence of legislation' (quoted in Moran, ibid., p.46).

Similarly, in 1977 *The Right Approach to the Economy*, a statement of party economic policy, rejected any simple attempt to ban closed shops; instead it suggested that they should only be established after a secret ballot. Throughout, the emphasis was upon voluntary agreement with a code of practice and ultimately legislation as a backstop. Mrs Thatcher backed Mr Prior's line, not because she supported it, but because it appeared the pragmatic option. The Winter of Discontent significantly altered the situation, although it didn't transform it.

The Winter of Discontent

The Winter of Discontent marked an important watershed for the Labour Government, the Conservative Opposition and the trade unions. As a result of this industrial unrest, and Jim Callaghan's decision not to call an election in Autumn 1978, the Conservatives won the election. In addition, the unrest strengthened the resolve of the Conservatives to reform the unions, hardened up their proposals and increased public support for such reform.

In essence, the conflict between the unions and the government began before the last pay restraint agreement between the TUC and the government expired on 31 July 1978. The TUC was opposed to any new agreement; indeed they argued that, even if an agreement was reached, it could not be honoured given the resentment building up on the shop floor. Labour ministers acknowledged the problem but couldn't live with the answer. As Dorfman puts it:

> The glue of comraderie had to be made to hold at least long enough to produce a victory at the election which was certain to be held within the next year.
>
> (Dorfman, 1983, p.61)

When no agreement appeared likely, the government issued a White Paper on 21 July 1978 which established a new pay norm of 5 per cent. The action surprised the TUC, who felt it would inevitably lead to confrontation, but they comforted themselves with the belief that it was nothing more than an election strategy; the government would fight the election on the policy but quietly defuse it after winning.

As such, while voicing their opposition to the White Paper, the TUC encouraged the Prime Minster to call an autumn election. Callaghan seemed to share this view and the TUC Congress in September 1978 resembled an election rally. However, only days later the Prime Minister announced there would be no election. This decision exacerbated relations between the unions and the Labour Government; the union leaders felt they had been deceived and used by Callaghan. Indeed, the General Council meeting of 25 October explicitly mandated its negotiating team not to agree a new pay deal in talks with Labour ministers (see Dorfman, 1983, p.68). An agreement did emerge from this meeting, but it was a paper agreement. The TUC merely agreed that it would send advice on 'responsible' bargaining to union negotiators. However, even this agreement was rejected by the General Council which indicated the strength of opposition to incomes policy. The main crunch would clearly come in the public sector when the government attempted to hold the line on the 5 per cent norm.

In fact, the first major industrial unrest occurred with a lorry drivers' strike, which involved extensive secondary picketing. Callaghan's reaction was predictable. He attempted to press Moss Evans, General Secretary of the union involved, the Transport and General Workers' Union (TGWU), to control the strikers, and the TUC to back his pressure. Once again, Dorfman makes the point:

> [Callaghan's] message was quite simply that the strikers, particularly the lorry drivers' strike, were literally killing the Government and playing into the hands of the Tories. And, the additional message was that unless they could act more vigorously to control secondary picketing the Government would have no recourse but to declare the State of Emergency that they had so far held off.
> (Dorfman, 1983, p.81).

The TUC leadership responded; it was afraid of the consequences of doing otherwise. What is more, Evans issued a new set of recommendations which controlled the picketing fairly effectively (Dorfman, 1983, p.92). Subsequently, the individual haulage companies settled, with most settlements around 15 per cent.

Once the lorry drivers' strike was settled the disputes over public sector pay came to the fore. Now, however, the TUC and the

Government were involved in serious negotiations (see Dorfman, 1983, pp.84–5 for a list of the contacts between 23 January and 9 February) about the crisis. The TUC's change of heart probably owed more to the effect the action was having on workers not engaged in disputes than to any desire to throw a lifebelt to the Labour Government. Nevertheless, the disputes dragged on, with rubbish on the streets and the dead unburied. The Prime Minister offered a compromise which involved the establishment of a Commission to study comparative pay in the private and public sectors. The TUC, and the leaderships of the four unions involved, were inclined to accept the offer. However, the Executive Committee of the National Union of Public Employees (NUPE), the largest union involved, recommended its membership to reject the offer and continue with the strike. The membership voted to reject the offer. As Dorfman argues:

> To the public at large the Government still seemed unable to get matters under control – right up until the day [28 March 1979] it lost the vote of censure in the House of Commons.
>
> (Dorfman, 1983, p.90)

Before we discuss the consequences of the Winter of Discontent, it is worth briefly dealing with its causes. Two points are particularly important because they have resonance elsewhere in this book. First, it is evident that the unrest resulted from the collapse of incomes policy. Incomes policies automatically invoke tensions for unions and for their relations with government. Unions' main *raison d'être* is wage negotiation; incomes policy removes that purpose and, over time, increases unrest among union members. It was clear that by 1978 the union leadership could not have delivered an incomes policy to the Labour Government, even if they had so wished. This observation raises two points discussed further elsewhere. Free collective bargaining clearly reduces the opportunities for tensions between government and unions, and the Conservatives have benefited from this fact since 1979. At the same time, any future Labour Government is also likely to flounder on the question of incomes policy.

Second, the Winter of Discontent revealed again the weakness of trade union leadership generally and of the TUC in particular. Dorfman perhaps overemphasises the importance of that weakness as it is a perennial theme of his work; in fact, it is not easy to see how other leaders could have defused the conflict in 1978–9 (Rodgers also emphasises weak union leadership, 1984, pp.172–3). Nevertheless, it is true that, with the retirement of Scanlon and Jones, the level of experience present on the General Council was significantly reduced and that changes in the structure and organisation of some unions, particularly the TGWU, had weakened the leadership's control over the membership (Dorfman, 1983, pp.72–3). In addition, the TUC, as always, was unable to mandate its members, given the limited sanctions it has over member unions. Certainly, as we shall see, failures in union leadership clearly affected Mrs Thatcher's strategic judgements about industrial relations legislation after her electoral victory.

The consequences of the Winter of Discontent were very significant. The views within the Conservative Party hardened (Riddell, 1983, p.37). Even Jim Prior concurred: 'During the winter of 1978–9, the Labour Government's 'Winter of Discontent', it became clear that the unions were far exceeding their proper role' (Prior, 1986, p.155).

Mrs Thatcher's reaction was not atypical; she 'made' policy on her feet without consultation with colleagues. In January, she proposed that the government: provide funds for postal votes for elections and strike ballots; withdraw social security payments from strikers; impose a picketing law; require secret ballots before strikes; restrict secondary picketing; deal with the closed shop; and end the right to strike in public utilities (see Dorfman, 1983, pp.77–9).

These were all ideas which had been present in Conservative thinking, but they were significantly more radical than the previous policy commitments. The point is easily made if we consider one of Moran's major conclusions, bearing in mind again that this was written in 1978:

> The direction of policy is thus apparently set: a steady retreat in the direction of voluntary collectivism, punctuated by occasional genuflections towards the individualist traditions. This progress will only be halted if the problem of party management becomes so acute that demands stimulated by individualism become irresistible. The likelihood of this happening depends very much on external events.
>
> (Moran, 1979, p.46)

The Winter of Discontent was clearly such an event. It allowed Mrs Thatcher to reveal more of her real views with less concern for the electoral consequences (see Young, 1989, p.117). It strengthened her resolve and her gut-reaction that the union issue could be a vote winner. Perhaps more importantly, it gave Conservative industrial relations policy a focus; they could claim, and did in the 1979 manifesto, that union reform was essential to prevent situations like the Winter of Discontent in which the country tore itself 'apart in increasingly bitter and calamitous industrial disputes' (Moran, 1979, p.284).

At the same time, the crisis weakened the credibility of the Labour Government and in so doing reduced a major electoral problem for the Conservatives. As Holmes argues:

> Up to the Winter of Discontent which helped to destroy the Callaghan administration electorally, the Conservatives faced a major political problem: how to convince the electorate, wearied by strikes and industrial disruption, that they could work with the unions...it was the unions who, unwittingly, came to the Conservatives' aid. By their highly unpopular industrial action in the winter of 1978–9 they destroyed Labour's claim to be the party who could 'work with' ...the unions and finally laid the ghosts of 1974 which the Conservatives had, themselves, failed to exorcise.
>
> (Holmes, 1985, pp.210–11)

The decline in the public perception of the governing competence of the Labour Government is clearly reflected in the opinion poll data. In June 1978 only 4 per cent of the population thought strikes were the most urgent problem facing the country; by November 1978 the figure rose to 17 per cent, and in January and February 1979 it topped 50 per cent. Similarly, while in October and November 1978 as many people thought the government were handling the economy correctly as thought it wasn't, by March 1979 almost 40 per cent more thought its policy was wrong than thought it right. At the same time, as Table 3.1 indicates, the unions became increasingly unpopular, while the government's handling of industrial relations increasingly became the focal point of criticism. The electorate believed that the Labour Government had mishandled the economy and the unions, and presumably that the Conservatives could hardly do worse. At the same time, as we shall see in the next section, the

Conservatives were offering the public the type of unions they had always wanted; apolitical unions unable to pursue pay claims by using unsavoury tactics.

The Conservatives in power: the triumph of individualism

The Conservatives clearly didn't have a coherent industrial relations policy in opposition which they carried through in power. They were divided in opposition and it was the Winter of Discontent which gave their policy a focus and credibility which it had previously lacked. Even so, the policy was initially stronger on rhetoric than content and still informed by a voluntary collectivist ideology, rather than an individualist one.

On her election Mrs Thatcher inherited a strong strategic position in relation to the trade unions. The economic situation and, in particular, rising unemployment and de-industrialisation, weakened the unions' position. The unions' standing was at a low ebb given the Winter of Discontent. Changes in the trade union leadership, together with the persistent failure of the TUC to exercise a leadership role, meant that the movement was likely to be weaker in its dealings with the new government than it had been in 1970 when Mr Heath was elected.

Mrs Thatcher was also aided by the fact that, while compliance was still a major problem, the majority of the population was even more strongly committed to trade union reform than they had been at the time of *In Place of Strife* or the 1971 Industrial Relations Act (see Table 3.1). In addition, as we have seen, the Winter of Discontent had reduced their credibility problem by destroying Labour's image of competence.

Mrs Thatcher was also able to learn from Mr Heath's mistakes; in particular, she was determined, despite her own preferences, to proceed slowly. Compliance remained the major problem. Here, the Conservatives were helped by two further factors. First, Mr Prior, the new Secretary of State for Employment, was widely respected in the trade union movement. He was known as a moderate within the Conservative Party who was committed to a continuance of the voluntary collectivist style of industrial relations. He also had been involved in discussions with trade union leaders in opposition and these were continued in office. Second, the existence of major divisions in the Conservative Party on industrial relations, rather perversely helped Mr Prior in his discussions with the TUC. Geoffrey Howe and Norman Tebbit could make speeches advocating tougher legislation while Prior was more conciliatory. As such, Prior was seen by the trade unions as by far the least of the evils available. It must also be remembered that industrial relations, while an important aspect of the incoming government's, plans was not as critical to Mrs Thatcher as it had been to Mr Heath. Economic policy was overwhelmingly the prime concern of the Conservatives in 1979; they aimed to transform the British economy, reducing inflation through the use of monetary control. This meant that in economic terms union reform was no more than an adjunct to monetary policy, although in political terms it was obviously more significant as a test of governing competence.

It is clear that, while the position in 1979 was fairly favourable to Mrs Thatcher and the Conservatives, they were inhibited from radical change by two main factors. First, the monetarists were not, as yet, totally dominant in the Cabinet and Prior and Whitelaw, in particular, were strongly opposed to sweeping union reforms. Second, they were still crucially concerned about the problem of compliance. The major thing they had learnt from the Heath years was that concerted union action, with tacit support from large employers, could prevent industrial relations legislation from being effective.

It was for those reasons that the manifesto commitment of 1979, and the 1980 Employment Act, proposed relatively small changes in industrial relations law. With hindsight this may appear to be the first step in an inevitably growing litany of legislation, and certainly each subsequent Act has, in important senses, built upon previous ones. However, it seems much more accurate to conclude that, while the Conservatives had other putative plans, the subsequent legislative development was not even predictable, let alone inevitable, in 1980. In fact, two crucial factors affected this subsequent development. First, Mrs Thatcher changed the composition of her Cabinet as soon as she felt able to assert her authority, so that individualism replaced voluntary collectivism as the dominant ideology underpinning industrial relations policy. Second, the trade unions' reaction to legislation was muted and, as such, the Conservatives' fear of compliance declined and their confidence in pushing ahead increased.

The Conservatives fought the 1979 election committed to trade union reform but their proposals were not radical; Mr Prior's cautious approach had been backed by Mrs Thatcher and the Cabinet. In fact, the manifesto contained a series of pledges: the law on picketing would be tightened up and, in particular, secondary picketing would be made unlawful; the law on secondary action would be reviewed and amended so that the immunity would be removed in cases where such action was involved; the operation of the closed shop would be restricted, in particular existing employees in closed shops who were dismissed should have the right of appeal to the courts and be entitled to compensation, while new closed shops could only be established after a vote by secret ballots; secret ballots for union elections and on other important issues should be encouraged by providing public funds for ballots; and unions should be made to bear their fair share of the cost of supporting members on strike.

As we have seen, industrial relations was not the first priority of the Thatcher Government. In addition, they were anxious to avoid Heath and Carr's mistakes so Prior was involved in a series of meetings with the TUC. For these reasons the government didn't rush into legislation.

Obviously, Prior's role was crucial. As Dorfman puts it:

> James Prior as Employment Minister became a kind of ambassador to the TUC. His position as it evolved was quite unique. Because of his personal relations with trade unionists, his role as a senior Tory, as a member of the Cabinet, and most importantly as an adversary of Mrs Thatcher, Prior gained credibility in a multi-faceted role.
>
> (Dorfman, 1983, p.113)

Prior strongly believed in the voluntary collectivist view of industrial relations. He was also firmly committed to consultation and met on a number of occasions with a team of 10 or 12 union leaders drawn from the TUC's Employment Committee and led by Len Murray, TUC General Secretary, and Harry Urwin of the TGWU (see Prior, 1986, p.157). Indeed, Prior's position is well summed up in a passage from his autobiography:

> Trying to keep our channels to the unions open and clear was an almost impossible task. At the Cabinet before the first TUC

Annual Conference after the May 1979 election, Margaret supported Geoffrey Howe's plan for a major speech. I took the
opportunity to advise colleagues on the need to exercise the
utmost caution over any comments before or during the TUC.
Union moderates were having a tough battle behind the scenes to
hold the union movement to a reasonable approach. Strident
statements by Ministers could only undermine them. I did not
want my consultations with the TUC on union reforms wrecked,
nor did I want to see the creation of a confrontationist atmosphere
on economic policy.

(Prior, 1986, p.156–7)

However, as this quote indicates, there was opposition in the Cabinet
notably from Geoffrey Howe, the Chancellor (see Prior, ibid.,
especially p.162), who made two strong public speeches in favour of
tougher legislation (see Prior, ibid., pp.157, and 164). Once again,
Prior's position was approved in Cabinet and the bill published in
December 1979 honoured the majority of the manifesto pledges and
reflected Prior's views:

The Employment Bill was introduced in December 1979. My
purpose was to bring about a lasting change in attitude by
changing the law gradually, with as little resistance, and therefore
as much by stealth, as was possible. There were also dangers in
having tougher legislation which employers might in practice be
afraid to use. It would be wrong to pass legislation which the
courts could not enforce, as had been the case with the 1971 Act.

(Prior, 1986, p.158)

The original bill didn't, however, contain any provisions dealing
with secondary action, largely because the government was awaiting
the House of Lords' decision in *Express Newspapers* v. *MacShane*
(see Prior, 1986, p.158). In December 1978 the Court of Appeal in
this case had established that unionists didn't enjoy an immunity
merely if they felt that their action was 'in furtherance' of a trade
dispute. The court should take into account 'objective criteria'; for
example, it might establish that the action was too far removed from,
or simply incapable of furthering, the original dispute. This decision,
putatively, gave the courts considerable discretion to declare secondary action unlawful, but on 13 December, the House of Lords

overturned the Court of Appeals' judgement. Subsequently, Prior introduced a new clause into the bill which restricted immunities in most, but not all, cases where secondary action was involved, although he had to fight off determined opposition from within the Cabinet, and from Conservative back-benchers, who wanted all secondary action banned (see Prior, 1986, pp.161–5). Once again, the crucial argument concerned compliance:

> Following the Lords' judgment I had been considering how best to tighten up the law on union immunities. The basic issue was whether to restrict immunities solely to the original dispute itself, as we were proposing on picketing with our plan in the Bill to limit picketing to a person's place of work. Or should we allow some scope for sympathetic, or 'secondary', industrial action by unions in furtherance of the original dispute?
>
> (Prior, 1986, pp.161–2)

Throughout the evolution and passage of the 1980 Employment Act, Prior was at pains to consult the unions. However, they had no significant influence on its contents. The consultations produced no concessions, while a demonstration and parliamentary lobby on 9 March 1980 and a 'Day of Action' against the policy on 14 May 1980 received limited support and had no noticeable effect. The TUC's problem was clear. The legislation was not particularly radical and was widely accepted by the public and many unionists. At the same time, the weakened union leadership was mainly concerned to prevent further, more radical, legislation and, at least in part, pursued a strategy designed to strengthen Prior's position:

> Congress House thus went out of its way to acquiesce in a complicated strategy which bolstered Jim Prior's position. For example, Len Murray and his colleagues loudly and repeatedly emphasized how threatened the movement would be by the terms of the existing bill. Their complaints were genuine but their vehemence served two other political purposes. It fulfilled their quite natural interest in using threatening Conservative policies in a traditional effort to rally union support for their own and the TUC's leadership. And just as importantly, it served their interests in helping Jim Prior to convince his Conservative doubters and adversaries that they could in good conscience support his

proposed legislation because it really would administer the kind of restrictive medicine against union power which they wanted.

(Dorfman, 1983, p.122)

Certainly, the unions' reaction after 1979 was hardly decisive and there can be little doubt that this reaction stiffened the Conservative resolve, given that, apart from Jim Prior and William Whitelaw, the majority of senior ministers favoured stronger legislation. Initially, there was little support in Cabinet because of the problem of compliance, but the unions' muted reaction made that appear much less of a problem. In fact, Dorfman gives considerable emphasis to the meeting between Mrs Thatcher and union leaders which took place on 25 June 1979 and revealed both Mrs Thatcher's combative style and the unions' weak response:

Everything changed, however, after Mrs Thatcher met with senior TUC leaders on 25th June. The Prime Minister and Sir Geoffrey Howe were 'amazed' by that session. Union leaders seemed surprisingly docile and confused and lacking in consensus about how to deal with them. Having lived through the Heath debacle, they had expected to find the unionists a 'tough lot'. Instead, they were surprised at how easily Mrs Thatcher dominated the meeting and even at moments when she did not, how poorly union leaders presented and persisted in their case. The breakdown of discipline at the end of the session when a number of unionists 'dropped in' their comments confirmed their disarray.

(Dorfman, 1983, p.220)

In general, the employers' reactions to the legislative proposals were favourable. In particular, the Engineering Employers Federation (EEF) and the Confederation of British Industry (CBI) gave the bill a broad welcome, although they were least happy with the closed shop provisions, which was not surprising given that large employers particularly have frequently favoured the closed shop because it tends to produce a more disciplined work-force.

After the passage of the 1980 legislation, and given the muted union response and Mrs Thatcher's increased authority within her Cabinet, it was not surprising that more legislation ensued. Prior, however, didn't see the need for radical change:

I was prepared to introduce new measures on the closed shop, including increased compensation and provision for regular reviews, by secret ballot of all those affected, of closed shop agreements. I would also have made it unlawful to refuse to include firms in tenders, or to offer or award contracts to them, on the grounds that they do not employ union members or recognise, negotiate or consult with unions of their officials, as 'union labour only contracts' were a particular problem identified in the consultations.

I would not, however, have curbed union immunities any further than they had already been restricted in the 1980 Act. I wanted to see the main provisions in our first Act given time to be accepted, and not to try to rush ahead too fast.

In my discussions with Margaret during the summer of 1981 I made my position clear.

(Prior, 1986, pp.170–71)

Prior was, thus, not surprised to be moved in Mrs Thatcher's first Cabinet reshuffle in September 1981:

I was not expecting to stay on as Secretary of State for Employment. I had been the Party's front bench spokesman on Employment and Industrial Relations, in Opposition or in Government, for seven years and I knew that, if I did stay there would be some enormous fights with Margaret.

(Prior, 1986, p.171)

Norman Tebbit, who succeeded Jim Prior, emphasises Mrs Thatcher's desire to establish her own position:

The Cabinet reshuffle was rightly seen as a turning point in Margaret Thatcher's premiership. She needed to strengthen the Cabinet with colleagues who believed that the policy of the Government was right and that it could be carried through. With the departure of Ian Gilmour, Christopher Soames and Mark Carlisle and the arrival of Cecil Parkinson and myself the balance in the Cabinet was decisively changed. The change from Jim Prior to myself was widely seen as significant.

(Tebbit, 1988, p.181)

Tebbit's appointment was significant and surprising. He had previously been a junior minister in the Department of Trade, so his promotion was accelerated. However, he had consistently expressed strong views on industrial relations. Indeed, his own 1979 election address only deviated from the party line on one issue, trade unions:

> We will protect people against the misuse of union power. Ordinary people damaged by unions should have a right of compensation. People denied work because of the closed shop should be able to sue the union for damages.
>
> (Quoted in Tebbit, 1988, p.162)

In fact, his appointment was clearly a statement of intent; Mrs Thatcher was anxious to assert her authority and push ahead with union reform. Certainly after 1981 the legislation became more radical, as we shall see later; so, for example, Tebbit's legislation was considerably more radical than Prior's 1981 Green Paper from which it was developed. In addition, once Prior had gone, the contact between the unions and government decreased. Indeed, Tebbit asserts, 'I scarcely saw them [the union leaders] at all except at meetings of "Neddy"' (Tebbit, 1988, p.193). Subsequently, the unions hardly talked to government about industrial relations for two years until after the TUC conference in September 1983. Even then, contacts ceased again a few months later when the Government Communications Headquarters (GCHQ) issue surfaced.

Overall, the TUC had little contact with government and virtually no influence over industrial relations policy. In fact, their only success was to persuade Tom King, who became Employment Secretary in October 1983 when Tebbit replaced Cecil Parkinson at the Department of Trade and Industry, to drop the contracting-in provision from the 1984 Trade Union Act. However, there were specific reasons for this concession which I shall deal with in Chapter 5.

The problem of compliance receded still further. No individual piece of legislation was sweeping; the emphasis remained upon enforceable legislation (see Tebbit, 1988, p.184). The TUC condemned each subsequent piece of legislation in turn. Indeed, at the 1982 Annual Conference the TUC passed a motion opposing government legislation and pledging that such opposition would be expressed without regard for legal consequences. However, at the next year's Conference it was decided to restart talks with Tebbit and there was a general move towards New Realism (see Bassett, 1987, pp.46–50) and in 1984 a National Graphical Association (NGA) motion committing the TUC to automatic support for unions in conflict with the new laws was defeated. Certainly, there was not a majority in the TUC in favour of defying the law; the general consensus among the TUC leadership remained that the laws were bad but should be obeyed.

In fact, the disintegration of opposition within the TUC was clearly reflected in their debate and decisions over the use of state funds for union ballots. By 1983 the Amalgamated Engineering Union (AEU) and the Electrical, Electronic, Telecommunication and Plumbing Union (EETPU), both unions which used secret ballots, were determined to apply for government money. In 1984, the government announced that no claims for money for ballots held since the legislation was introduced in 1980 would be met unless they were lodged before February 1985. The AEU members voted overwhelmingly in a ballot to accept funds and, in June 1985, the union received over £1 million to cover its balloting costs. At the same time, the EETPU applied for government funds. The General Council voted to discipline the AEU. However, the 1985 Congress reached a compromise by which the unions agreed to reballot their members on the issue making it clear that TUC policy was opposed to such applications. Both unions voted overwhelmingly in favour of accepting government money. In response, a Special TUC Conference in February 1986 voted to drop the boycott on unions applying for government funds. As McIlroy argues: 'This conference set the final seal on the demise of any TUC defiance of the new legislation' (McIlroy, 1988, p.91). It also indicated once more that the government had little to worry about in terms of compliance.

As the problem of union compliance receded so employers' support for the legislation increased. In this way the CBI, the Engineering Employer's Federation (EEF) and the Institute of Directors gave a warm welcome to the 1982 Employment Act and the 1984 Trade Union Act. While, as we shall see in the next chapter, the large employers who tend to dominate these organisations were not particularly anxious to use the new legislation, they were well aware that its existence was bound, to some extent, to weaken the bargaining position of unions. So, if there was no major problem of compliance and, in particular, if employers not directly involved in a strike were unlikely to be affected by secondary action, then the existence of the legislation could only help them in their bargaining with their own unions.

As the legislation accumulated and the government's concern about compliance dropped, so did the political importance of the issue to the Conservatives. This is reflected in the changes in the importance of the position of Secretary of State for Employment. During the Labour Government, Michael Foot, who was a key figure in the party and later party leader, was in charge of industrial relations. When Mrs Thatcher came to power, Jim Prior, the Secretary of State, was clearly a major politician, albeit one whose views were very different from the Prime Minister. Norman Tebbit, who was hardly a major figure when he was appointed, was clearly appointed to toughen up industrial relations policy and he became an important member of the Cabinet. Subsequently, when the problems of compliance faded so the importance of the Employment Secretary receded. Thus, Tom King, who replaced Tebbit in 1983, had a much more marginal position in the Cabinet. Similarly, Lord Young, although he was one of Mrs Thatcher's favoured ministers, was not a member of the House of Commons. In an earlier period it is difficult to imagine such a sensitive department being given to a member of the House of Lords. The decline in the importance of the position was further highlighted by the appointment of Norman Fowler to succeed Lord Young in 1987. His move from the Social Services to take over at Employment was widely seen at the time as a demotion.

Before we examine the legislation it is important to examine why the problem of compliance has receded. Obviously the legislation was harder to oppose than the Industrial Relations Act, both because it was initially much narrower in scope, and because the government was less actively involved in its operation which, in an important sense, depoliticised it. At the same time, union leaders were increasingly conscious that a majority of unionists supported the legislation (see Table 6.2). In addition, and possibly most important, the weakening economic position of unions due to rising unemployment, deindustrialisation and, more parochially, falling union membership left unions much less strong. They were ill-prepared to fight a long, costly and probably ultimately unsuccessful, rearguard action against a determined government, particularly given that the 1982 Employment Act made union funds, for the first time since

1906, liable to claims for damages from employers for losses occurred as a result of an illegitimate trade dispute.

The legislative onslaught: its scope and content

There have been five major pieces of trade union legislation passed since 1979. These five Acts – the 1980 Employment Act, the 1982 Employment Act, the 1984 Trade Union Act, the 1988 Employment Act and the 1990 Employment Act – have significantly changed the legal position of unions. In addition, a whole series of other Acts have also affected unions. Table 3.2 outlines the major features of each of the pieces of major trade union legislation.

There have been eight major elements in the Conservative legislation: the blanket immunity enjoyed by unions, as distinct from unionists, was removed by the Employment Act 1982; the definition of a legitimate trade dispute has been successively narrowed so as to reduce the immunities enjoyed by unionists (and now unions); the legal basis of the closed shop was initially restricted by the 1980 and 1982 Employment Acts and subsequently removed in the Employment Acts of 1988 and 1990; under the Trade Union Act 1984 unions are required to hold secret ballots for the election of officers; this legislation also requires unions to conduct political fund ballots; the Employment Act 1988 gives individual unionists a series of rights *vis-à-vis* their unions; the 1988 Act also prevents unions from disciplining members who refuse to go on strike or cross picket lines; and the 1990 Act makes unions responsible for their members' unofficial action unless the unions repudiate the strike, or make it official after a ballot.

The first two are the most important elements. The removal of the blanket immunity, which unions had enjoyed since the 1906 Trade Disputes Act, made unions liable for civil actions in tort and, as such, claims for damages for losses incurred in 'an illegitimate strike' could be pursued against the funds of the unions. As we shall see in the next chapter, once the 1982 Employment Act came into force, employers overwhelmingly took out injunctions against trade unions rather than unionists. Nevertheless, it is the removal of immunities which gave unionists, and now unions, protection against civil actions in tort which has been the crucial development. The so-called 'golden formula' has been much restricted. In particular, unions and unionists now no longer enjoy any protection for industrial action involving secondary action, on which there has not been a prior secret ballot, or involving support for workers selectively dismissed.

The 1980s legislation differs from the Industrial Relations Act and the *In Place of Strife* proposals as Table 1.1 indicates. In fact, it differs from the Industrial Relations Act in four respects. First, and most obviously, the changes in the 1980s have been cumulative, involving five stages rather than one. Second, the 1971 legislation included some positive gains for unions, on employment protection, the disclosure of information and the encouragement of collective bargaining. The current legislation contains no such provisions. Third, the 1980s legislation has a different structure from, and omits certain provisions which were included in, the 1971 Act. All the legislation has involved amending existing laws. The government has not proposed an entirely new system of law, rather it has altered the existing rules. No separate judicial system has been established, there is no equivalent of the National Industrial Relations Court (NIRC); instead the amended laws are operated by the existing legal structure, the industrial tribunals and the courts. The Secretary of State is not involved at all in the legal process, everything is left to the parties to the action and the courts so that the government plays no direct role in the operation of the legislation; and there has been no attempt to make collective agreements between employers and unions legally binding. The 1980s legislation has also included restrictions on unions not included in the Industrial Relations Act and, to that extent, is much more radical. In particular, the current laws: remove more of the immunities unions and unionists enjoyed; intervene much more in the internal affairs of the union, requiring ballots on the election of all officers and on the unions' political funds; place more restrictions on picketing; constrain all secondary action rather than just some; give union members more rights in relation to their unions; and outlaw labour-only clauses in contracts and tenders.

Many of these differences result from conscious decisions by the Conservative Government based upon the experience of the Heath Government, although, as already indicated, we must be cautious before suggesting that a deliberate step-by-step policy has been pursued. It all depends upon what step-by-step is taken to mean. Certainly, the Conservatives' approach has been cautious, largely

Table 3.2 *The main features of the Thatcher Government legislation*

	1980 Employment Act	1982 Employment Act	1984 Trade Union Act	1988 Employment Act	1990 Employment Act
1.	Restricted closed shop	Removed blanket immunity for trade unions as distinct from trade-unionists	Members of principal executive committees of unions and Presidents and Gen. Secretaries to be elected by secret ballot every 5 years	Abolition of all legal protection for post-entry closed shop	Abolition of all legal protection for pre-entry closed shop
2.	Secondary picketing unlawful – picketing protected only at strikers' own place of work	Outlawed union labour – only clauses in contracts and tenders	Unions lose immunity unless a secret ballot is conducted before strike action	Establishment of union members' right not to be disciplined for refusing to strike or crossing picket-line	Requires unions to repudiate or adopt unofficial strikes
3.	Removed immunity in most cases where secondary action involved	Further restrictions on closed shop	Unions which operate political funds must ballot their members every 10 years	Establishment of union members' right not to be called out on strike without secret ballot	Allows selective dismissal of unofficial strikers

4.	Allocated public funds for union ballots	Provided compensation for workers dismissed from closed shops between 1974 and 1980	Establishment of union members right to postal vote in union elections and ballots	Immunity removed for official organised action in support of people selectively dismissed for taking part in unofficial action
5.	Union recruitment tactics using coercive sanctions against employers ('blacking') made illegal	Made industrial action against non-unionised companies unlawful	Establishment of Commissioner for rights of trade union members with task of helping trade union members with legal action – providing advice and legal aid	All immunity for all forms of secondary action removed
6.		Facilitated selective dismissal of strikers		
7.		Redefined meaning of a trade dispute		

Table 3.3 *The step-by-step approach: a cumulative process*

Legislative Change	1980 Employment Act	1982 Employment Act	1984 Trade Union Act	1988 Employment Act	1990 Employment Act
Restriction closed shop	Restricted closed shop	Further restriction closed shop; compensation for workers dismissed from closed shop 1974–80		Abolition of all legal protection for post-entry closed shop	Abolition of all legal protection for pre-entry closed shop
Picketing restrictions	Secondary picketing made unlawful				
Removal of immunities	Immunity removed in most cases where secondary industrial action involved	Blanket immunity for trade unions removed; definition of trade dispute changed and limited action	Union loses immunity if no secret ballot before strike action		Immunities removed from all disputes involving secondary action

Democratising trade unions	Public funds allocated for union secret ballots	Members of Executive Committee of trade union to be elected by secret ballots. Political Fund ballots required	Union members given a right to vote in all union ballots
Establishment of rights for union members			Union members to have right to be disciplined for refusing to strike; not be called out on strike without ballot

because of the perceived problems of compliance. At the same time, each piece of legislation has, in important senses, built upon previous legislation, as Table 3.3 indicates. So, for example, the outlawing of the closed shop has occurred in four distinct stages. Similarly, the immunity enjoyed where secondary action was involved was removed in two steps. Undoubtedly then, the process has been a cumulative one. However, in 1978 Moran, and most other observers, were unsure of the shape of future legislation, and even in 1980 it was far from certain how things would develop. Certainly, it would appear mistaken to see the legislative approach of the Conservatives as a coherent approach developed in Opposition and followed through in power. Rather the Conservative Party wanted to curb the unions, and Mrs Thatcher loathed them, but was unsure how to proceed, particularly given the problem of compliance. However, once it became increasingly clear after 1981 that compliance was not a major problem, Mrs Thatcher's ideological aversion to unions coincided with her pragmatic political judgement. Unions could be successfully curbed which would, in her terms, remove a crucial constraint upon the operation of the market. In addition, the curbing of union power could be portrayed as evidence of the Conservatives' governing competence while, at the same time, proving electorally popular.

Conclusion

Four main conclusions emerge from this analysis of the development of the Conservative legislation:

1. The Conservative legislation was not meticulously planned in opposition and pushed through in power as part of a grand Thatcherite strategic plan.
2. Even late in 1978 it was impossible to predict the future shape of Conservative industrial relations policy. The Winter of Discontent was crucial in stiffening the resolve of the Conservatives, largely because they saw the clear electoral advantage of playing the 'union card'.
3. In power the Conservatives were circumspect and their step-by-step approach was much less a clever strategy devised in Opposition than a short-term tactic to cope with the problem of

compliance. Once the problem of compliance receded the
legislative programme gathered pace.
4. The legislative programme to date has been considerably more
radical than any previously seriously contemplated. The legal
balance between unions and employers has been significantly
changed; most importantly, unions rather than just unionists are
now liable for actions in tort and the immunities which unions
and unionists enjoy from such actions have been significantly
reduced.

The future

In 1991 the Government introduced another Gren Paper on industrial
relations law , *Industrial Relations in the 1990s*. It proposed certain
significant changes. It would give customers of public services a right
to bring proceedings to prevent or restrain a strike affecting those
services if the employer failed to take action against the union; require
unions to give seven days' notice of official strike action; tighten up
various aspects of the balloting provisions; extend the rights of union
members; and extend the powers of the Certification Officer. In
addition, it would change the law to encourage unions and employers to
make collective agreements legally binding. Legislation based on these
proposals would only be introduced after the 1992 General Election, if
the Conservatives won.

In the event of a Labour Government coming to power we could
expect significant changes. These are dealt with at length in Chapter 6.
The Labour Party is pledged to retain the requirement for ballots before
industrial action and for the election of union executives, and not to
legalise the closed shop. However, it will restore to unions the right to
take limited secondary action and give individuals the right not to be
dismissed for lawful strike action. Overall, then, the Labour Party
proposes to restore some protection to unions and unionists, in mpart by
moving to a system of positive rights rather than by restoring
immunities.

4

Using the Legislation: An Employer's Onslaught?

Any analysis of the role of the law in industrial relations which exclusively, or even mainly, concentrated upon the operations of the Conservative Government's trade union legislation would be, at best, very limited. There has been a clear increase in the juridification of industrial relations which can be traced back at least two decades; that is to well before the election of Mrs Thatcher (Clark, 1985). This process has found an expression in the passage of the new legislation but cannot be reduced to it.

The move towards juridification which began in the 1960s was obviously also reflected in previous attempts to legislate; to put unions on a legal footing. However, such legislative initiatives were only a part of a broader picture. The 1960s also saw a resurgence of judicial creativity, with the judges extending the common law liabilities of those taking or encouraging action particularly through the development of a series of new economic torts (Elias and Ewing, 1982). Of course, to the extent that the Conservative legislation removes most of the immunities from civil action liabilities which unions and unionists enjoyed, this has provided additional scope for such judicial creativity.

In the more recent period, other changes have also contributed to the increased use of the law in the regulation of industrial relations. First, one relatively recent development in the operation of the law has had a major effect on the conduct of disputes. Since a House of Lords decision in 1975, injunctions have become easier to obtain and are now the major legal weapon used by employers in the conduct of industrial disputes. Second, there has been a significant increase in the use of the law of contract by employers and individual unionists. Third, the use of the criminal law has become a common feature of the policing of industrial disputes.

This chapter will deal with all of these developments. It is divided into four substantive sections. In the first section I shall examine the operation of the recent legislation. I will pay particular attention to the injunctions which have become the dominant tactic involved in employers' use of the legislation. However, a subsection will also consider the significance and use of the legislation to restrict the closed shop. The second section will then deal with the changes which have occurred in the use of the law of contract in the industrial relations field. The third section will consider the role of the police and the use of the criminal law in policing industrial disputes, particularly the miners' strike. The fourth section will examine how the existence of the legislation restricts the autonomy of unions in their conduct of industrial disputes. In each of these sections I will be dealing mainly with the aggregate patterns although I shall also consider some of the major cases and disputes since 1979. It is only by examining such cases that we can fully appreciate the changes which have occurred.

The overall pattern is clear. Many of these important developments pre-date, and don't merely depend upon the Conservative legislation. The legislation has altered the climate for industrial relations and the views of the employers and the courts. In addition, it is evident that the legislation itself, and the case law which has developed from it, has severely restricted the autonomy of unions, particularly in relation to the conduct of disputes. Nevertheless, it is important to recognise that these developments have accentuated, albeit significantly, trends which already existed.

The operation of the Conservative Government's legislation

The period since the election of the Conservative Government in 1979 has seen a marked increase in the number of legal actions brought by employers against unions or unions members, (see Evans, 1985, 1988; *Labour Research*, October 1985, October 1987, September 1988, October 1989). The vast majority of these cases which were brought under legislation introduced by the Conservative Government involved applications for injunctions. In fact, *Labour Research* calculated that of the 46 cases they identified which were brought between January 1983 and July 1985, 38 (83 per cent) involved such applications (*Labour Research*, 1985). For this reason a major emphasis in this section will be on the use of injunctions.

The injunction

As I indicated in the introduction to this chapter, the general principles covering the granting of interlocutory injunctions were laid down by a decision of the House of Lords in 1975 in the case of *American Cyanamid and Co* v. *Ethican Limited*. This decision established that an applicant for an injunction didn't have to show that they had a prima facie case, as had previously been thought. At present an applicant merely needs to establish that he has an arguable case and that there is a serious issue to be tried. Once this has been established the court will consider the 'balance of convenience between the parties'.

The decision in the *American Cyanamid* case suggested that the court should not go into the facts of the case any more than was necessary to ensure temporary justice as between the parties. However, it was assumed that this principle didn't apply to labour dispute cases where the granting of an interlocutory injunction effectively decided the action. Indeed, section 17(2) of the Trade Union and Labour Relations Act (TULRA), as amended in 1976, confirmed this by declaring that if, in interlocutory proceedings, the defendant claims to be pursing a legitimate trade dispute, then the court shall take into consideration the likelihood of his being able to establish such a defence. It was the Conservative Government's legislation which changed the position:

The right to organise a strike was intended to be protected by section 17 of TULRA (as amended) which restricts the court's power to grant interlocutory injunctions in labour disputes. However, like other parts of TULRA, the section has been robbed of much of its practical effect by the Employment Act 1980, and 1982, the Trade Union Act 1984 and the Employment Act 1988. In essence, as the definition of legitimate trade dispute has been limited, then the protection afforded by section 17 of TULRA has been severely restricted.

Rogers and Fodder sum up the concept of 'balance of convenience', as currently interpreted, very well:

The balance of convenience (which has perhaps more accurately been described as the balance of injustice) involves weighing all the circumstances of the case; the desirability of maintaining the status quo (where it is possible to determine what that is); whether if the injunction were granted the plaintiff's undertakings as to damages would be sufficient to compensate the defendant for loss suffered in the meantime; and, most important, comparing the magnitude of the loss on one side with that likely to occur to the other. In industrial action cases the balance of convenience will almost always be decided in the plaintiff's favour because he can point to certain and definable pecuniary loss if the industrial action is allowed to continue whereas the defendant union can point only to the unquantifiable loss of a tactical advantage in the dispute if the action is restrained.

(Rogers and Fodder, 1987, p.90)

The key point is clear. In the vast majority of instances, injunctions are granted to the employer in industrial relations cases. As Table 4.1 indicates, over 90 per cent of the injunctions requested by employers between 1980 and 1988 were granted. What is more, such injunctions are usually granted quickly. Indeed, an injunction can be granted without the union being present; these are called ex-parte injunctions. In fact a *Labour Research* study indicated that employers were involved in a maximum wait of 24 hours, with hearings sometimes lasting less than 15 minutes (*Labour Research*, 1985, p.259).

Of course, an injunction is just a temporary legal remedy designed to preserve the status quo until the case is resolved at a full trial. However, in industrial relations cases it is very rare for an action to proceed to trial. The granting of an injunction, if it is obeyed, suspends, or rather in effect ends, the industrial action and renders further action by the employer unnecessary, unless he wishes to pursue a claim for damages. As we shall see later, such claims by an employer are rare. Employers don't generally pursue a claim for damages because they calculate that the granting of an injunction is sufficient to achieve their main aim, the suspension of the industrial action. The employer's judgement appears accurate.

In most cases unions do comply with the injunction and suspend their industrial action. As Table 4.1 shows, in the period up to the passage of the 1982 Employment Act almost 90 per cent of the

Table 4.1   *The use of injunctions in industrial relations cases, 1980–89 (in all instances number of cases are reported with percentage in brackets)*

| Years | Grounds for injunction | | | | |
	Picket-ing	Secondary action	Strike	Other Ballots	Total
Sept. 1980–Sept. 1982	11 (52%)	5 (24%)	–	5 (24%)	21
Oct. 1982–Aug. 1984		7 (47%)	6 (40%)	2 (13%)	15
Sept. 1984–July 1989	11 (12%)	20 (21%)	53 (56%)	10 (11%)	94

| | Outcome of injunction | | Target of injunction | | Union response to injunction | |
	Granted	Not granted	Indiv-idual	Unions	Complied	Resisted
1980–2	19 (90%)	2 (10%)	21 (100%)	0	17 (89%)	2 (11%)
1982–4	14 (93%)	1 (7%)	3 (20%)	12 (80%)	4 (31%)	9 (69%)
1984–9	85 (93%)	6 (7%)	14 (16%)	75 (84%)	41 (77%)	12 (23%)

| | Subsequent action by employers/court | | | |
	Contempt proceedings initiated		Damages pursued	Sequestration of union assets
1980–2	2	(100%)	2	–
1982–4	3	(33%)	3	2
1984–9	10	(83%)	8	2

Source: Adapted and updated from Evans 1985, 1988 using *Labour Research* figures.

injunctions awarded were complied with, a figure which is not surprising given that until 1982, when unions' immunity from liability in civil law actions was removed, injunctions were taken out against individual unionists not against unions. Such individuals rarely have the resources to risk any claim for damages which might be pursued by an employer for non-compliance.

In the subsequent period, more than 80 per cent of injunctions were sought against unions rather than unionists (see Table 4.1). The pattern of compliance in this period was less uniform; between the passage of the 1982 Employment Act and the 1984 Trade Union Act, resistance to the injunctions was much more common. The majority of this resistance occurred in the printing and publishing industry which is, as we shall see later, the area in which conflict between employers and unions has been most marked in the whole period under study.

The printing employers were successful in imposing restructuring on the union and the work-force despite this resistance. It is perhaps not surprising that the failure of the print unions' strategy of non-compliance with the injunctions, together with the other putative costs of that strategy – contempt proceedings, damages and sequestration of unions' assets – appears to have acted as a strong disincentive for unions to resist the injunctions after 1984. Certainly, in the last of the three periods dealt with in Table 4.1, the period after the passage of the 1984 Trade Union Act, compliance again became the norm.

Table 4.1 also indicates that, although it was usual for employers to initiate proceedings for contempt if a union resisted an injunction (in 64 per cent of the cases between 1980 and 1988), it is unusual for employers to pursue damages. As Stephen Evans concisely argues: 'The law is being used, in the majority of cases, to seek relief through the injunction rather than damages' (Evans, 1985, p.135).

The excellent study by Weekes, *et al.* of the operation of the 1971 Industrial Relations Act emphasised that the reluctance of employers, particularly large employers, to use that legislation played a major role in rendering it ineffective:

Managers were especially reluctant to see bargaining arrangements disturbed by the new individual rights, and combined effectively with unions to draw the sting from the law's attack on closed shops. Nor were they keen to use the law to enforce procedures or prevent costly disputes. They did not expect procedures always to be followed and they believed the use of the law could only make disputes more intractable. Managers were aware that legally enforceable agreements, attempts to end the closed shop and restrictions on the right to take industrial action were strongly opposed by unions and the members. They were reluctant, therefore, either to enforce the legal rights of others or to use legal sanctions that were designed to enhance their own authority.
(Weekes *et al.*, 1975, p.223)

To what extent does the conclusion of Weekes, *et al.* hold for the Conservative Government's legislation? Are employers, including large employers, more ready to use the law than they were between 1971 and 1974? Table 4.1 suggests that, at most, the answer is a *very qualified 'yes'*. As we've seen, the injunction is the legal remedy most often used by employers, but it is infrequently used. Evans's figures suggest that, on average, less than one injunction a month was applied for between September 1980 and August 1984. After the passage of the 1984 Trade Union Act the number more than doubled, with 60 per cent of the injunctions in this later period being sought, under the 1984 legislation, against a union not conducting a ballot before calling a strike. Even so, the number of injunctions sought was still small and concentrated in a few sectors.

As Table 4.2 shows, in the more recent period, 77 per cent of the injunctions were sought in three sectors – printing, shipping/transport and the public sector; indeed, a third of the cases were in the printing and publishing field. The explanation of this pattern is clear. Employers are most willing to use the legislation in sectors marked by a high degree of conflict and poor management – union relations where, in their own terms, they have little to lose. Such conflict is particularly accentuated when there are strong economic pressures pushing management towards a reorganisation of production, thus further undermining employer-union relations. Evans makes this point very well with particular reference to the printing sector:

> Use of injunctions in the printing sector can also be associated with the radical change in business strategies and firms' movement out of old, craft technologies into, if not always new, certainly more semi-skilled labour processes in which employers have tried to evade detailed craft union regulations and recognition. These employer strategies have exposed the printing unions' dependence on regulating the labour market and labour process through the pre-entry closed shop and blacking. This has made them especially vulnerable to the new legal restrictions. It is in printing where reorganisation of production has posed a particularly radical challenge to the unions, and where unions have put up notable (overt) resistance. It is in printing, too, where employers have most readily and effectively demonstrated the potency of the law in subordinating labour to the narrow boundaries of legitimate industrial action now determined by economic restructuring.
>
> (Evans, 1988, p.425)

Table 4.2 *Sectoral distribution of injunctions, 1980–87 (nos, % in brackets)*

Sector	Time Sept. '80–Apr.' 84		Period May '84–Apr. '87	
Printing	9	(26)	29	(36)
Shipping/transport	3	(9)	18	(23)
Public services			14	(18)
Engineering/shipbuilding			5	(6)
Professional			3	(4)
Chemicals			3	(4)
Communications	3	(9)	3	(4)
Retail/distribution			2	(3)
Construction			2	(3)
Coal	2	(6)	1	(1)
Unknown	17	(50)	–	
Total	34		80	

Source: Adapted from Evans, 1985, 1988.

Some large companies have used the legislation, notably British Telecom, Shell, General Electric Company and Austin Rover. However, as Table 4.3 indicates, of the 67 private sector companies which sought injunctions under the Conservative Government legislation between September 1980 and July 1988, only 7(10 per cent) were top 100 companies, and 24 (37 per cent) top 1000 companies. What is more, 14 of these top 1000 companies (56 per cent) were in the printing or transport industries. Overall, it is clear that in most sectors the large majority of companies, and particularly the larger companies, prefer not to take legal action. A combination of pragmatism and a continuing commitment to existing bargaining procedures and the, often informal, 'rules of the game', seems to indicate that this will remain the usual response of most employers. At the same time, some employers, particularly in industries marked by a history of poor industrial relations, have used, and will continue to use, the new legislation ruthlessly as a key element in their industrial relations strategy.

Table 4.3   *Injunctions brought by size of company, 1980–88*

Time period	Number of injunctions brought by top 100 companies (% in brackets)	Number of injunctions brought by top 1000 companies (% in brackets)	Number of injunctions brought by other companies (% in brackets)
Sept. '80–April '84	3 (13%)	9 (39%)	14 (61%)
May '84–July '88	4 (14%)	15 (34%)	29 (66%)

Notes: 1. Column 2 includes cases in column 1
         2. Any company which applied for more than one injunction in period is only counted once.
Source: Constructed using the cases noted in Evans, 1985, 1988.

The use of the Conservative Governments' employment law: some cases

No legal cases are typical. However, it is evident that a number of cases decided in the early 1980s have had a significant resonance for subsequent industrial relations. In particular, and not surprisingly given Evans's figures, the printing industry offers a number of examples which indicate the readiness of small entrepreneurial employers to use the legislation. The dispute which led to litigation in *Dimbleby & Sons Ltd* v. *National Union of Journalists* (NUJ) had its origins in the growth of free news sheets and the resultant declining profitability of local newspapers, (see Shrubsall, 1984). The Dimbleby group in response to this pressure looked for a reduction in their production costs. The Dimbleby newspapers were not in fact printed by the company itself but by an associated company, Dimbleby Printers Ltd.

After six months inconclusive negotiation with the National Graphical Association (NGA) two redundancies were announced at Dimbleby Printers Ltd, which led to a strike and brought Dimbleby Printers Ltd to a standstill. In order to resume publication of its local newspapers Dimbleby had to find an alternative printer and TBF (Printers) Ltd at Nottingham was contracted to print copy supplied by Dimbleby and to publish the local newspapers. However, TBF (Printers) Ltd was an associated company of T. Bailey Forman Ltd, the publishers of the Nottingham Evening Post, with whom the NUJ had been engaged in a dispute since 1979. In pursuance of that dispute the NUJ instructed their member journalists employed by Dimbleby to refuse to provide copy for printing by TBF. Dimbleby sought an interlocutory injunction against the NUJ, restraining the union from issuing such instructions to its members because this was 'secondary action' as defined in the 1980 Act.

The High Court granted the interlocutory injunction, and the Court of Appeal and the House of Lords dismissed the union's appeal. The NUJ argued that the instruction was not unlawful and that a defence under section 13 of the 1976 Trade Union and Labour Relations Act (TULRA) was likely to succeed. First, it contended that there was a trade dispute between the NUJ and Dimbleby and so the action was not 'secondary action' as defined by section 17 of the 1980 Employment Act but was primary action protected by section 13 of TULRA. Second, it argued that the trade dispute was between the NUJ and T. Bailey Forman Ltd but the action against Dimbleby & Sons Ltd was 'protected secondary action' under section 17(3) of the 1980 Act.

The Court of Appeal and the House of Lords held that there was no trade dispute between Dimbleby and the journalists. The row that had blown up had nothing to do with the Dimbleby journalists' terms or conditions of employment which were not in dispute. The journalists' refusal to provide copy was to put pressure on Dimbleby not to deal with TBF.

The two courts also rejected the second argument. It was accepted that there was a trade dispute between the NUJ and T. Bailey Forman Ltd, but action against Dimbleby & Sons Ltd, which interfered with the printing contract it had with TBF (Printers) Ltd, was not held to be 'protected secondary action'. The Court argued that secondary action would only be 'protected' by section 18(3) of the 1980 Employment Act where there was a contractual link between a party to the dispute and the party against whom the action was taken. In this case there was no contractual link between T. Bailey Forman Ltd and Dimbleby & Sons Ltd, as TBF (Printers) Ltd could not be said to be the same party as T. Bailey Forman Ltd. Although a wholly-owned subsidiary company, it was a separate entity. In the House of Lords, Lord Diplock took the view that it was impossible to 'pierce the corporate veil' and treat the two companies as being the same employer.

Here we see how legislation can be and is being used to restrict the activities of unions. In addition, the interpretation by the House of Lords which established T. Bailey Forman Ltd and TBF (Printers) Ltd as totally separate entities even if right in law indicates the scope of the legislation. The decision clearly provides an easy way for employers to remove any immunities unions still enjoy by diverting contracts affected by industrial action to newly-established subsidiaries.

In the printing field the Messenger case was another to indicate the effect the legislation can have on a union's actions. Early in 1982 a dispute arose between Fineward Ltd, a subsidiary of the Messenger Group, and the National Graphical Association (NGA), over a new wage agreement. Technological developments in the late 1970s and 1980s have stimulated the growth of:

> an alternative printing industry based on art and advertising studios, in-plant printing, instant print shops, and the growth of a communications world based on television, telecommunications and computer based technology, in which the NGA has little or no presence.
>
> (Gennard, 1984, pp.7–8)

These developments have led to the growth of free sheets which depend on advertising to meet costs and generate a profit. This has become a very large market; indeed Gennard calculates that between 1974 and 1982 advertising revenue for free sheets grew from £17m to £136m.

Mr Shah, the chairman of the Messenger Newspaper Group, published six free newspapers and employed 120 staff in offices in Stockport, Bury and Warrington. About half of his employees were in jobs traditionally organised by the NGA. In 1979 Mr Shah opened his own typesetting company, Fineword Ltd, in Stockport, employing eight NGA members. He signed a closed-shop agreement with the NGA for a new typesetting plant in Bury. However, no agreement was reached as to pay and conditions. The management offered £40 less in Bury and, when the NGA refused to agree, they cancelled the closed-shop agreement and began employing non-union labour. The company also opened a printing plant in Warrington again recruiting non-union labour. After a series of negotiations the union wrote to the Group in June 1983 saying that, if agreement was not reached, they would declare an official dispute, withdraw their members from Stockport, and instruct their members to black all work from, or for, companies in the group. In fact, on 4 July 1983 six NGA members at Fineward Ltd. went on strike and then were dismissed by the management. The company brought a series of actions against the NGA under the Government Employment Acts. On 14 October the High Court granted the company two injunctions. The first ordered the NGA not to put pressure on the company's advertisers to withdraw advertising from the group's papers and to stop 'blacking' the company's work (unlawful under the 1982 Employment Act). The second was granted against secondary picketing by NGA members at Bury and Warrington as they were not picketing their workplace (unlawful under the 1980 Employment Act). When the union ignored these rulings it was judged to be in contempt and fined £50,000. After the union refused to pay this fine, the Advisory, Conciliation, and Arbitration Service (ACAS) intervened and a settlement was reached between the two sides. However, the Messenger Group refused to reinstate the six dismissed NGA members. Despite intensified mass picketing, the free sheets were still produced and distributed.

The conflict shifted gear again when the Group issued a writ for sequestration against the NGA for its contempt of the Court orders. The Court fined the union £100,000 and ordered the sequestration of all its funds to ensure payment of this and any subsequent fines. The NGA's response was to organise 'spontaneous' action in Fleet Street. Despite renewed negotiations no agreement was made and on 9 December another action brought by the company led to a further contempt of court fine of £525,000. This time the NGA National Committee's response was to call a 24-hour national stoppage of the printing industry on Wednesday 14 December. However, this strike call was met by the granting of a series of High Court injunctions to employers ordering the NGA to withdraw its strike call. The General Council of the Trades Union Congress (TUC) refused to support the NGA action and the NGA called off the proposed strike.

Subsequently, in January 1984, the NGA National Council voted to purge its contempt in order to regain control of the union funds. In

June 1984 the NGA decided to call off all picketing and the six dismissed NGA members were found work elsewhere. The NGA, which had been seen by many to be one of the strong unions well capable of protecting its members' interests, had been badly beaten. In addition, the Messenger Group continued its action and obtained £124,000 damages against the NGA.

The lessons from this dispute are clear as Gennard indicates:

> Had [the Government Employment laws] not existed, the outcome of the dispute might have been different. The group may then have had no alternative but to negotiate with the NGA. However, the Messenger was different in that it represents a new type of employer coming into a growing alternative printing industry. These firms are not steeped in the traditions and practices of conventional newspaper production. If the NGA is to control them it will have to continue to develop its new recruitment policies being used in other non-traditional sectors of printing, e.g. non-manual employment. To continue traditional methods of recruitment may lead to more Messenger situations.
>
> (Gennard, 1984, p.13)

The dispute also showed the imbalance of the picketing laws as an employer can, and in this case did, transfer work to another establishment which it then becomes unlawful for the union to picket. Indeed, the Messenger dispute confirmed the success of the Employment Acts in their own terms. As Gennard says:

> it showed that they can be used to curtail substantially [sic] the degree to which unions can ask other trade unionists to take sympathetic action, and how the boundaries of lawful action have been successfully redrawn in the favour of the employer.
>
> (Gennard, 1984, pp.18–19)

The *Mercury Communications Ltd* v. *Scott-Garner* case in 1983/4 is also revealing. In this case Mercury, a private communications company, sought an interlocutory injunction against the Post Office Engineering Union (POEU) and its President. The company asked for an injunction to prevent the POEU instructing its members not to connect the Mercury system to the British Telecommunications (BT) system. The union was also blacking Mercury, refusing to carry out maintenance at its headquarters and threatening industrial action against Mercury's subscribers. The unions' action resulted from its opposition to the government's decision to allow private companies to compete with BT. The union argued that its action against Mercury was in furtherance of a trade dispute and, as such, was protected under TULRA. Mercury contended that it was not involved in a trade dispute with the POEU whose action was against the government. As such, the union's action was secondary action, illegal under the 1980 Employment Act.

Initially, a High Court judge refused to grant Mercury an injunction arguing that the union's argument was likely to succeed if the case went to full trial. However, the Court of Appeal allowed Mercury's appeal arguing that there was 'massive evidence' that the union was involved in a political struggle against privatisation. The case never came to full trial and this reflects two important points. First, the side which loses this initial action is reluctant to proceed to trial given the costs involved and the probability of defeat. Second, once industrial action is postponed, it is difficult to revive it to any effect, thus, if the union complies with any injunction, it removes the strike threat as a bargaining counter.

The Mercury case reveals how the legislation has been used to render ineffective any broad-based industrial action against privatisation. At the same time, it indicates the importance of the interlocutory action. Industrial action can be curtailed by employers without recourse to full trial and at relatively little cost.

The Austin-Rover (A-R) case in 1984 represents a variation on the main pattern. Here a large employer used the law as a tool in its industrial relations strategy in order to 'discipline' its work-force. The 1984 Trade Union Act requires unions to hold a secret ballot *before* industrial action. When the six unions which comprised the joint negotiating committee in A-R called a strike on the basis of a vote at a mass meeting, the management sought injunctions against the six unions individually requiring them to withdraw support from the strike until and unless a secret ballot was held.

In response the Electrical, Electronic, Telecommunication and Plumbing Union (EETPU) made it clear that it wouldn't endorse the strike by its members at A-R unless they complied with the law and held a secret ballot. As a result, Austin Rover withdrew their action against the EETPU. In contrast, the Transport and General Workers' Union (TGWU) continued to support the strike action even after the

High Court granted A-R an injunction. Subsequently, the TGWU was fined £200,000 for contempt of court which it refused to pay. Following the granting of the injunctions, all the other unions involved disowned the strike action and there was a return to work. In the event, A-R didn't pursue its contempt proceeding against the TGWU but proceeded with a claim for damages against the union.

Here a large company, albeit an unusual one with a macho-style of leadership, felt able to use the legislation with little fear of the consequences its action might have for future industrial relations. Most of the unions involved, mindful of the threat of damages or even the sequestration of their funds, and weakened by the recession, were unwilling to confront the company.

The closed shop

The legislative assault on the closed shop in the 1980, 1982, 1988 and 1990 Employment Acts accelerated the closed shops decline; a decline which, as Dunn and Gennard indicate, was already under way, largely because of changes in the economic structure associated with technological changes and managerial opportunism (Dunn and Gennard, 1984).

However, few closed shop cases were in fact brought between 1982 and 1988. *Labour Research* could identify only ten closed shop cases pursued between November 1983 and July 1985. In seven cases the industrial tribunal found against the union. Perhaps more significantly, seven of the ten plaintiffs were supported by the right-wing Freedom Association (*Labour Research*, 1985, p.260). Overall, employers and unionists showed little interest in this legislation.

The use of the law of contract

The law of contract has played an important role in a number of recent major industrial disputes. First, working miners made extensive use of it in the so-called rule-book cases which were a significant feature of the miners' strike. Second, Rupert Murdoch used the fact that, in striking, an employee breaches his contract of employment to dismiss 5000 workers during the Wapping dispute.

The rule-book cases

The union rule book provides the basis of a contract between the union and the member. As such, if a union fails to adhere to its rules it can be liable for breach of contract. In fact, over the course of the miners' strike working miners brought actions against both the national NUM and every striking area branch with the exception of Kent; the majority of the actions revolved around the contention that the strike was unlawful because it was called in breach of the union rules (Ewing, 1985).

The two significant rules were rule 41, which provides that no strike is to take place in any area of the union without the sanction of the National Executive Committee (NEC), and rule 43, which declared:

> a national strike shall only be entered upon as the result of a ballot vote of the members taken in pursuance of a resolution of Conference, and a strike shall not be declared unless 55 per cent of those voting in the ballot vote in favour of a strike.

No national ballot was held; rather the NEC legitimised area strikes under rule 41. The two points at issue in the cases under consideration were thus, firstly, whether the area rules had been complied with, and, secondly, whether the NEC was in breach of its rules for not holding a ballot before organising a national strike.

In a series of cases the courts decided that the area strikes were unlawful, both because they were in breach of area rules and because they were, in fact, part of a national strike unsupported by a ballot. Once the strike was established as unlawful a series of consequences followed. First, in most cases it exposed unions to injunctions which prevented them calling upon members to support the strike and not to cross picket lines. Second, it meant that unions' funds could be restrained to prevent their use in support of the strike. Third, it meant that NUM members could not be disciplined for failing to join the strike.

In fact, the NUM did not always obey the court orders. As such, the union and Mr Scargill were fined for contempt of court and, subsequently, union funds were sequestrated. Such moves have become fairly common in recent years. However, there were a number of new points which emerged in the miners' strike.

First, when the sequestrators found it difficult to locate the union's funds, a receiver was appointed following another application by working miners. The court took such an action on the grounds that the union's trustees, including its three leading officials, were 'not fit and proper people to be in charge of other people's money', in large part because they had continued 'serious and deliberate contempts of orders which place the funds that they hold for the union in jeopardy'. Second, in *Taylor* v. *NUM (Derbyshire Area)(No. 3)*, the court found that union officials are, in principle, liable to make good any payments from union funds which have been made in breach of union rules. If this decision is upheld in future cases, union leaders may be reluctant to take action which might breach the union rule book.

Despite all this, Ewing points to what is perhaps the key lesson of the miners' strike:

> One lesson of the strike for both trade unionists and lawyers is that in appropriate cases the courts are willing to go a long way to maintain both their dignity, and ... the rule of law.
>
> (Ewing, 1985, p.175)

This position was clear in Nicholls J. judgment when fining the NUM and Mr Scargill for contempt. He asserted:

> A great and powerful union with a large membership has decided to regard itself as above the law...if orders of court are set at nought in this way – openly and repeatedly defied by such a body with impunity – where is the rule of law?
>
> (Quoted in Ewing, 1985, p.170)

Overall then, the Conservative legislation and the law of tort played little direct role in the miners' strike (see Benedictus, 1985). However, again it must be emphasised that there was probably an indirect effect. The legislative constraints on trade unions introduced by the Thatcher Government, and the restrictive interpretation of the new laws by the workers, clearly affected the atmosphere within which relations between unionists and their unions, as well as between unions and employers, took place. Such an atmosphere can only have encouraged individual union members, often supported by anti-union organisations, to challenge their unions in the courts.

Wapping and the law of contract: there is no right to strike

As we have seen, trade union opposition to the introduction of new technology and the recruitment of non-union labour was greatly limited by the provisions of the 1980 and 1982 Employment Acts which made illegal most action to protect the closed shop and, in particular, made the taking of secondary action by unions unlawful in most circumstances. Outside London, a variety of attempts were made in the 1980s to break the control of the NGA over newspaper production; the most successful action, as we have seen, being taken by Mr Shah. Rupert Murdoch was determined to achieve a similar success in Fleet Street (see Ewing and Napier, 1986).

Mr Murdoch had plans to develop a new site in Wapping where the new technology would be used; although he claimed, at the outset, that his intention was to publish a new London evening paper on the site, rather than to move the production of his existing titles. As this was a new operation, union recognition was a matter for negotiations which took place between union officials and News International throughout 1985. The unions made significant concessions; they were willing to accommodate the new technology by accepting flexible job definitions and to agree to a disputes procedure which involved binding arbitration. However, the unions would not abandon the pre-entry closed shop.

The outcome of the negotiations was predictable. News International broke off negotiations at the end of 1988. In the meantime, however, they had prepared their ground to withstand the industrial action which would be inevitable when their true plans, to move the production of *The Times*, the *Sun*, and their other titles, to Wapping, were revealed. In order to exploit fully the restrictions on secondary activity, and bearing in mind the outcome of the Dimbleby case, News International set up a large number of associate companies, each a separate entity, during 1985. Such companies could act as a buffer between News International and the union, and union action against the 'buffer company' would be illegal, secondary, action.

The company also sought advice from its legal advisers about how to dismiss its Fleet Street employees at minimum cost.

In January 1986 the move was made and, following the call by the NGA and the Society of Graphical and Allied Trusts (SOGAT '82) for industrial action on 24 January, more than 5000 printing and other workers were dismissed. Of course, such a strategy would have been costly for the employer if the dismissed employees could claim unfair dismissal, or were entitled to redundancy payments. Similarly, it could be not have been successful unless the dismissed workers could be replaced. As I have said, however, News International were well prepared.

As Ewing and Napier point out, there is no right to strike in English labour law, and in striking, an employee breaches his contract of employment. More specifically:

> Section 62 of the Employment Protection (Consolidation) Act 1978 provides that, if an employee was taking part in a strike or other industrial action at the date of dismissal, then an industrial tribunal is not empowered to determine whether the dismissal was fair or unfair – unless the employer discriminated in the dismissal of those taking part in the industrial action.
>
> (Ewing and Napier, 1986, p.291)

Although the law relating to redundancy rights is more complex the effect is similar. Participation in a strike is a misconduct which disqualifies the employee who is dismissed from any entitlement to redundancy payments. Armed with legal advice to this effect, the costs of the move to News International were consequently limited.

At the same time News International did need to man the new plant and here they pursued a classic policy of divide and rule to some effect. Of course, News International could have chosen to recruit a non-unionised work-force, as did Eddie Shah, but that may have proved difficult in a field marked by high levels of unionisation, particularly given the existence of a continuing acrimonious dispute. Instead, they reached an agreement with the EETPU which agreed to accept the new working practices and a 'strike-free' deal. Relations between the print unions and the EETPU had already been strained when the electricians signed a single union agreement with Mr Shah's News (UK) which publishes *Today*. However, the problem was exacerbated when the union not only signed an agreement with

Mr Murdoch but secretly assisted News International to recruit staff for printers' jobs. This led to a complaint to the TUC by the four other unions involved that the electricians had breached TUC rules and marked an important stage in the process which led ultimately in 1988 to the EETPU's expulsion from the TUC. In the meantime, however, Mr Murdoch had his work-force.

The policing of industrial relations and the use of the criminal law

The actions of the police have become a significant feature of recent industrial relations disputes. This has meant that the criminal law has played an increasing role in strikes. In particular, the massive scale of police deployment in the 1984–5 miners' strike ensured that it was their use of the criminal law relating to public order offences which rendered mass picketing ineffective (see Wallington, 1985; De Friend and Rubin, 1985). As Wallington argues:

> Effectively they filled the vacuum created by the failure of the NCB and others to use the civil law; effectively they became, wittingly or otherwise, the agency by which the strike was contained and eventually broken.
>
> (Wallington, 1985, p.159)

Before we examine the police action, and the use of the criminal law, in more detail, it is important to recognise that a number of changes occurred after the 1972 miners' strike which enabled the police to play such a decisive role. After the 1972 strike, a National Reporting Centre (NRC) was created to improve co-ordination between the police forces; to establish effective mutual aid under Section 14 of the Police Act, 1964. The NRC monitored all law enforcement aspects of the miners' dispute. Indeed, it co-ordinated the movement of police between forces in the strike to such effect that during one week in June 1984, 8100 officers were deployed outside their home area under the mutual aid arrangements.

Of course, while weight of numbers are important, they are not sufficient in themselves. However, the urban riots in Brixton and Toxteth in 1981 led to the systematic retraining and operational restructuring of police forces in order to deal with public order problems. All police forces established Police Support Groups to tackle public disorder problems and these groups were equipped with, and trained in the use of, riot gear . So, when mass picketing became a feature of the miners' strike, especially in Nottingham-shire, the police were well prepared for the ensuing confrontations.

Even so, although the police were better prepared, this would have been of little consequence unless they had been given sufficient resources to preserve law and order and access to the pits. As Wallington emphasises:

> This enabled them to make the choice to preserve order by containment or prevention of picketing. With fewer resources it might, in some cases, have been necessary, and would certainly have been lawful, to preserve the peace by preventing individual returning miners from attempting to pass through picket lines. Resources enabled a choice to be made as to whose activities were to be curtailed.
>
> (Wallington, 1985, p.159)

The government's industrial relations legislation was little used in the miners' strike. It was the law of contract, in the so-called 'rule-book' cases, and the criminal law which were of much more importance. The criminal law was extensively used by the police to restrict the effect of picketing in the interests of public order.

As Table 4.4 indicates 9808 people were arrested in England and Wales, of whom 7917 (81 per cent) were charged with 10 272 offences. The vast majority of the offences were minor and arose from picketing (7655 or 75 per cent). In addition, 643 charges were brought under section 7 of the Conspiracy and Protection of Property Act 1875. These mainly dealt with 'watching and besetting' the homes of working miners. Of the more serious offences, the vast majority involved unlawful assembly and riot, charges which stemmed in the main from picket-line confrontations.

The police were mainly concerned to contain and disperse pickets to preserve order and access. However, they also made extensive use of their common law powers to keep pickets and supporters away from picketed areas. In particular, road blocks were widely used; mostly in Nottinghamshire 164 508 'presumed pickets' were turned back in the first 27 weeks of the strike (Wallington, 1985, p.154; see also Percy-Smith and Hillyard, 1985). The legal basis for such road

Table 4.4   *The use of the criminal law in the 1984–5 miners' strike in England and Wales*

Number of people arrested	Number of people charged (% of those arrested in brackets)	Number of offences	Minor charges arising from picketing expressed as % of total charges (Nos in brackets)			
			Breach of Peace	Obstruction of police	Criminal damage	Obstructing the highway
9808	7917 (81%)	10272	42% (4314)	16% (1682)	10% (1019)	6% (640)

Note   *These charges were brought under section 7 of the Conspiracy and Protection of Property Act, the vast majority of them were for watching and besetting, but a minority were not.
Source: Adapted from Wallington, 1985.

blocks was never tested but rested upon the police officers' powers to stop vehicles under the 1972 Road Traffic Act. However, the powers of the police in this area were strengthened by the 1984 Police and Criminal Evidence Act and senior police officers are clearly convinced that such road blocks have considerable value in preventing breaches of public order.

Overall, the major point is clear and is well made by Wallington:

> It is clearly established that the police may prevent *even lawful activity*, including picketing within the statutory immunity, if it is necessary to do so to prevent a breach of the peace.
>
> (Wallington, 1985, p.155)

What is more, it is the police who judge what is likely to cause a breach of the peace:

> The courts also played a major role in restricting picketing. A large number of the arrests occurred in Nottinghamshire (2,417 or ?? per cent of the total) and most were dealt with by Mansfield Magistrates Court.
>
> (Wallington, 1985, p.150)

It was this court which initiated the use of restrictive bail conditions to prevent those charged from further picketing. Indeed the Mansfield Court went as far as to prepare pro-forma slips noting the bail condition:

> Not to visit any premises or place for the purpose of picketing or demonstrating in connection with the current trade dispute between the NUM and the NCB other than peacefully to picket or demonstrate at his usual place of employment.

These forms were stapled upon the bail forms of miners before their bail application was heard.

These 'usual conditions' were increasingly used outside Nottinghamshire and were upheld in *R. v. Mansfield Justices, ex P. Sharkey* (see Wallington, 1985, p.156). The key point with this decision is that it legitimised the use of additional weapons in the prevention of secondary picketing.

The indirect effect of legislation

Of course, the Conservative legislation has an indirect effect on the conduct of industrial relations and, particularly, on the way in which trade unions pursue a dispute. Given that if an employer seeks an injunction the courts are almost certain to grant it, a union leader has to be circumspect in the conduct of a dispute; as such, unions are very concerned to ensure that they comply with the law so as not to lose their immunity from an action in tort. This means that a union has to think carefully before taking industrial action. A *Labour Research* survey of union representatives in 53 workplaces gives some indication of the indirect effect of the legislation. Only three of the union representatives reported that legal action had been taken by employers. However, the survey also found that: in one in three workplaces employers had threatened to use the law during negotiations; in 20 per cent of workplaces industrial actions had been called for as a result of such threats; in nearly a third of workplaces union members were unwilling to strike for fear of the law; two-thirds of all representatives felt that the law had affected how they negotiated. None of this meant that unions were emasculated; there had been industrial action in the last three years in over 50 per cent of the workplaces. However, the legislation had a significant effect on both the union's decision on industrial action and their conduct of collective bargaining (*Labour Research*, September 1990, pp.11–12).

The TGWU's action against the abolition of the National Dock Labour Scheme in 1989 provides an excellent example of how the legislation can constrain a union leadership seeking to take industrial action. On 6 April 1989, the government announced that it intended to introduce a bill quickly into Parliament which would dismantle the National Dock Labour Scheme (NDLS). Under the Scheme, which was introduced in 1947 to do away with casual labour, employers in 63 ports were required by law to use registered dock-workers. These registered dock-workers all belonged to a TGWU closed shop. As soon as the announcement was made unofficial strikes brought seven ports to a standstill. However, Ron Todd, the TGWU's General Secretary, was clearly concerned to ensure that any action taken was within the law, thus avoiding legal action by the employers (see *The Times*, 10 April 1989).

The 1982 Employment Act stipulates that a legitimate trade dispute must be 'wholly or mainly' concerned with an industrial issue. As such, a strike in defence of the NDLS would almost certainly have been challenged in the courts as a political strike and, most likely, ruled illegal. A strike in defiance of the law would necessarily lead to an injunction; if this was not complied with then there would be a fine for contempt and, possibly, sequestration of the union's assets. Not surprisingly in these circumstances, the union and the National Association of Port Employers (NAPE) sought legal advice. Even less surprisingly, the union's response was circumspect.

On 10 April, the union decided in principle to call a national strike ballot, but a decision on industrial action was delayed while further legal advice was sought. The situation was fraught with problems for the union. Norman Fowler, then Secretary of State for Employment, commented that a strike against the NDLS would be a political strike and he would expect the NAPE to take the matter to court. At the same time the union was aware that any attempt to extend industrial action to dock-workers in ports not covered by the NDLS would involve secondary action and thus break the law. In addition, Ken Cooper, the Chairman of the NAPE, warned the union that he would consider the wording on the ballot paper very carefully before deciding how to pursue the matter in court. Overall, it was clear that the union needed to ballot for a strike in defence of the employment terms and conditions laid down under NDLS itself. Certainly, the conduct of the industrial action in this case was much more complicated than it would have been prior to 1979.

The dock-workers' leaders voted on 11 April to proceed with a national strike ballot against the advice of RonTodd. However, by 14 April Todd had won support from his Executive to delay a strike ballot until attempts had been made to negotiate a new national agreement with the NAPE. Finally, on 20 April the TGWU called a national strike ballot against the employers' refusal to negotiate a new agreement to replace NDLS. At this stage, the union had no hopes of saving the Scheme but was pushing for a new national agreement covering all employers in the industry.

Associated British Ports (ABP), which covered 19 Scheme ports, started proceedings on 8 May seeking an injunction from the High Court to prevent the unions inducing their members to take illegal action; they argued that the action was against the government decision to abolish the NDLS and, as such, was not covered by the immunity from actions in tort. They were subsequently joined in this action by the Port of London Authority (PLA) and the Mersey Dock and Harbour Corporation (MDHC). In addition, on 11 May the NAPE was granted an injunction to stop the TGWU encouraging the continuation of unofficial action in Hull.

When the High Court hearing into the ABP, PLA and MDHC case began on 18 May, the employers were claiming at least £250,000 damages from the TGWU. They accused the union of manufacturing a dispute. Despite this, the dockers voted overwhelmingly to strike; on a 90 per cent turnout, 74 per cent supported industrial action and 26 per cent opposed it. Subsequently, on 1 June the High Court ruled against the employers, confirming that the union was pursuing a legitimate trade dispute and was, thus, protected by the immunity. Even so, the union decided to wait for the Court of Appeal decision in the case before calling a national stoppage. Once again, the fear of legal action ensured the union was circumspect in its conduct of the dispute.

In fact, the Court of Appeal overturned the High Court's decision and granted an injunction to the port employers restraining the TGWU from calling a strike. The decision was based upon the 'balance of convenience' argument which was dealt with earlier in this chapter. The court argued that the employers would suffer a greater loss and inconvenience if an injunction was not granted than would the union if it was granted. However, the TGWU was granted leave to appeal to the House of Lords.

The Court of Appeal decision presented the union with an additional problem. Under the 1984 Trade Union Act, any strike must be called within 28 days of the ballot which supports it. This meant that the mandate for strike action, which resulted from the ballot, would run out on 15 June, before the House of Lords decision was known. The position for the TGWU was further complicated because, as a result of the judges' decision, a number of ports were paralysed by unofficial action. In effect, the strike was being held up by a point of law, but Ron Todd continued to emphasise that, despite the problems this involved for the unions in pursuing its dispute and the pressure he was under from sections of his membership, the TGWU intended to stay within the law at all times.

On 20 June the Law Lords ruled in favour of the union and overturned the Court of Appeal decision. However, given that the mandate provided by the initial strike ballot had expired, the union was required to conduct a second ballot. At the same time, the situation was soon significantly changed because on 3 July the government's Bill received Royal Assent and the NDLS ceased to exist. Despite this, the dock-workers confirmed their earlier decision and voted in the second ballot by a 3 to 1 majority in favour of a strike. The strike began on 14 July but, while it received initial support from the majority of dockers, it was called off on 1 August. Merseyside dockers remained on strike for some time, but the action ended in a major defeat for the union. They were forced to accept local wage bargaining at best; indeed, the PLA decided to issue personal contracts to its work-force, thus effectively de-recognising the union.

This case presents a graphic, and perhaps fairly extreme, illustration of how the government legislation can affect the conduct of a strike, even though the courts ultimately upheld the legitimacy of the unions' actions. Of course, once the government had decided to abolish the NDLS, it was virtually impossible, given their parliamentary majority and antipathy to trade unions, that any industrial action would have led them to reconsider. However, if the legislation of the 1980s had not been passed, the TGWU would have had a much freer hand to use a variety of tactics in support of its attempts to persuade the port employers to accept a new national agreement to replace the Scheme. If they had been able earlier to pursue more decisive action without any fear of legal consequences, then it is quite possible that they could have achieved this aim. As it was, they were forced to delay industrial action in order to stay within the new laws. Such delay clearly significantly weakened the TGWU's bargaining position with employers. In the end, they emerged from the aborted strike in a much weaker position.

Conclusion

This review of the operation of the Conservative legislation suggests a number of clear conclusions:

1. The Conservative legislation has not been widely used. Few employers resort to the law when conducting their industrial relations.
2. However, when an employer seeks an injunction it is granted in the vast majority of the cases; few employers pursue the matter any further.
3. The law is used most in two sectors; printing and shipping. These were also the sectors in which employers used the 1971 Industrial Relations Act. Clearly the legislation is used most in industries with a history of poor industrial relations.
4. When legal action has been taken to resolve industrial relations disputes since 1979 it has often involved laws, and legal recourses, which existed prior to the election of the Thatcher Government. The key tactic available to employers in industrial disputes is the application for an interlocutory injunction and this recourse has been available, and almost inevitably successful, in industrial relations cases since 1975. In addition, the Wapping case showed that the absence of a right to strike, and the fact that employees can therefore be dismissed for striking, is a crucial weapon available to employers in industries marked by poor industrial relations; this tactic has always been available to employers, but rarely used. The key tactic available to individual unionists, at least until the 1988 Employment Act, was the use of the law of contract to hold unions, and union officials, to the letter of their rule books; this tactic has also been available for a long time. Similarly, although since 1979 the criminal law has played a more central role in industrial

disputes, and was crucially important in the Messenger dispute, the Wapping dispute and, particularly, the miners' strike, the police previously had the powers they used in these disputes.

5. In fact, the major role the legislation passed since 1979 has played has been indirect. It has clearly restricted extended industrial action, although, as Chapter 8 indicates later, 'cut price' or shorter industrial action is still very common. Unions, union leaders and unionists are now much more conscious of the consequences of stepping outside the increasingly restricted protection of the 'golden formula' and this affects the strategic judgements they make in the pursuit of a trade dispute particularly, and in the conduct of, industrial relations generally. At the very least, union leaders have to prepare the ground very carefully before they take industrial action and this delays action and weakens their bargaining position.

6. One other point needs to be made and it is not one which should surprise any student of industrial relations. The courts since 1979, as throughout the history of British industrial relations, have interpreted the legislation in a way which restricts the protection unions and unionists enjoy under the 'golden formula' to a minimum.

The future

Little is likely to change in the future if a Conservative Government remains in office. Employers are unlikely to use the legislation much more frequently. It will still be most used in certain industries. Its chief effect is likely to remain an indirect one. Union leaders will remain circumspect in their use of industrial action. If a Labour Government is elected some of the legislation is likely to be repealed, injunctions will be more difficult to obtain and a new Industrial Court will be created. As such, one would expect less use of the law in industrial relations.

5

The Unions' Political Role: Relations with the Conservative Government, 1979-90

There is no doubt that the unions' political role has reduced significantly since 1979. There are a number of related reasons for this change. First, the unions have always had a closer relationship, if not always a total harmonious one, with Labour governments. The election of the Conservatives in 1979 inevitably meant that the relationship between the unions and government would deteriorate, particularly because, as we have seen, the newly-elected government was committed to trade union reform and that commitment had played a significant part in their manifesto and election campaign.

Second, the Conservatives were also committed to market, rather than corporatist, solutions to economic problems. No attempt at a corporatist solution is feasible without union involvement because such a strategy is based upon supply-side management and government intervention in the relationship between capital and labour. In contrast, while market solutions may involve some less direct government intervention, for example, by establishing cash limits in the public sector which affect wages, such intervention is not negotiated with unions – there is no exchange involved – but rather imposed upon them.

Third, the Conservatives were strongly influenced by the government-overload thesis, which suggested that one of the major reasons for Britain's economic decline was the proliferation of demands placed upon government resources. For many observers this was a consequence of incorporating interest groups into the policy-making process (see King, 1975). It was implicit in much of the literature on government overload, but explicit in Conservative rhetoric, that foremost among these powerful, constraining, over-demanding interests were the trade unions.

Fourth, and in many ways most importantly, as we saw earlier, much of the policy of the incoming government, and even more of its rhetoric, was a conscious response to the failures of Mr Heath. If Mr Heath became the spectre at the feast, the trade unions remained the devil to be invoked and held responsible for the failure of both Mr Heath and the Labour Government. As such to negotiate with the unions would have been to sup with the devil.

This chapter deals mainly with the relationship between the trade unions and the Conservative Government, although the last section looks briefly at the European dimension. It is divided into four sections. The first section looks at an attempt to quantify the decline in the Trades Unions Congress (TUC) access to government. Subsequently, I will briefly re-examine the role of the unions in the evolution, passage and implementation of the Conservatives' industrial relations legislation through a consideration of the unions' one major success – the removal of the proposal for the restoration of contracting in from the 1984 Trade Union Act. The third section deals with the major strike with political resonance in the period – the miners' strike of 1984–5. The fourth part of the chapter will present a case study of the operation of the Manpower Services Commission (MSC), now the Training Agency (TA), since 1979. The fate of the MSC, and in particular of the unions' role upon it, represents an excellent example of the unions' changed political role. The final section pursues a slightly different tack. It examines the changing relations between the British trade unions and Europe.

The unions' access to government

It is the TUC which co-ordinates and undertakes most of the contacts between the government and the unions. Neil Mitchell presents an interesting attempt to quantify the extent, quality and effect of the TUC access to government between 1976 and 1984. The tables I present merely partially update his analysis using the same method. Mitchell's tables are based upon an analysis of the reports by the General Council of the TUC to each Annual Conference. As Mitchell says:

> These reports provide a detailed account of the TUC's relations with government and Parliament, and a comprehensive record of the TUC's policy positions and its written and personal contacts

with government on these positions. From these reports it is possible to extract information on frequencies of contact, methods of contact (meeting, correspondence), levels of contact (prime ministerial, ministerial, etc.), types of contact (bipartite or tripartite), and the effectiveness of a contact.

(Mitchell, 1987, p.510)

The picture which emerges from Mitchell's analysis is clear (see Table 5.1). The number of contacts between the government and the unions did not decrease but the pattern and quality of those contacts changed significantly. In particular, after 1979 there were fewer meetings (10 per cent) than before (27 per cent), so less personal contact. In addition, fewer of the contacts were initiated by the government after 1979 (8 per cent) than previously (18 per cent). What is more, the number of contacts initiated by the government fell from fifteen in the first year of the Conservative Government to six in both 1983 and 1984.

Mitchell also reports a clear decline in the effectiveness of the contacts. The TUC Annual Reports claimed 'success' when the TUC advocated a particular policy position to the government (or a government agency) and the government agreed to take the appropriate action. Obviously, there is a major problem with this data. The TUC's assessments clearly overestimates its effectiveness; any interest group does so in order to justify its own existence and importance. However, as we are mainly interested in the comparative reports of success in the periods of Labour and Conservative Government, the figures can be used with care, given that we have no reason to believe that the level of the TUC's overestimate of its success has changed significantly. Mitchell's figures confirm the widely-held view that the TUC has had significantly less influence over the Conservative Government (8 per cent) than it did over the Labour Government (19 per cent).

Mitchell's analysis also suggests that tripartite contacts have become more important to the TUC since 1979, despite the anti-corporatist attitudes of the Conservatives. According to the TUC, 38 per cent of the 'successes' under the Thatcher government were achieved as a result of tripartite contacts, as compared with 17 per cent in the 1976–9 period. As Mitchell points out:

Table 5.1 Number and type of contact between government and unions, 1976–84 and 1988

		Labour				Conservative						
		1976	1977	1978	1979	1979	1980	1981	1982	1983	1984	1988
Initiated	TUC	61	58	62	60	63	66	68	69	74	70	60
By	Govt.	17	19	17	17	15	11	11	10	6	6	17
	Parl	1	1	2	1	0	4	6	5	4	3	4
	Other*	21	21	20	22	23	19	15	15	17	21	1
Method	Meeting	25	35	26	28	23	17	14	14	16	16	16
	Writing	49	39	50	45	46	50	52	55	60	52	45
	Other**	27	26	24	27	31	33	35	31	31	32	39
Type	Bipartite	75	73	73	74	67	66	62	64	66	64	73
	Tripartite	18	16	17	15	17	16	14	13	16	18	13
	Other***	6	11	10	11	17	18	23	23	18	18	14
	Total N	279	205	242	187	48	252	281	280	248	264	245

Notes:
* Includes contacts initiated by bodies like the Manpower Services Commission, the Health & Safety Commission and other tripartite organisations, as well as cases where the initiator was unspecified.

** Includes tripartite, Royal Commission, parliamentary and other cases where the method of contact was unclear.

*** Includes Royal Commission, parliamentary and public opinion contacts and other cases where the type of contact was unclear.

Sources: Years 1976–84 taken from Mitchell (1987); 1988 calculated from the TUC Annual Report using Mitchell's criteria.

This result is not really surprising as tripartite contacts are institutionalized, not impromptu, and inherently less susceptible to partisan or ideological change than bipartite contacts, as long as tripartite institutions themselves survive. The TUC understand this difference, hence their tenacious attachment to the principle of tripartism.

(Mitchell, 1987, pp.514–15)

Unfortunately for the TUC, while the Advisory, Conciliation and Arbitration Services (ACAS) and the Health and Safety Commission (HSC) survived, the MSC, probably the most important of these institutions to the TUC, did not.

Influencing government legislation

There are, then, major problems with assessing the influence of an interest group over policy. However, as we saw in Chapter 3, it is difficult to escape the conclusion that the TUC had little influence upon the shape of the government industrial relations legislation; yet it is in this area where, prior to 1979, many observers saw the trade unions as omnipotent. The government's cautious approach to industrial relations reform clearly owed a great deal to their assessment of the unions success in curtailing the effect of Heath's Industrial Relations Act; they were obviously wary that something similar might happen. In fact, as we saw above, the unions response to the 1980 and 1982 Employment Acts was weaker and less concerted than the government had expected, partly because the unions thought that if they behaved 'responsibly' it was less likely that further more radical changes would follow, and partly because a large percentage of unions' own members supported the legislative changes. What is more, it soon became clear that it was of little use, and very expensive, to resist the law. Such acquiescence ensured they had little influence over the policy. Only on one occasion did the government make a significant concession to the TUC, when it agreed to drop its commitment to 'contracting in' from the 1984 Trade Union Act, and it is worth examining this case because it is revealing about the limits of trade unions' influence.

Before the 1984 Act, trade unions' political finance was based upon the 1913 Trade Unions Act which re-established the legal basis of trade union political action, undermined by the 1909 Osborne judgment, subject to a number of constraints (see A.Taylor, 1987, pp.205–6). A ballot was necessary before a political fund could be established but, of course, most ballots had been held soon after the 1913 Act became law and no subsequent ballot was required. Any union member who didn't wish to pay the political levy could contract out, although between 1927 and 1946 this was replaced by the requirement that those who wished to pay should contract in. The difference between contracting in and contracting out is very significant; when contracting out was reintroduced in 1947 those paying the political levy increased from 39 per cent to 60 per cent in eighteen months.

The government's Green Paper, *Democracy in Trade Unions*, published before the 1983 election, strongly attacked the political levy. As Steel *et al.* indicate, two arguments were advanced against the contracting-out rules. It was suggested that the high proportion of members paying the political levy in some unions contradicted psephological studies which indicated a decline in the number of trade unionists voting Labour. At the same time, the Green Paper argued that the unions failed to inform their members about the political fund and the opportunities to contract out:

> there is evidence that many trade unions do not take adequate steps to ensure that their members know that they can contract-out or how they can do so. Independent research indicates that rank and file union members are often not aware that they are in fact paying a political levy and have no knowledge of the procedure for contracting-out.
>
> (Quoted in Steel *et al.*, 1987, p.445)

The government's overall strategy in the 1984 Act was clear. They wished to depoliticise the trade union movement; to weaken its link to the Labour Party and force it to concentrate on economic, not political, activity. It claimed a mandate for the reform, especially as public opinion polls indicated widespread antipathy to the political levy and union political, particularly party political, activity. Soon after the election, Norman Tebbit, the Employment Secretary, announced that the political levy would be reformed so that, once again, contracting in replaced contracting out (A.Taylor, 1987, p.207). However, when the Trade Union Bill was published it didn't include any such provision, rather it contained a redefinition of political objects and a requirement that ballots be held for the continuation of political funds. Why?

Tebbit did talk to the TUC before the election or, rather, he listened to their proposals. However, the change came with the appointment of Tom King as Employment Secretary in the reshuffle after the 1983 election. King was not so identified with the confrontational style of government-union relations as Tebbit. However, the change in policy owed more to a series of strategic political judgements by the government than to the change in personnel. On 19 October 1983, the TUC had a 90 minute meeting with Tom King at which they agreed to prepare a code of practice on the operation of political funds once the Trade Union Bill was published; in return King clearly promised not to proceed with the contracting out proposal as long as the TUC promises were firmed up. However, even after the bill was published, King was under considerable pressure from some of his back-benchers and he announced that the government was drawing up a contracting out amendment; of course, this threat was a useful bargaining counter in his negotiations with the TUC. In fact, on 15 November the TUC agreed to provide more information on contracting out and stricter supervision of political fund accounts. This *Code of Practice* was approved by the TUC's Employment Committee and then by the General Council. It was accepted by the government and any plans to introduce a contracting in amendment were dropped (Steel *et al.*, 1987, pp.445–6). Even so, certain Conservative backbenchers, with support from the Alliance parties, tried, but failed, to introduce such a clause (Steel *et al.*, 1987, p.446).

It is easy to see why the TUC were keen to negotiate on this issue. Contracting in, as we have seen, would have seriously restricted the size of the political fund; which unions saw as particularly important in a cold climate. The 1983 TUC Annual Conference had embraced New Realism and given approval for renewed contacts with government. Indeed, these negotiations, conducted on the TUC side by Len Murray, the General Secretary, and Bill Keys, Chairman of the TUC's Employment Committee, provided a brief window in an extended period of strained relations, given that a fortnight after the deal was concluded all contacts between the TUC and the government ceased because of the Government Communications Headquarters (GCHQ) case.

Why did the government negotiate and make a fairly major concession to the unions? A number of explanations have been offered. Taylor suggests that the government were unwilling to see the Labour Party bankrupted (A.Taylor, 1987, p.215). As this stands, it is superficial. Actually, Grant appears much nearer the mark when he argues:

By tampering with union political funds the Conservatives also knew they had placed the Act in the party political spectrum and again became worried about public opinion. There is little doubt that the Conservatives felt that contracting in was a far more contentious and open act of aggression on the Labour Party than the covert tactic of ballots which left union members to do the government's work for it. The Conservatives did not wish to be seen openly attempting to bankrupt their political rivals, thereby providing more ammunition for the unions. They feared that the effects would rebound on them in a wave of pro-Labour sympathy.
(Grant, 1987, p.62)

Taylor also suggests that the government believed that the concession would strengthen New Realism in the trade union movement and lead to a more responsible attitude to government legislation and to collective bargaining. There may be an element of truth here. However, the government's action in the GCHQ case which quickly followed put back the cause of New Realism until it was resuscitated by the miners' strike.

Both Grant and Taylor argue that Conservatives were reluctant to damage the Labour Party too much for fear that it might result in a stronger Alliance (see A Taylor, 1987, p.215; Grant, 1987, p.63). On this reading, the Conservatives were keen to keep a divided, and therefore weak, Opposition. Indeed, Grant also suggests that the government's failure to play any role in the political fund ballots which followed reflected the fact that, at that time, they wanted Labour to 'win' the ballots, because they feared the Alliance more. He even argues:

Their inconsistency over the political funds issue has therefore tended to fluctuate in accordance with whichever of these two parties presented the predominant challenge to Conservative popularity. By the end of 1983 the Conservatives had come to regard the Alliance as a major threat: to have bankrupted the Labour Party would have increased the Alliance's electoral potential.

(Grant, 1987, p.63)

There may be something in each of these explanations but two other factors seem to me to be more important. First, as Taylor points out, the government was well aware that any extended legislative battle on contracting in would have focused attention on the methods by which the Conservative Party was financed (A. Taylor, 1987, p.216). Although trade union contributions to the Labour Party are greater than company contributions to the Conservatives, and make up a much greater proportion of the Labour Party's income, nevertheless company contributions are a significant element in Conservative finance.

Second, and most important, the government was conscious of its image of governing competence and responsiveness to public opinion on the industrial relations issue. It wished to ensure that the legislation was not only passed, but also accepted and complied with, in order to preserve its reputation for governing competence. In addition, it was aware that, with the TUC embracing New Realism and expressing a willingness to talk, such action might result in the government losing the battle for the hearts and minds of the electorate and, particularly, of unionists. As Grant puts it:

The Conservatives therefore felt that a further hard-line piece of legislation, implemented without consultation, might in fact make them appear to be too insensitive and inaccessible about the issue of trade union reform. This was underlined by a change in public opinion on the issue of trade union reform, perhaps on the basis of 'we don't believe in kicking them when they are down'. A Gallup poll showed a decline in the belief amongst the public that 'trade unions are too powerful', from 77 per cent in 1979 to 53 per cent by 1985, while a MORI poll, asking the same question, showed a steep decline amongst trade unionists themselves, from 73 per cent in 1978 to 40 per cent in 1985. This trend worried the government because it relied on high levels of union unpopularity, especially amongst trade unionists, in order to implement its legislation successfully.

(Grant, 1987, p.62)

The exclusion of the contracting in proposal from the 1984 Trade Union Act probably represents the major political concession achieved by the TUC since 1979. However, it occurred more because of a series of judgements made by the government about the political, and in particular, electoral, consequences of pursuing the proposal. At the same time, the government shifted responsibility to the TUC and the unions for informing members of their rights as regards contracting out and the threat was always present that further legislation to introduce contracting in might be introduced. Certainly, this 'success' was quantitatively and qualitatively different from that achieved in relation to *In Place of Strife* or the 1971 Industrial Relations Act.

A strike with political resonance

As we will see in Chapter 8, although the number of strikes has fallen markedly since 1979, the pattern is not a straightforward one. However, the miners' strike was clearly the most significant industrial dispute since 1979 and had broader political resonance. It deserves consideration for this reason. Not surprisingly, an immense literature on the strike has emerged. There is no space to do that material justice here and, indeed, some of it is dealt with in other chapters of this book. However, it is important briefly to examine the causes, outcome and consequences of the strike for a number of reasons. First, the confrontation with the miners was an important symbolic event for the Conservative Government; Mrs Thatcher 'succeeded' where Mr Heath 'failed', a very important contrast for those who felt humiliated by the outcome of the 1973–4 miners' strike. Second, the outcome of the strike removed the National Union of Mineworkers (NUM) as a crucial factor in the politics of the TUC and had a significant effect on establishing the ascendancy, perhaps only the temporary ascendancy, of New Realism in the Labour movement. I obviously cannot review the literature here so, instead, I will critically assess Adeney and Lloyd's analysis of the causes, outcomes and consequences of the strike, in *Loss Without Limit*, widely viewed as the best general account of the strike (Adeney and Lloyd, 1986). Fortunately, Gibbon has produced an excellent review of the material on the strike which I will use extensively in this section (Gibbon, 1988).

In Adeney and Lloyd's view, when the Conservatives were

elected in 1979 their commitment to market forces and the manager's 'right' to manage struck a chord with the emerging top management strata in the National Coal Board (NCB), particularly the mining engineers. At the same time, the government was prepared; it had a plan to defeat the public sector unions. Of course, for the Conservatives the NUM was a prime target, partly because it was seen as a particularly powerful union, but mainly because of the embarrassing defeat Mr Heath had suffered at their hands in 1974.

To Adeney and Lloyd, the NUM was lured into a strike it couldn't win; in the spring of 1984 the government deliberately closed a Yorkshire pit, Cortonwood Colliery, at a time when there were high coal stocks and a falling world price. The government's overall strategy was informed by the Ridley Report prepared in 1978, which recommended:

(a) a build-up of maximum coal stocks, especially at the power stations;

(b) the establishment of contingency plans for the import of coal;

(c) the encouragement of the recruitment of non-union lorry drivers by haulage companies;

(d) the introduction of dual coal/oil firing in all power-stations;

(e) a large, mobile police squad should be created and equipped to prevent mass picketing;

(f) return on capital figures should be adjusted so that above-average claims could be paid to vulnerable industries, especially electricity supply;

(g) social security benefits should be withdrawn from strikers – so forcing the union to finance them.

Adeney and Lloyd argue that, on the basis of this plan, the Conservatives had prepared for a fight on their own terms. In 1981 they hadn't been ready and so had backed away from a confrontation. By 1984 everything was in place: coal stocks were high and it was spring; there were contingency plans to import cheaper foreign coal; the electricity industry's dependence on coal had been reduced; the urban riots in 1981 had established the National Reporting Centre as an effective means of co-ordinating police actions; and under the 1980 Social Security Act it was assumed that all official strikers received £25 from union funds, so that their benefits were reduced by that amount.

Adeney and Lloyd's account is fairly favourable to both management and the government. The management merely wanted to get on with their job, managing unfettered by the constraints which a privileged NUM placed upon them. The government wished to make the coal industry more efficient; to introduce market disciplines into the nationalised industries. More importantly, as any government should, it asserted its governing competence by carefully planning a certain victory before entering into the field. In contrast, the NUM leadership, and Arthur Scargill in particular, were committed to an outdated style of unionism. According to Adeney and Lloyd, Scargill was committed to the use of the miners' power to challenge the elected government, and to undermine the New Realism of the TUC and replace it with a commitment to rank and file militancy. They argue that this strategy was bankrupt and conclude that the days of 'heroic' trade unions are at an end; the way forward is the New Realism of the EETPU.

It is difficult to know where to start in criticising Adeney and Lloyd's work, which is strong on facts and opinion but weak on analysis. In particular, they fail to situate the miners' strike in its historical context; fail to understand Arthur Scargill's role in the NUM and hence in the strike; place too much emphasis on the governing competence of the Thatcher government; and over-estimate the deleterious effect of the strike on the trade union movement. Fortunately, Gibbon's review provides an excellent antidote and I shall use it extensively, if critically, in what follows.

It is impossible to understand the strike if it is not seen as a reaction by the rank and file of the NUM to the disappointments of almost 40 years of nationalisation and, in particular, to the corporatist strategies pursued between 1974 and 1979 (see G.Taylor, 1991). As Gibbon points out, corporatism operated in British nationalised industries through two quite separate relationships:

> Firstly, a relationship between the state and the industry, in which the state more or less actively supports or obstructs investment decisions, regulates demand, manipulates prices and more or less directly controls manpower levels. Secondly, a relationship between management and union(s) within the industry, whose character reflects not only pre-existing traditions and broader trends in the class struggle, but also the specific room for compromise (formal and informal) made available by the character of the first

relation. Occasionally a direct relationship between the state and the union has also existed, but this has been the exception rather than the rule.

(Gibbon, 1988, p.145)

To a large extent, Gibbon is correct. However, there is little doubt that, during the Labour Government between 1974 and 1979, the relationship between the government and the NUM was crucial. The Labour Government failed to deliver the co-ordinated energy policy, in which coal played the key role, that the NUM wanted and expected. At the same time, the NUM, expecting to be rewarded by such an energy policy, acquiesced in a series of pit closures while its members watched as Joe Gormley endorsed the Social Contract which, after 1975, as we saw in Chapter 2, became little more than an incomes policy.

During the 1974–9 period a clear gap emerged between the policies pursued by the NUM leadership and the views and interest of their members. As we saw, the Labour Government failed to deliver its part of the implicit corporatist bargain with Joe Gormley. At the same time, as Adeney and Lloyd argue, the NCB management began to reject the corporatist link with the NUM and were also increasingly subject to government intervention. Against this background we can see the true significance of the rise of Arthur Scargill.

In fact, Scargill won the Presidential Election in 1984 because he was not Joe Gormley; he offered the membership an alternative based upon a withdrawal from the corporatist embrace and an assertion of the bargaining power of the union. In Gibbon's terms:

> Scargill's election campaign had centred around a rejection of managerial authority (and, he might have added, of corporatist politics) and in the process he mobilised nationally the pit tradition for the first time in living memory.

(Gibbon, 1988, p.190 – my comment in brackets)

As Gibbon shows, it is misguided to see Scargill as some sort of authoritarian leading the NUM into the industrial equivalent of the Valley of Death. He was elected by an overwhelming majority and he remained popular in, and even after, the strike. The tactics the NUM used, particularly flying pickets and mass picketing were used by the NUM in previous strikes and by other unions; they failed, as we saw in

Chapter 4, largely because of the strategies adopted by the police. The decision not to hold a national ballot was, with hindsight, a mistake, but it was understandable given the failure to achieve a majority in the previous ballots on the issue of pit closures. In addition, Gibbon persuasively argues that the view that the vast majority of miners in Nottingham would have accepted the result of a ballot to strike is misguided given that: 'the type of trade unionism which existed there at pit level was even more narrowly corporatist than the tradition of national mineworkers' politics' (Gibbon, 1988, p.176).

Overall, the tactics pursued in the strike reflected, in large part, a rejection of the failed corporatist politics of the 1970s and a reassertion of the view that the union must rely on its industrial strength in an increasingly hostile economic and political climate. Not surprisingly, in that situation, the union used those tactics which had proved successful in 1974.

Gibbon tends to play down the government's role in the strike. In particular, he is rightly dismissive of the view of Adeney and Lloyd that the Ridley Report provided a blueprint for the strike and represented one element of a consciously-planned government strategy. Gibbon argues that the government's position was strengthened by factors over which they, or indeed anyone else, had little control, particularly the development of an international coal trade which led to a dramatic fall in the price of coal. In addition, he makes much of the appointment of Peter Walker as Secretary of State for Energy in 1983. In Gibbon's view, Walker was not the man the government would have chosen if they had intended from the outset to confront the NUM:

> While Walker was no opponent of the nuclear and/or privatisation lobbies, he was still one of the most potentially unreliable 'representatives' they could have chosen – particularly in the light of the supposed fact that a major confrontation with the NUM was planned in the immediate future.
>
> (Gibbon, 1988, p.146)

Gibbon perhaps underplays the importance of the government's role, while Adeney and Lloyd certainly overemphasise it. The Conservatives were clearly concerned to assert their authority in relation to trade unions and had particular reason to feel that the NUM should feel the brunt of this exercise of authority as we saw in Chapter 2.

The government was clearly thinking about the possibility of a confrontation and Gibbon is surely wrong to dismiss the Ridley Report. However, as we saw in Chapter 3, the Conservatives were unsure in Opposition of how to deal with the unions. They proceeded slowly, taking advantage of those chances which arose. In essence, the Conservative Government built upon the unpopularity of the unions and used the fall in world coal prices and the media's portrayal of the issues and events in the strike, rather than deliberately creating them.

Adeney and Lloyd's assessment of the consequence of the strike is also simplistic. They argue that for the NUM and the miners it was, in the title of their book, *Loss Without Limit*, while for the trade unions it pointed the way to a future based on New Realism. The picture is more complicated. Certainly, the consequences for the NUM as a national union have been dire. The membership has shrunk to about 65 000 and employment in the industry has fallen from 187 000 in 1983 to 85 000 in February 1989, with a planned decrease to 70 000 by mid-1990 (Gibbon and Bromley, 1990, p.64).

However, as Gibbon and Bromley point out, industrial relations at the pit level, like industrial relations on the shop floor in industry more generally, reflect the relative strengths of management and labour in the pit and will always fluctuate (ibid, pp.75–82). In addition, Gibbon and Bromley indicate that local conflicts have flared up as the NCB pushes for increased flexibility in working practices, increased production, lower manning levels and reduced allowances. Such a management offensive attempts to impose basic changes in the labour process and is certain to provoke opposition at the pit level. Certainly the number of disputes in the coal industry has risen steadily since March 1985. In 1986 the number of days lost lost per 1000 workers was 1200 and in 1987 2212. This compares with 1840 and 3160 in 1982 and 1983 respectively.

One other point, which Gibbon neglects, is also worth making. Historically, the national and regional NUM has attempted, with limited success, to control local politics, and assert the primacy of the central union. However, by weakening the national NUM, the strike has ensured that local pit politics, which in Thatcherite terms is extremely disruptive, will be the dominant political strategy in the NUM for the foreseeable future.

Gibbon is less sound when dealing with the wider effect of the strike:

Outside the coalfield the outcome of the strike has been largely demoralising in the long run. While not ending large, long strikes as a phenomenon (cf. Wapping) it has certainly restricted their likelihood, especially in the public sector where the predominant feeling appears to be 'if the miners can't do it, then how the hell can we?' Furthermore, it has speeded up the forward march of New Realism inside both the TUC and the Labour Party (where its most obvious effect has been to secure the position of Neil Kinnock). All this is widely recognised. What is less easy to grasp is that the strike appears to have had rather less of an effect on industrial relations in coal. The disparity between coal and other industries is in this respect wider than ever.

(Gibbon, 1989, p.189)

In the first place the NUR's industrial action in 1989 showed that extended action by public sector unions is not only possible but can be successful. More importantly, however, Gibbon's implication that the strike had a major effect on industrial relations outside the coal industry is surely wrong. As we shall see in Chapter 8, it is often suggested that even the full weight of the government's industrial relations legislation since 1979 has had limited effect on industrial relations in the workplace. Workplace industrial relations in all industries, not just in the coal industry, are largely determined by the history and current strength of capital and labour within individual companies, and even workplaces, not by broad political events like the miners' strike.

The unions' role in policy-making and implementation: the case of youth employment policy

The decline of the position of the trade unions in relation to youth unemployment policy presents an excellent example of the shrinking political role of the unions generally since 1979. The Manpower Services Commission (MSC) was established in 1973. Obviously, I haven't the space here to deal with the whole history of the MSC. However, it is essential to establish how the various periods differ in order to identify the changes since 1979. (For more details see Marsh, 1992.)

1973–9: the creation and growth of the MSC

At the beginning of the 1970s, as Britain moved into a deeper economic recession, the employment prospects for young and old alike worsened; although in 1973 only 5 per cent of the unemployed were under 18. The 1973 Employment and Training Act established the MSC which provided the institutional setting within which future policies on unemployment, particularly youth unemployment, were developed and implementation planned. The MSC was a semi-autonomous specialist agency hived off from the Department of Employment (DEmp) and staffed by civil servants. It was tripartite; the CBI and the TUC had three representatives on the Commission, the local authorities two, with one nominee of professional education interests. The original role envisaged for the MSC was as a source of labour market intelligence but as unemployment increased it was given responsibility for special schemes designed to reduce unemployment.

The period between 1976 and 1979 was marked by two major changes. First, the scale of youth unemployment grew rapidly. By 1976 12 per cent of the total unemployed were under 18 while in 1978 this figure peaked at 22 per cent: that is 328 000 young people. Second, the policy process became increasingly centralised around the MSC with strong bilateral contacts between the government and the TUC.

The role of the TUC was clearly crucial and during the late 1970s the bilateral contacts between the TUC and the government were most important. Of course, the 1974–9 Labour Government claimed a close relationship with the TUC, institutionalised in the Trade Union-Labour Party Liaison Committee and reflected in the Social Contract. In the youth employment policy field this relationship bore fruit for the Labour Party. The TUC were closely involved in the evolution of policy and co-operated with its implementation, despite the fact that the details of the Youth Opportunities Programme (YOP) appeared more geared to the interests of employers than those of unions.

The participants in policy-making were the DEmp, the MSC, the TUC and the Confederation of British Industry (CBI). They shared a changed consensus broadly agreed on policy and all backed YOP, the new, larger scheme introduced in 1978 which had 162 000 participants in its first year and 553 000 in its last year, 1982–3.

However, there were signs of instability in this policy network. The MSC was a tripartite body associated with the corporatism of the Labour Government and might be expected to play a more limited role under a Conservative Government committed to market forces. In addition, the TUC's position was far from easy; it accepted a number of elements within YOP which it disliked because it saw YOP as the first step to a future with a broader-based, more high-quality, training programme. As such, its strategy was based upon the re-election of a Labour Government which would fulfil its promises on training. At the same time, a number of actors excluded from the policy network, particularly some of the individual unions which were required to co-operate in the delivery of youth training, were strongly opposed to YOP. In the next period such tensions were exacerbated, not eased.

1979–1987: direction and control

When the Conservatives were elected in 1979 the MSC's expanded role in policy-making appeared under threat. The Conservatives disliked the corporatist overtones of the MSC and were strongly committed to less government intervention in the economy. However, after a brief period of hostility, the new government embraced the MSC and this period was marked by an intensification and extension of earlier trends. This is not to say that nothing changed. In particular, the position of the TUC and the unions significantly weakened. In part, of course, the decline in the role of the TUC was a reflection of their growing weakness in an era of high unemployment. At the same time, however, the Conservative Government was anxious to reduce the policy-making role of the trade unions; beer and sandwiches in Downing Street were very much a thing of the past.

The government initially saw the MSC as part of a public sector which acted as a drag upon the wealth-creating private sector. Given the government's deflationary policies and its initial antipathy to the MSC, it is not surprising that in the first two years of the Thatcher government MSC expenditure remained static in real terms. However, things quickly changed. Youth unemployment rose rapidly. In January 1980, 20 per cent of those under 18 were unemployed. In addition, by the middle of 1980, unemployment had replaced inflation as the most important problem facing the government according to the Gallup opinion polls. So the Conservatives were faced with the same political imperative which had helped to shape the policy of the Labour Government; they needed to be seen to be doing something about youth unemployment. The MSC's special programmes had the advantage of providing a relatively cheap means of keeping down the unemployment figures. By Christmas 1980 the government had issued a White Paper which promised to invest £1 billion in the creation of a comprehensive, one year Youth Training Scheme (YTS).

It was against this background that the decision to establish the YTS was taken. There is little doubt that political considerations were the crucial factor which shaped outcomes or that the government was the key actor in the policy network, particularly as regards the decision to create YTS (for much fuller discussions see Marsh, 1992; Keep, 1986; and Stringer and Richardson, 1984). In contrast, the MSC was still strongly committed to a consensual style of policy-making. It believed that sensible and lasting change could only be achieved through an extensive process of consultation which served to develop agreement on both the objectives to be achieved and the means to be used.

While the government stressed the responsibility of individual firms for training, its main concern was to develop a scheme which would quickly reduce the level of youth unemployment. This reduction became imperative as an election approached. In contrast, the MSC wanted a more rational, extensive and consultative policy-making process which would produce a more effective scheme.

Two other interests played a key role in the evolution of YTS, the CBI and the TUC. As the MSC argued, 'the key to the new scheme lies with employers in both private and public sectors' (MSC, 1982, para.3.9). The CBI position, however, was not easy because its members had divergent interests and views. Despite this, the CBI pushed for a comprehensive review of the integration of training and educational provision for those aged between 14 and 19. However, it was rebuffed on this crucial point because, for the government, time was of the essence. Keep (1986, p.14) makes the key point; the outcome was a 'triumph of short-term pressures'. Faced with this time constraint, the CBI concentrated upon minimising those aspects of the new scheme opposed by sections of its membership.

During this period, the network role of the TUC changed dramatically. It had agreed to YOP as a step towards a comprehensive training policy. When the Conservatives were elected there was little chance of achieving such a policy and the TUC was forced to pursue a difficult two-pronged strategy. On the one hand, they criticised the Thatcher government's economic policy, calling for reflation. At the same time, they remained a loyal supporter of the MSC despite the fact that there was growing antipathy to it among individual unions (see Keep, 1986, p.10; Eversley, 1980, pp.200–26). The TUC, like the CBI, wanted an integrated education and training policy for the young. However, they were even less likely than the CBI to convince the Conservative Government of the merits of a broader view, given that in abolishing the majority of the Industrial Training Boards (ITBs), the government had made clear that it would reduce the unions' participation in training policy formulation (Keep, 1986, p.11).

After the YTS was established, the TUC continued to urge unions and the unemployed to participate in the scheme. It saw YTS as a step toward the development of a comprehensive training policy. Its strategy was to reform from within. The strategy led increasingly to tensions within the trade union movement as a series of unions spoke out against YTS and refused to co-operate with its administration. The TUC's influence on youth employment policy was declining.

The attitudes of individual unions towards the special programmes has always been more ambivalent than the view of the TUC, and hostility has grown over time. In particular, unions have been unhappy about: job substitution; the relaxation of health and safety protection; and the use of allowances which, in effect, reduce wages. Many unions were strongly opposed to at least some elements of YTS, while an even larger number of unions bestowed 'conditional approval' on training policy, endorsing particular schemes provided that they met certain criteria laid down by the unions. Overall, response was diverse and there was little co-ordination between unions (Eversley, 1980, especially 216–17).

Although the government rejected the views of the MSC, the CBI and the TUC on the need for extensive consultation and a broad review of training and education, it is too simplistic to say that the government was never constrained by other members in the policy network, even though the process became more centralised. Indeed, the government made a number of important concessions in the discussions which led to the creation of YTS.

The main difference between the rest of the policy network and the government lay in three areas. The MSC, the TUC and the CBI all wanted the allowance for YTS to be kept at the same level as for the YOP and for the scheme to be open to all school-leavers. In addition, it opposed the notion that the scheme should be compulsory and that supplementary benefits should be withdrawn from those who refused a suitable YTS place. In contrast, the government wanted a lower allowance and the scheme to be restricted to unemployed school-leavers and to be compulsory. A process of consultation in the end produced a compromise; the CBI agreed that the employers would fund the extra costs of the MSC proposals from the grants they were given for each trainee. In addition, the government withdrew the threat of compulsion.

The government's change of attitude is not difficult to explain. The CBI and the TUC presented a joint position to Norman Tebbit, the Employment Secretary, against compulsion. In addition, Tebbit was aware that it was likely that if the government didn't concede the point, the TUC would have been forced by its member unions to resign from the MSC and oppose the implementation of YTS. Against this background, the CBI held a series of separate meetings with the DEmp which culminated in a meeting with Norman Tebbit. Subsequently, the Secretary of State announced that the government intended to withdraw the provisions on compulsion. Keep (1986, p.19) concludes:

> The precise thinking behind the government's climbdown is impossible to verify, but it seems reasonable to presume that, in the face of united...opposition, the government concluded that the prospects for the successful implementation of YTS were threatened and that its commencement before the general election was held to be of paramount importance.
>
> (Keep, 1986, p.19)

Certainly, on this issue the other actors in the policy network constrained government policy.

There is little doubt then that during this period the policy network became more exclusive. The dominant axis had changed with the link between the Department of Employment, the MSC, and to a lesser extent the CBI, now crucial. All other groups, *including the TUC*, had no role to play in policy formulation. In effect, the TUC's role was to legitimise the MSC's implementation of YTS. There was a dominant core to the network which shared clear policy preferences which emphasised training, the needs of industry and lower wages or allowances. This ideology runs through the programmes introduced between 1979 and 1987 (see Marsh, 1992).

1988 onwards: consensus, who needs consensus?

The third term of the Thatcher government has been marked by major changes in the policy network and the collapse of any broad consensus. Training is now run by employers for employers and, to a considerable extent, paid for by the state. The MSC became the Training Commission and then the Training Agency and the role of the TUC in the formulation of training policy is virtually non-existent.

There has been a growing antipathy to the special programmes generally and to YTS, particularly in the trade union movement. A number of individual unions refused to co-operate with the operation of YTS and pushed within the TUC for a general condemnation of, and withdrawal from, the scheme. Despite this opposition the TUC reaffirmed its critical commitment to the MSC after the 1987 elections. However, the government was determined to reduce the role of the unions and strengthen the role of employers. As such, Part 2 of the 1987 Employment Bill transferred the MSC broader employment services to the DEmp and consequently renamed the Manpower Services Commission as the Training Commission (TC). The new TC's prime responsibility was thus to administer the special programmes. In addition, the new bill allowed the Secretary of State for Employment to increase the representation of employers on the TC by six, so that employers now had nine representatives, as compared with three for the unions, two for the local authorities and one for the educational interests. As such, the employers had a clear majority.

The Employment Bill also finally established another cherished aim of government policy. Supplementary benefits would be withheld from those who refused a YTS place, who lose a YTS place because of misconduct, or who leave a placement without good cause. This development was confirmed in the 1987 Social Security Act. It was estimated that this measure would save the government £95 million per year on supplementary benefits.

The government also introduced a new special measure, the Employment Training scheme (ET) in 1988. The scheme was aimed to recruit 600 000 participants per year and all those unemployed for more than six months were eligible, although priority was given to 18 to 25-year-olds unemployed for more than six months, or older people unemployed for over two years. Initially, the TUC gave conditional support to ET but it raised a series of issues with the Secretary of State which reiterated past concerns: the quality of training; the level of allowances; the arrangements for Trade Union involvement; and the question of employment protection. Norman Fowler, the Secretary of State for Employment, made minor concessions which placated the TUC, but a number of individual unions were strongly opposed to ET. In fact, the Transport and General Workers Union's conference voted not to co-operate with the scheme and its General Secretary, Ron Todd, resigned as a TUC-nominated member of the TC. Subsequently, in August 1988 the TGWU, National Association of Local Government Officers (NALGO) and National Unions of Public Employees (NUPE) launched a joint campaign against ET, and the TUC Conference in September voted to withdraw from ET over a two-year period.

Norman Fowler's response was instant and seemed to suggest an opportunity grasped, if not manufactured. He announced that the Training Commission would be abolished and its functions temporarily transferred to the DEmp. A new Training Agency (TA) would be established nationally, together with a network of local Training and Enterprise Councils (TECs). Two-thirds of the TA were to be leading figures in industry and commerce, while at least two-thirds of TEC members were to be senior employers. The remaining members of the TEC would be senior figures from local education and training and representatives of voluntary bodies and trade unions *who support the aims of the council* (DEmp, 1990). As Cassels points out: 'So far has the representation of trade union interests dwindled from its customary parity with employers interest' (Cassels, 1989, p.4). Each TEC would have independent legal entity and would be set up and led by local employers and driven by local labour market needs. The TECs would run all the government's existing programmes, including YTS, ET and the Enterprise Allowance Scheme.

By the beginning of 1990 13 TECs were operating. Their membership included 122 private sector representatives, 15 from local authorities, nine trade unionists, six representatives from voluntary organisations and six from Local Education Authorities (*Employment Gazette*, July 1990, p.366). In May 1990 the YTS became Youth Training (YT). The name change was designed to reflect the government's aim to make training provision for young people more flexible and more rigorous, leading to a National Vocational Qualification.

The structural changes in the policy network have thus been considerable. The system is now decentralised and totally employer-led. The government shapes broad policy through its control of the TA, but employers largely control the implementation of policy and the delivery of the special programmes. The needs of industry clearly determine policy and, in this sense, the current structure is a natural result of prior developments. All other interests, including the trade unions, are effectively excluded from policy-making. As yet we have no thorough study of the operation of the TA or the TECs. However, Ashby (1990, pp.31–3) emphasises that the TA operates in a very different manner from the MSC. In particular, the intermediary organisations, the CBI and the TUC, play no role, reflecting the mood of the times. As Cassels (1989, p.14) stresses:

The mood of the times is to be suspicious of representative bodies like the CBI and TUC. Employers' organisations and trade unions are seen as intermediaries between government and either companies or individual workers (who are also citizens and electors) and the fear is that the institutional, bureaucratic and perhaps political views of the intermediating organisations will weaken or distort communications and generate power relationships which hinder good government.

In this policy area, then, we now have a narrow policy network involving the DEmp, the TA and individual employers. However, this putative community may not persist for two reasons. First, if a Labour Government is elected, policy is likely to change and certainly the TUC will be reincorporated into the policy-making process. Second, while the government has removed the TUC from the youth employment policy network, it still needs individual unions to co-operate in the delivery of the policies, both in the local TECs and, particularly, at the company level. As such, the unions have an influence on the delivery of policy. In addition, and in return, the unions are likely increasingly to negotiate membership of the TECs and, thus, influence over local policy. As yet we have no detailed studies of the operation of the TECs, but it appears likely that in many local areas unions will be incorporated into the local policy networks because, without their involvement, implementation will be very difficult.

The European dimension

The unions' attitude to Europe has changed significantly over time, in large part because they have turned to Europe as a means of removing some of the constraints which the Conservative Government has placed upon them. As Teague points out there have always been three distinct views on Europe within the union movement: pro-European, anti-European and pragmatic (Teague, 1989a; see also Teague, 1989b). Before 1972, the TUC took no position on European membership but rather adopted a wait-and-see policy (Teague, 1989b, pp.31– 2). However, the TUC moved towards opposition when the Conservative government published a White Paper outlining the negotiated terms for UK membership in 1971. Despite this, Britain became a full member of the EC on 1 January 1973. The 1972 TUC Congress voted to oppose the principle of EC membership and refused to participate in any EC institutions, against the wishes of the General Council. This policy was endorsed by votes taken at the next two Congresses. When the Labour Party returned to power in 1974, it renegotiated membership terms and put them to a referendum. The TUC didn't organise a campaign of its own, although it did participate in a number of anti-EC rallies, largely because unions and unionists were to be found on both sides of the argument.

As Teague again points out:

> The policy change in 1976 had nothing to do with any divisions within the TUC. What forced it to adopt a more conciliatory approach to Europe was the sheer scale of the 'Yes' vote in the referendum. To have ignored this vote and continued with an anti-EC policy would have run the risk of the TUC's reputation being seriously discredited in the public eye. Thus, the TUC acquiesced and adopted a more positive stance.
>
> (Teague, 1989b, p.33)

During the 1976–9 period, the pragmatists and the pro-marketeers together made up a clear majority in support of membership. The TUC increasingly recognised that the Commission's authority could affect the operation of British unions and become increasingly involved in EC institutions, notably the Economic and Social Council (ESC). In particular, they pressed for an EC employment initiative to reduce unemployment. However, it didn't take the British unions long to become disillusioned by what Teague calls the 'labyrinth of EC institutions' and in particular the ESC's lack of power. The TUC had no success in persuading the Commission to adopt an employment initiative and Teague suggests that it was these 'dispiriting experiences in Brussels [which] allowed the issue of British withdrawal to surface' (Teague, 1989b, p.35). In effect, the pragmatists were changing sides again.

The result was that the TUC became firmly anti-European during the early 1980s. Indeed, the 1981 Congress passed a resolution calling on a future Labour Government to withdraw from Europe without a referendum. This policy was re-endorsed at the 1983 Congress. By this time a clear gap was emerging between the TUC and the Labour Party, which was starting to adopt a more conciliatory attitude towards the EC. In fact, the TUC reaction to the EC during this period was very muted.

However, the union position changed gradually; largely because the EC provided a putative alternative avenue by which to influence policy. Initially, as Teague points out, a change occurred among the TUC Secretariat. Indeed, writing in 1988, Teague argues that a crucial division exists between the TUC officials and the General Council and Congress:

> The crux of the division is that the Secretariat wants the TUC to adopt a position similar to that of the Labour Party, while the General Council wants to maintain the status quo.
>
> (Teague, 1989b, p.36)

This is much less true than it was, largely due to the fairly vigorous promotion by the EC of the Social Charter (for more details see Teague, 1989b). This is one product of a process which began in 1985 when the European Commission produced a policy document which set out a series of measures intended to help facilitate the establishment of a Single European Market by 1992. In order to speed along this process, the 1987 Single European Act introduced the principal of qualified majority voting; so, in effect, no two countries, even the largest, can halt Single Market legislation approved by the others. However, the Act specifically states that provisions relating to the rights and interests of workers require unanimity before they can be binding on member states.

The Social Charter establishes: a right of freedom of movement for employees; the necessity of an improvement in workers' conditions by, among other things, establishing a shorter working week and improving the position of part-time and temporary workers; a right to belong, or not to belong, to a union; a right to strike; the right of unions to negotiate and the need to encourage collective bargaining; the right of workers to receive information and be consulted about the operation of companies, particularly multi-national companies; protection of the position of particular sections of the workforce, young people, the disabled and those who have retired.

The Social Charter then is a radical programme the implementation of which would necessitate major changes in British law. It is not surprising that it has been embraced by the Labour Party and the TUC. The changing TUC attitude was reflected when the 1988 Congress reversed its policy of opposition to Britain's membership of the EC. In addition, the President of the European Commission, Jacques Delors, was invited to address that year's Congress. It also called upon the British union movement to become more involved in the European Trade Union Confederation and to adapt its own internal policy-making processes to take account of the growing importance of the European dimension.

Once again the position of the unions on the EC has changed because the bulk of unions have pragmatically seen the Social Charter as a means by which some of the changes introduced by the Conservative government can be reversed.

If it is hardly surprising that the TUC have endorsed the Social Charter, it is even less surprising that the Conservative Government have rejected most of its provisions. Mrs Thatcher re-christened the Social Charter a 'Socialist Charter' and argued that it is full of unnecessary controls and regulations which will constrain the operation of the market. As such, the government has worked within the Community to defuse the Commission plans and, in particular, has opposed most of the Social Charter's proposals (see Teague,

1989b, pp.318–326). So, as *Labour Research* points out, most of the Commission's plans which affect unions have been deradicalised:

> It is significant that a number of draft directives (legally binding instructions) on part-time work, temporary work and rights to information and consultation for workers' representatives are missing from the list. This is despite the fact that in every case the commission has produced detailed proposals for their implementation. Also missing is a proposed Council recommendation on the reduction and reorganisation of working time.
>
> *(Labour Research*, September 1988, p.10)

The Conservative Government couldn't prevent the development of the Social Charter but it has strongly opposed almost all its provisions with regard to employment rights *(Labour Research*, December 1989, p.16). It has consistently argued that such matters are the concern of national governments and that any change would alter for the worse the balance between employers and unions. As such, it will clearly not adopt the Charter as a declaration, despite the fact that it has broad political support in the European Parliament and the European Economic and Social Committee. Of course, it might be argued that the British government will be embarrassed if it alone doesn't ratify the Charter, but, given the history of the Thatcher government, that appears unlikely. On the other hand, the Labour Party is strongly committed to the Social Charter and would be likely to accept its provisions if it were re-elected. Again, it is clear that the fate of the unions turns to a large extent on the re-election of a Labour government.

Conclusion

In this chapter I have examined various aspects of the changing political relations between the trade unions and government since 1979. Three conclusions are clear:

1. The unions have much less of a political role at the beginning of the 1990s than they did at the end of the 1970s. They are rarely consulted in the policy-making process, as Mitchell's aggregate figures, and the brief analysis of the politics of the coal industry

presented earlier, indicate. Even in areas in which the unions previously played an important role, they have been marginalised by the government, as the case study of the politics of youth unemployment clearly demonstrates.

2. Unions have had virtually no influence on legislation since 1979; their one major success in relation to the 1984 Trade Union Act is very much the exception which proves the rule.

3. The unions' attitude to the EC has changed significantly. They see it as a putative alternative avenue by which to influence policy. However, the Social Charter is not likely to have a major effect on British industrial relations unless a Labour Government comes to power.

The future

The future of the unions' political role is uncertain. It could change quickly once again. The election of a Labour Government would inevitably mean closer relations between government and unions and significant legislative change, as we will see in the next chapter. Similarly, it would mean that the European dimension, and particularly the Social Charter, would play a greater role in British industrial relations. At the same time, any incoming government which pursued a different economic policy based on supply-side management would need to reintroduce consultation and allow unions a role in policy-making.

At the same time it must be appreciated that while a government can extend or restrict the consultation process and push through legislative change, it cannot control policy outcomes; it often needs the co-operation of the unions. So, while the government has removed the TUC from the youth employment policy network, if the new policy is to work it will need the co-operation of the unions at the local level. As such, the unions will have an influence on the delivery of the policy. There is an important general point here. Much of the literature on Thatcherism ignores the crucial problem of implementation: governments always find it easier to enact policy than to implement it in a way which produces the required effect (see Marsh and Rhodes, 1990). I shall return to this point in the conclusion to this book.

6

Trade Unions and the Labour Party

The link between the trade unions and the Labour Party is crucial to any understanding of the past, present and future of the unions. As Andrew Taylor emphasises, this link has always involved contradictions which stem from the different roles which the unions play. Taylor's primary concern has been the contradiction between the unions' sectional interest group role and their role in boosting the electoral chances of the Labour Party (A.Taylor, 1986, p.15). However, as he would acknowledge, the situation is considerably more complicated. In particular, the relationship between the two branches of the Labour Movement is clearly different in opposition than in power.

When Labour is in power the key problem is the one identified by Taylor. Normally, the unions have been a stabilising force within the Labour Party, together with the Party leadership, exercising control over the Party in general and the Conference in particular. The unions have been essentially concerned with pursuing their sectional interests through free collective bargaining; politics has been left to the Labour Party. As such, as we saw in Chapter 2, the period between 1968 and 1979 was unusual. It was marked by significant conflicts between the Parliamentary Labour Party (PLP) leadership and the unions, in particular over *In Place of Strife* and the 'Winter of Discontent', and by the politicisation of the unions and their relationship with the Labour Party. This was inevitable because, for the first time, Labour governments attempted to impose incomes policy and trade union reform. Or, to put it another way, for the first time the political wing of the Labour Movement intervened overtly to constrain the activities of the economic wing. However, such a tension is much more important when Labour is in power. When the

Conservatives won in 1979, the role of the unions in the Labour Party, and the main tensions they faced, changed. This chapter examines the changing relations between the trade unions and the Labour Party since 1979.

In opposition, the trade union-Labour Party link takes on a different character. The tension between the political and economic role of the unions in relation to the Labour Party is reduced, although not removed as it re-emerges when an election approaches and the unions and the Party try to construct a plausible economic strategy, with electoral appeal, which the unions can accept. However, a new problem comes to the fore in opposition. Almost always an election defeat results in an upsurge in political recriminations and a critical, and often acrimonious, review of policy. This was certainly the case after 1979. In such circumstances, the trade unions, because of their key role at Conference, are inevitably at the centre of these debates. At such times, there is a clear tension between their role as a stabilising force in the party and their desire to support the PLP leadership and ensure the re-election of a government.

After the 1979 election defeat, however, the future of the union-Labour Party relationship was complicated by a number of other factors. First, the electoral future of the Labour Party began to look very bleak, particularly after the 1983 election performance. Second, it became increasingly clear that the proportion of trade unionists voting Labour was dropping and, perhaps more surprisingly, the attitudes of trade unionists to the Conservative's trade unions reforms were relatively favourable. Third, because historically trade unions had a limited political purpose, the links between the party and the unions were in fact very weak, particularly, although not exclusively, at the constituency level. Fourth, the overall decline in union membership was accompanied by a major shift in the sectoral composition of that membership which had begun in the 1970s. This shift led to a significant change in the structure, composition and political views of the General Council of the Trade Union Congress (TUC). Such changes appeared to make the triumph of new realism inevitable. Fifth, after their 1983 election victory the Conservatives pushed ahead with union reform with a proposal, the 1984 Trade Union Act, designed to test, and perhaps break, the link between the Labour Party and the trade unions, by requiring periodic political fund ballots.

In such circumstances, a major dislocation in the trade union-

Labour Party link might have been expected. However, it has not occurred. Why? In large part this chapter will address this question. In fact, the chapter has two themes. First, I shall examine how the unions' stabilising role in the Labour Party was reasserted after 1983. Second, I shall suggest that the victories in the union ballots, required under the 1984 Trade Union Act, played a major role in reinforcing the trade union–Labour Party link which in 1983 seemed under threat. Increasingly, the 1984 Trade Union Act looks an even bigger own goal by the Conservative Government than previously acknowledged. However, it is also important to recognise that since the ballots the link has changed and is likely to change still further.

In order to address these two themes this chapter is divided into seven sections. The first section examines the trade union role in the constitutional debates in the Labour Party in 1979–81 and the reassertion of the unions' role as a stabilising force after 1982. The second section considers the psephological and the public opinion poll evidence on the relationship between the unions and the Labour Party. The third section identifies the paucity of links between the two organisations, particularly at the local level. The fourth section looks at the changes in the sectoral composition of the union movement and how this has been reflected in changes in the General Council to the TUC. The fifth section then examines the outcome and significance of the political fund ballots. The sixth section looks at the role of the unions in the run up to the 1987 General Election. Finally, the last section considers the trade unions' role in the Labour Party Policy Review and the likely changes in industrial relations which would occur if a Labour Government was elected.

Trade unions and constitutional reform, 1979–83

The failures and disappointments of the Labour Government between 1974 and 1979 led directly to increased demands for the democratisation of the Labour Party. In fact, the Campaign for Labour Party Democracy (CLPD) was established in 1973. It had three specific goals intended to ensure that the PLP leadership was more responsive to the policies passed by Conference:

1. The election of the Party leader by an electoral college rather than by the PLP alone;

2. The mandatory reselection of all MPs during the lifetime of each Parliament;
3. Sole control over the election manifesto to lie with the National Executive Committee (NEC), rather than control being shared between the PLP leadership and the NEC, a procedure which effectively gave the parliamentarians control.

Most unions were not greatly interested in constitutional reform. Indeed, the unions used their dominance upon the Conference Arrangements Committee, which has formal responsibility for controlling the Conference agenda, to prevent the discussion of mandatory reselection of MPs for a considerable period. As Minkin puts it:

> Supporters of reform had to fight through a range of delaying filters... In spite of the weight of support for mandatory reselection it took five years of concerted pressure for this constitutional amendment to clear all the obstacles.
>
> (Minkin, 1986, p.355)

Even when, after the 1979 Election defeat, the issue of constitution reform dominated discussion in the run up to the 1980 Party Conference, the unions were to be found on all sides of the debate; they demonstrated little unity. In 1976 eight trade union branches were affiliated to the CLPD; by 1980 the number had risen to 112. The CLPD received national support from seven unions including Association of Cinematograph, Television and Allied Technicians (ACTT), Association of Scientific, Technical and Managerial Staff (ASTMS), Amalgamated Unions of Engineering Workers (AUEW)/ Construction, AUEW/Management, Fire Brigade Union (FBU), and National Union of Public Employees (NUPE). It also had support from sections of other unions (A.Taylor, 1987, p.132).

Surprisingly, almost everyone believed that some reform was necessary. However, both the Campaign for Labour Victory (CLV) and Trade Unions for Labour Victory (TULV) opposed the CLPD proposals and both had significant trade union support. The CLV was committed to 'one person, one vote' and had strong support from the National Union of Railwaymen (NUR), the AUEW and the Electrical, Electronic, Telecommunication and Plumbing Union (EETPU). The TULV's preferred option was less clear; in essence they wanted the minimum amount of reform necessary to ensure unity, their support came mainly from the TGWU, General, Municipal Boilermakers and Allied Trades Union (GMBAT), Confederation of Health Service Employees (COHSE) and Associated Society of Locomotive Engineers and Firemen (ASLEF). The voting at the 1980 Conference reflected these divisions among the unions. Unions such as the Transport and General Workers Union (TGWU), NUPE, ACTT, ASTMS, and FBU supported the proposals. In contrast, the AUEW, GMBATU, the NUR and the EETPU opposed them. As Fatchett says: 'The divisions between unions were such as almost to cancel out the vote cast for or against change' (Fatchett, 1987, p.53). In the end the CLPD achieved its first two aims but failed to remove control of the election manifesto from the PLP leadership.

Of course, the battle for constitutional reform did not end at this point. In 1981 a Special Conference was called to decide on the composition of the electoral college for leadership elections. Again, the unions were not united on their preferred option. More importantly, the final decision, in which the unions obtained 40 per cent of the electoral college (with 30 per cent each going to the PLP and the CLPs) was an option preferred by a minority of the voting strength at the Conference. Taylor explains this strange outcome:

the maverick behaviour of the AUEW and USDAW [Union of Shop Distributive and Allied Workers] determined the outcome. The AUEW moved amendment 105 which sought a 75 per cent proportion for the PLP; if this was defeated (which was inevitable) the AUEW would abstain because of its mandate that in any electoral college a majority should go to the PLP. The Right were aghast as they expected the AUEW block vote to move to the GMWU's resolution seeking 50 per cent for the PLP. The loss of so many votes opened the possibility of reducing the PLP to below 50 per cent and this was made possible by USDAW's resolution seeking a 30/30/40 split, with 40 per cent for the unions. For Basnett's resolution to be defeated there had to be unity on the Left: the NEC's option was dropped and the Left's supporters were persuaded to support USDAW whose resolution was approved. So the AUEW's purism and USDAW's belief that its amendment would be defeated (USDAW is traditionally right wing) gave victory to the Left, so precipitating the founding of the SDP.

(A. Taylor, 1987, pp.138–9)

The 1981 Deputy Leadership election between Benn and Healey marks the end of this period of constitutional wrangling. The Constituency Labour Parties (CLPs) strongly favoured Benn, and his supporters lobbied hard within the unions. However, in the end Healey won narrowly. Benn's defeat, together with the departure of the 'Gang of Four' to the Social Democratic Party (SDP), and particularly the approach of a General Election, meant that the unions began to look to Labour's election prospects and focus on the need to establish unity.

Even before the 1979 defeat, the unions felt the need for greater co-ordination in their help for the Labour Party and so TULV was launched in the autumn of 1978. As Taylor says:

> TULV as an organisational pressure group, sought to revive Labour's grass-roots and transmit Labour's message specifically to trade unionists counteracting a growing tendency for trade unions not to vote Labour.
>
> (A.Taylor, 1987, p.124)

TULV had a limited impact on the 1979 election, although it did play a role in the Labour Party enquiry into the election defeat (see A.Taylor, 1987, pp. 126–8). However, after TULV was constituted on a permanent basis in 1981, it grew in importance, particularly once the dust of constitutional battle began to settle. Indeed, in 1982 it had an income of £240,000 (A.Taylor, 1987, p.131) and took part in two meetings with the National Executive Committee designed to reduce internal party strife and establish what help the unions could give the party at the next election. Certainly Minkin argues that the unions' effort was larger, more organised and much better co-ordinated in 1983 than in 1979 (Minkin, 1986). However, the outcome was the Labour Party's worst result since 1918.

During the entire period of constitutional struggle, the trade unions were hardly a radical force. Most had not wanted the constitutional debate; the pressure for constitutional reform had come from the CLP and, in particular, from the CLPD, in which unions played a minor role. Throughout the dispute most unions wanted minimal change, even though there were important divisions among them. As usual then, the unions were a conservative, stabilising force within the Party. However, the inevitable involvement of the unions in the process legitimised the reforms and the conflict and made a Labour election victory less likely. In a sense, the unions, in acting as a stabilising force in the party and 'resolving' the constitutional issue, as they were bound to do given their preponderance at Conference, had made it less likely that the Party would be elected in 1983, given the image of disunity which the constitutional wrangle projected. When the unions reasserted the primacy of party unity and electoral success in 1982, it had a limited effect in the short run.

Trade unionists' voting behaviour and political attitudes

As we shall see later in this chapter, there has been a major decline in union membership since 1979 (See Tables 2.1 and 2.2). There has also been a major decline in the Labour vote since 1974. However, as Crewe points out (Crewe, 1990, p.22), the de-unionisation of the electorate doesn't account for Labour's electoral decline. The proportion of the electorate belonging to a union fell by 6 per cent between 1964 and 1987. If the proportion of unionists voting Labour had remained constant this would have accounted for a 6.5 per cent fall in the Labour vote. In fact, the Labour vote fell by 13 per cent over this period. More specifically, the Labour vote fell by 17.3 per cent among blue-collar workers, while it remained constant among white-collar unionists. As Crewe emphasises, 'Almost the whole of Labour's electoral losses occurred within this group – its traditional base of support' (Crewe, 1990, p.23).

As Table 6.1 indicates, Labour's support among manual trade unionists dropped by a staggering 25 per cent between 1964 and 1987, while it only dropped by 7 per cent among manual non-unionists. It is also noticeable that it was the centre parties, rather than the Conservatives, which benefited. Webb also points out that there has been a parallel decline in the strength of Labour Party identification and working class identification among blue-collar unionists (Webb, 1987). Crewe concludes:

> By the late 1980s union membership appeared no longer to be an agent of class or partisan socialisation: among the working class, at least, it was more or less a non-partisan matter.
>
> (Crewe, 1990, p.22)

The weakening of the manual trade unionist Labour vote is

Table 6.1 *Class, union membership and vote, 1964–87*

	Union members			Non-members		
			Change			Change
	1964	*1987*	*1964–87*	*1964*	*1987*	*1964–87*
	(%)	*(%)*	*(%)*	*(%)*	*(%)*	*(%)*
Manual workers:						
Conservative	23	28	+5	41	39	–2
Lib/SDP/Other	5	24	+19	15	24	+9
Labour	73	48	–25	44	37	–7
Non-manual workers:						
Conservative	46	37	–9	65	63	–2
Lib/SDP/Other	23	33	+10	15	24	+9
Labour	31	30	–1	20	13	–7

Source: Crewe, 1990.

accentuated by other developments in the economy. Large manufacturing plants are in decline; growth in the service sector and in the high-tech sector is not associated with trade union membership, let alone with Labour voting. The importance of such trends is clearly evident in the regional variation in the relationship between union membership and voting. By 1987 the Labour majority among unionists in the North was still significant, while in the South it was non-existent (Crewe, 1990, pp.25–8).

It is clear then, that there has been a major decline in the percentage of unionists voting Labour. However, Labour's link with the trade unions is also an electoral liability with the broader electorate. Labour lost the 1979 election partly because of the 'Winter of Discontent'. Certainly, the three issues central to that election – unemployment, prices and industrial relations – all centred on the question of trade union power. More broadly, Sarlvik and Crewe see the image of trade union power as a key factor in Labour's decline in the 1970s (Sarlvik and Crewe, 1983, pp.140–149).

Unionists are less likely to vote Labour and its trade union link is an electoral liability. In addition, trade unionists are not even inevitably sympathetic towards unions. A Marplan poll conducted among unionists in 1983 revealed a worrying pattern for the unions. There was general support for the proposals enshrined in the first three pieces of Conservative legislation. Overall, only 37 per cent of unionists thought the legislation had gone too far; 39 per cent thought it was about right; 14 per cent thought it hadn't gone far enough and 10 per cent didn't know. More specifically a MORI poll found that 55 per cent of unionists thought unions who disobeyed the new law should be punished; 76 per cent thought there should be secret ballots in all union elections; and 69 per cent supported secret ballots before strike action (see Table 6.2).

Links between the Labour Party and the trade unions

Faced with the weakening of unionist support for the Labour Party, the unions became more conscious of the paucity of the links between the two organisations, particularly at the constituency level. Indeed, there is a clear divergence between the involvement of the unions at the national level of the Labour Party and their lack of involvement at the local level.

I have already dealt with the linkages at the national level in Chapter 2 and these have not changed significantly since 1979. As Fatchett shows (Fatchett, 1987, pp.46–9), the unions' contribution to the Labour Party's income has fluctuated, but remains around 80 per cent. What is more, trade union affiliation fees to Labour Party Head Office have been on the increase recently. They rose from £2.9 m in 1984 to £4.2 m in 1987; an increase of 21 per cent in real terms.

The majority of this income comes from the largest unions. Indeed, in 1974 58 per cent of trade union affiliation fees came from four unions: TGWU, GMWU, NUPE and AUEW. In addition, the unions made major financial contributions to both the 1983 and the 1987 election campaigns: £2.25 m in 1983 and £3.8 m in 1987. Once again, the majority of those contributions came from a limited number of unions. In 1987 half came from two unions, TGWU and GMWU, and two-thirds from five unions. As Pinto-Duschinsky rightly points out:

Labour's heavy reliance on the Transport and General Workers' Union which organised Trade Unionists for Labour, and on the General and Municipal Workers, for which Larry Whitty (now General Secretary of the Labour Party) formerly worked, emerges clearly from these statistics.

(Pinto-Duschinsky, 1989, p.20)

148   *The New Politics of British Trade Unionism*

Table 6.2   *Attitudes of trade unionists (MORI poll, September 1983)*

Questions and Answers		Questions and Answers	
1. As far as you know, is your union affiliated to the Labour Party?		5. Do you think that trade union members should or should not be regularly asked whether or not the union should have a political fund?	
Is	64		
Is not	17		
Don't know	19		
		Should	63
		Should not	18
2. Do you believe your union should or should not be affiliated to the Labour Party? (This sample is based on trade union members only)		Don't know	18
		6. Do you believe your union's main national decision-making body should or should not be elected by secret ballot?	
Should	36		
Should not	53	Should	58
Don't know	11	Should not	28
		Don't know	15
3. Do you presently pay the political levy or do you contract out of paying the political levy?		7. Before there is a strike, do you think there should not be a secret ballot of members?	
Pay	55	Should	69
Contract out	18	Should not	17
Not necessary	18	Don't know	14
Don't know	9		
4. In future, would you continue to pay the political levy if, to do so, you had to contract in each year?			
Would continue	45		
Would not	31		
Don't know	24		

Indeed, 42 per cent of the affiliation fees and the contributions to the General Election Fund came from these two unions: 28 per cent came from the TGWU. The unions also have the potential to dominate the organisational structures of the Labour Party. This position has not changed since 1979; indeed, as we have already seen, since the 1981 reforms the unions cast the largest number of votes in the electoral college. The unions dominate the Annual Conference, casting 90 per cent of the votes. In fact, the five largest unions, TGWU, AUEW, GMBATU, NUPE and USDAW control well over 50 per cent of the total vote. In addition, the NEC which is elected at Conference could be dominated by the unions. They nominate and directly elect the 12 members of the trade union section. In addition, they could, because of their voting strength, determine the outcome of the elections for Treasurer and those of the five members of the women's section, and strongly influence the election of Leader and Deputy Leader. In theory then, the unions control eighteen of the thirty-one seats on the NEC and have a major influence upon two others. In practice, however, as we saw in Chapter 2, the NEC is dominated by the PLP. Indeed, the trade unions rarely act as a block in NEC elections, as Fatchett argues:

> An illustration of the point that it is grossly mistaken to see the union votes acting as a block is provided by the 1984 election for the post of Party Treasurer, an office determined by the vote of the whole of Conference. In 1984, there was a contest between what were largely regarded as right-wing and left-wing candidates. According to the Annual Conference records, 2.867m votes were cast by the trade unions for one candidate, with 3.207m for the other. The unions almost divided down the middle.
>
> (Fatchett, 1987, p.53)

Between 1972 and 1979 the Trade Union-Labour Party Liaison Committee was the major link between the two organisations, although as we saw in Chapter 2, its importance declined after 1975. In opposition, the Liaison Committee has remained in existence but its role has been significantly downgraded. After the 1979 election, as Taylor points out:

> The Liaison Committee went on to examine taxation, public spending, financial institutions, Ulster, the EEC and the effects of

> government economic policy. The importance of the Liaison
> Committee declined in proportion to the breadth of its remit.
>
> (A.Taylor, 1987, p.118)

In contrast, the links between the Labour Party and the unions at
local level are weak, as Fatchett indicates. His survey of Labour
Party constituency parties reveals a clear pattern. The trade unions
contribute very little money to the constituencies; those who
responded to Fatchett's questionnaire had received less than £500.
More over, 87 per cent of the constituencies reported that the trade
union contribution to their total income was less than 25 per cent. At
the same time, the unions also played a limited role in the constituency organisations. The trade unions provided a majority of the
General Committee in less than 10 per cent and of the Executive
Committee in less than 5 per cent of the constituencies. Indeed, in
more than one-third of the constituencies the affiliated unions were
unable to find enough delegates to fill all the places available to
them. Similarly, only 31 per cent of constituency parties had a
chairman, and 23 per cent a secretary, who was a trade union
delegate.

There has been one significant change in the role of the unions in
the constituency associations recently. One of the first acts of Neil
Kinnock when he became party leader was to press the 1984 Party
Conference to introduce a one person-one vote system for candidate
selection. However, this proposal was rejected by almost 1 million
votes, given that the unions were not prepared to see their role in the
selection process removed. In 1986 the NEC established a working
party to re-examine the issue and in 1987, by a narrow majority, the
constituencies backed its proposal for a one person-one vote system.
Once again, however, the unions were unhappy and the TGWU and
the GMBATU supported a compromise which was approved by the
1987 Conference. This established an electoral college system which
gave both individual members and the trade unions a role. In the
college the unions have up to 40 per cent of the vote on a sliding
scale related to the number of union branches affiliated to the
constituency party. The individual members cast the remaining
votes.

The electoral college is open to manipulation as any union branch
can affiliate to a constituency providing that it has a levy-paying
member in that branch who lives or is registered in that constituency.

The unions do abuse this procedure, despite the fact that Fatchett's evidence would suggest they are ill-prepared to do so. For example, when Frank Field, Labour MP for Birkenhead, was initially deselected in December 1989, he was replaced as candidate by a TGWU full-time official, Paul Davies. There appears little doubt that Mr Davies had campaigned to encourage TGWU branches to affiliate and, in fact, the number of TGWU branches affiliated increased from four in 1987 to nineteen in 1989. Nevertheless, Fatchett's conclusion appears valid:

> There is a certain intriguing similarity in the data concerned both with finances, and with involvement, at constituency level. There is, in both contexts, little to suggest that, at local level, the Labour Party is dominated by trade unions.
>
> (Fatchett, 1987, p.54)

In fact, the trade unions, like the Labour Party itself, have been dominated by a leadership view of politics which, while at odds with the organisation's democratic origins, fits very well with the British political system which lacks any strong participatory tradition (Tant, 1987). As Fatchett points out, the emphasis has been upon decentralised collective bargaining and centralised politics:

> The picture then which emerges is of a trade union movement committed to a leadership-dominated form of politics, which is reinforced, somewhat paradoxically, by the post-war changes in industrial relations and trade union organisation.
>
> (Fatchett, 1987, p.43)

In the 1980s the Labour Party and the unions have come to question such centralisation both because it is thought that it has been a major factor in the depoliticisation of individual unionists, and because the absence of strong links at the local level makes it very difficult to do much about depoliticisation. For that reason, the party and the unions have attempted to strengthen local links. In this way, TULV was specifically formed to overcome the lack of co-ordination in the unions' efforts to help Labour's electoral prospects and improve the limited contact between the unions and the constituencies. As we shall see later, this effort was stepped up after the successful

campaign on the political fund ballots with the creation of Trade
Unions for a Labour Victory (TULV).

The changing sectoral composition of the TUC

As Table 2.1 indicated, trade union membership has declined significantly since 1979: by 28 per cent between 1979 and 1987. Kelly
argues that the decline has been less significant than in previous
recessions (Kelly, 1987, p.11). Certainly, Cronin's figures indicate
that trade union membership fell by 40 per cent between 1890 and
1893 and 35 per cent between 1920 and 1923 (Cronin, 1979, Table
B.10); in contrast it fell by only 15 per cent between 1979 and 1982.
However, the decline has continued and shows little sign of
reversing, indeed, it fell by 5 per cent in 1987.

As Table 2.1 also indicated, there were clear sectoral patterns in
both the growth of unions in the 1970s and their decline in the 1980s.
In the 1970s the bulk of the union growth was in the public sector
and, to a lesser extent, among white-collar unions. So the National
Association of Local Government Officers (NALGO) grew by 66 per
cent between 1970–8, while NUPE grew by 91 per cent and COHSE
by a staggering 139 per cent in the same period. Among white-collar
unions ASTMS more than doubled in size, The Technical Administrative and Supervisor Section of the AUEW (TASS) grew by 90
per cent and Banking, Insurance and Finance Union (BIFU) by 42 per
cent. In general terms, the same sectors have held up best as union
membership has declined in the 1980s. As such, NALGO, NUPE and
COHSE have hardly contracted, while the larger private sector
unions, especially the TGWU and the AUEW, have been very hard
hit, the TGWU shrinking by 31 per cent and the AUEW by 20 per
cent since 1979. More significantly, white-collar private-sector
membership has generally increased; TASS by 25 per cent and BIFU
by 19 per cent, although ASTMS membership has contracted by 21
per cent. Indeed, in 1988–9 Metcalf estimates that union density in
the private sector was 28.3 per cent while in the public sector it was
62.9 per cent (Metcalf, 1990b, Table 2).

These sectoral changes over the last two decades have had
considerable effect on the TUC and upon the relationship with the
Labour Party. As Taylor emphasises:

The implication of these changes for the relationship between the unions and the party are considerable. Hitherto, union representation in both the TUC and Labour Party corresponded: both were dominated by blue-collar manual workers unions; so smoothing the relationship between the two. However, the TUC has always insisted that it speaks equally for all unions whether or not they are affiliated to the Labour Party. The changing occupational composition of the TUC away from blue-collar to white-collar implies a loosening of the connection between the TUC and the Labour Party.

(A.Taylor, 1987, pp.154–5)

By the end of the 1970s a number of unions were campaigning for a change in the method by which the General Council of the TUC was elected. The top ten unions had automatic representation while the other unions divided into trade groups were, in effect, elected by the grace and favour of these larger unions. This system tended to favour the blue-collar, private sector, unions rather than the rapidly expanding white-collar and public sector ones. After considerable debate, and not a little acrimony, the automatic representation of unions with a membership of 100,000+, 'automaticity', was approved at the 1982 Congress by a narrow majority. Automaticity was introduced for elections at the 1983 Annual Congress; it marked a significant political change. The white-collar unions who benefited were, with the exception of ASTMS, not radical and none were affiliated to the Labour Party. The members of these unions were less likely to vote Labour and more likely to support the Conservative Government's industrial relations legislation (see A.Taylor, 1987, pp.161–4). The leaders of these unions played a key role in the move at the 1983 Congress, after the 1983 Election defeat, towards New Realism and the TUC's decision to reconsider its political strategy. As Taylor puts it:

The concept of political trade unionism integral to post-war British politics is under attack from a government which has successfully set the agenda for union reform. The TUC's initial response was to pretend nothing had happened but after 1983 it began a hesitant reappraisal.

(ibid., p.168)

Overall, trends in the economy and in the trade union movement seem to point towards a loosening of the ties between the unions and the Labour Party.

The political fund ballots

In the period immediately before the political fund ballots, the trade union-Labour Party link was, thus, under some threat. Fewer unionists were voting Labour, the connections between the unions and the Labour Party at the local level were poor, and the changing composition of the work-force and the TUC seemed to suggest that New Realism and weaker union-party connections were inevitable. It was against this background that the government introduced legislation to require the unions to conduct political fund ballots. The omens were not good and, indeed, most predictions were that few unions would vote to retain their political funds. As Table 6.2 indicates, a MORI poll found massive hostility among unionists to unions giving money to any political party and opposition to sponsoring MPs, local political activity and the provision of general political support (see A.Taylor, 1987, p.212). In addition, the chances of union success were not helped by the fact that few had centralised membership lists or any real history of communicating effectively with their members.

Despite all this the ballot campaign was a total success. Between May 1985 and March 1986, 37 TUC affiliated unions with potential funds held successful ballots for their retention, as did one union which was not a member of the TUC. What is more, two additional unions, the Inland Revenue Staffs Federation and the National Union of Hosiery and Knitwear Workers, voted to establish a political fund for the first time. In most cases, the votes were overwhelming. Indeed, in 35 of the 37 ballots more than 70 per cent of those voting supported a political fund. The turnout figures were also high compared with other union ballots (see Fatchett, 1987, p.63). Why did the gloomy predictions prove so wrong?

In essence, the answer is simple. The unions chose the right strategy and pursued it effectively, while the opposition was silent. Senior union leaders met in early November 1983 to discuss how the political fund ballot campaigns might be conducted. Their preferred strategy was to allow those unions who were sympathetic to the party to hold their ballots first and hope to establish a bandwagon effect. However, no one was sure which unions were likely to be sympathetic to political funds so TULV commissioned MORI to produce an opinion poll on union attendances. The Labour Party was also unsure how to proceed, but in February the NEC's organisational subcommittee decided that the party should not mount a high-profile 'yes' campaign. In fact, the union leaders on the committee argued that a high party profile would be counterproductive.

The final strategy was crucially influenced by the results of the TULV's poll. The poll revealed that unionist opinion was divided upon political action; they opposed affiliation to the Labour Party but supported the sponsoring of MPs. Only six of the 15 unions polled supported action and only three, the NUM, the UCW and the EETPU, were in favour of affiliation to the Labour Party, although a majority in all unions believed the union should sponsor MPs. Not surprisingly, the unions were horrified at this result. As Taylor emphasises:

> the poll prompted an instant rethink of strategy. Instead of using the ballots to generate support for Labour the aim was to persuade the membership that they had a legitimate political role *distinct* from affiliation to the party.
>
> (A.Taylor, 1987, p.220)

The Trade Union Co-ordinating Committee (TUCC) was established in October 1984 as a result of a meeting between the NEC and 34 union leaders. The Committee was chaired by Bill Keys of SOGAT '82 and made up of members drawn from the largest unions. It was financed by a 3p levy on each union member and directed by Graham Allen, the ex-director of the Greater London Council's Campaign Unit. The TUCC's strategy was based upon playing down the Labour link but emphasising that unions need to take political action to defend their members' interests. It also relied very heavily upon proselytising in the workplace rather than glossy media campaigns; the emphasis was upon the unions communicating with their members, quite a novel idea in the history of British unions. In addition, the ballot timetable was co-ordinated to ensure that those unions who balloted first were those most likely to return a 'Yes' vote.

Ironically, the unions were also helped by a major weakness in the 1984 Act. Sub-sections (e) and (f) of Section 17 of the Act state that unless a union has a political fund it cannot spend money on conferences or publicity material designed to persuade people to vote for a political party or candidate. The unions argued that this would prevent unions without political funds campaigning against public spending cuts. They cited as evidence a statement by Alan Clarke, an Employment Minister, that the 1984 Act would make 'unlawful' any campaign such as the £1m one conducted by NALGO in 1983 against spending cuts.

The lack of opposition also played a role. The Conservative Party and its union organisation, the Conservative Trade Unionists (CTU), played virtually no role in the ballots, while the Alliance parties were ineffective. Initially, Tom King, then Secretary of State for Employment, attempted, but failed, to inject a party political dimension when he stressed what he saw as the basic question:

> Do union members want their leaders not only to spend money but also to dissipate time and energy in playing party politics; or do they want them to get on with the important job which trade unions were set up to do – representing their members' interests?
> (King, quoted in Fatchett, 1987, p.79)

Subsequently, however, the government withdrew from the debate. Fatchett's conclusion seems accurate:

> By changing the definition of political, the government had offered a campaigning opportunity which was legitimately and effectively taken up by the unions. It is inconsistent to complain about that, when one claims, as the government did, that the sole purpose of the exercise was not to attack your main political opponent but simply to offer trade unionists the opportunity of deciding whether they wanted to continue with a political role for their union.
> (Fatchett, 1987, pp.79-80)

The unions' success in the political fund ballots had a number of significant effects. First, it legitimised the unions' political role and thus, inevitably, their link with the Labour Party. This gave a boost to the link at a time when it was under considerable threat.

However, it is worth noting Taylor's qualification. He suggests that the results legitimised the nature of the existing link at a time when it needed significant reform:

> The danger of a series of 'yes' votes which leaves the financial link with the unions unmodernised is that the movement will again face enervation. Dependence on union funds remains a weakness for Labour which can only prosper if it can attract a mass following. Union finance has been a substitute for a mass base.
>
> (A.Taylor, 1987, p.234)

Second, as we saw earlier, it encouraged non-fund-holders to consider holding a ballot. Third, it politicised the unions in a way which was unusual. In particular, it significantly improved the links between the leadership and the membership. Fourth, there were major organisation spin-offs. Many unions for the first time produced a central membership list and developed an effective network of workplace contacts and activists. Finally, and perhaps most important, it improved union morale and confidence at a time when it was at a low ebb.

Overall, the political fund ballots provided a window in the gloom. As one author claims, the unions' success represented a major own goal for the Conservative Government (Grant, 1987). More surprisingly, and despite Taylor's fears, they appear not only to have led unions to reaffirm but also to reassess their links with the Labour Party.

Beyond the ballots

Before all the ballots were conducted there were two meetings between TUCC and TULV to discuss a merger, and Trade Unions for Labour (TUFL) was formed in February 1986. The aim was to increase co-ordination and at the same time avoid the criticism experienced by TULV which, to many unionists, had been too involved in the sectional conflicts, particularly over constitutional reform. As such, TUFL was to play no role in policy-making, its aim was to improve the links between the unions and the Labour Party in order to help to achieve an election victory. TUFL played a major role in the 1987 election campaign as Minkin shows:

The integration was quite striking. There had never been an organisation to rival TUFL in its breadth and co-ordination of union support for the Labour Party, both at national and local level. During the campaign, the Trade Union Unit was more integrated as a functional unit into head office campaigning and feedback processes than any previous trade union effort. Personnel from the unions were also more integrated. A range of union officials were formally seconded to positions in the party's national campaign aiding Walworth Road, the front bench and the party's leader in a much more systematic way than previously. At a more symbolic level, the Leader's Campaign Committee included five union leaders – an effective point of influence had this committee played the role expected of it.

(Minkin, 1989, pp.268–9)

Alongside this increased co-ordination, there was a change in strategy which reflected a desire to establish a distance between the party and the unions. Minkin suggests that this occurred for three main reasons. First, the Labour Party had to appeal beyond its shrinking union base. Second, it was felt that Kinnock needed to appear strong and independent of union influence. Third, the party felt it needed to associate itself from unpopular unionism, particularly from the picket-line violence associated with the miners' strike. Of course, the Labour Party still lost the election, but this attempt to distance the party from the unions in electoral terms has continued since, and is reflected in some of the outcomes of the Labour Party Policy Review.

The Labour Party Policy Review

Even in its 1986 policy document, *People and Work*, the Party was still committed to 'repeal the legislation enacted since 1979' (*Labour Party*, 1986, p.45). However, things changed significantly as a result of the 1987 election defeat. In fact, the impetus behind the establishment of the Policy Review came from within the union movement. Tom Sawyer, NUPE's Deputy General Secretary, in September 1987, presented a paper to the Home Policy Committee of the NEC entitled 'An Approach to Policy Making' which proved to be the basis of the Review. There were two key reasons for Sawyer's proposal. First, he suggested that the Labour Party needed to develop policies which would have broader appeal to the electorate. Second, he was anxious to avoid another round of post-election recriminations (see Shaw, 1989). The Review had three stages. The first stage produced a statement of values and the main policy themes for the 1988 Party Conference. The second stage saw the drawing up of a series of major policy statements for the 1989 Conference. The final stage involved the finalisation and revision of these policies in preparation for a 1992 election. There were seven Policy Review Groups (PRGs) entitled: A Productive and Competitive Economy; People at Work; Economic Equality; Consumers and the Community; Britain in the World; and Physical and Social Environment. The *People at Work* PRG dealt with industrial relations. Each group had seven to ten members and was chaired jointly by a member of the Shadow Cabinet and a representative from the NEC. In the case of the *People at Work* group they were Michael Meacher, the Party Employment spokesman and Eddie Haigh, a TGWU official. The other members were drawn from the Shadow Cabinet, the NEC and the trade unions. A small number of advisers were added to this list who, although they were not formerly members, took part in all discussions. In addition, a much larger number of experts, particularly academics, interest group leaders and unionists, were consulted, being asked to submit papers or joint study groups. As such, the unions were closely involved in the production of the new Labour Party policy on industrial relations, although they didn't dominate it.

The key theme in the report of the *People at Work* group was the need to balance the interests of unions and their members. So the party pledged to remove many of the constraints which the Conservatives had placed on union activity while retaining the rights of individual unionists to have more say in the running of the unions. There were clear differences of interest and view between the Shadow Cabinet and the unions on this point. As Shaw points out, most union leaders would have preferred the retention of the party's 1986 commitment to total repeal of the Conservative's legislation. However, most were aware of the electoral consequences of such a commitment. In addition, Shaw suggests that Michael Meacher and, in particular, Neil Kinnock, were strongly committed to the retention of secret ballots for union elections and before strike action (Shaw, 1989). The Shadow Cabinet view triumphed, although the policy document still contained considerable ambiguity. As an example, although a pledge to increase worker participation in the running of companies was included, no details were given because there was considerable disagreement between Michael Meacher, who favoured a Works Council directly elected by all employees, and Eddie Haigh who was committed to indirect representation through the trade unions.

The publication of the Policy Review final report in 1989, as *Meet the Challenge – Make the Change*, was followed by *Looking to the Future*, in 1990. The party committed themselves to retain pre-strike ballots and ballots for the election of union leaderships and not to restore the closed shop. However, they did propose major reforms. The centrepiece of a new legal framework would be an Industrial Court which would deal with industrial disputes. It would be headed by a senior High Court judge and replace the Employment Appeal Tribunal. It is evident from the proposals that the Labour Party has learnt lessons from a number of the most contentious cases dealt with in Chapter 4. So, they are committed to giving unions the right to take secondary action where: the primary employer has contracted out work to avoid strike action; the outcome of the primary dispute will affect the terms and conditions of another employer's employees; where corporate legal identity is manipulated to make secondary action unlawful. These plans are clearly designed to overcome the problems unions face as a result of the decisions in the Messenger and Dimbleby cases. Similarly, Labour proposes to ensure that individuals have the right not to be dismissed for lawful strike action. This deals with the weakness in the position of individual unionists which was revealed in the Wapping case. Three other proposals are worthy of note. First, there would be a right to picket peacefully, in limited numbers, in accordance with a statutory code of practice. Second, the law in relation to injunctions would be changed. Ex-parte injunctions, which allow an employer to get a court order without the union being able to argue its case, would be prohibited. In addition, if an injunction was granted, either party could immediately request a full hearing on the case. If this happened, the employer would have to prove his case, rather than merely demonstrate the union has a case to answer, a much more difficult task. Third, a right to union recognition could be enforced through the new Industrial Court if substantial support existed for such recognition in the workplace.

Overall then, the Labour Party proposes to restore some protection to unions and unionists, in large part by moving to a system of positive rights rather than restoring immunities. However, it is not committed to as extensive a system of rights as proposed by some labour lawyers. In addition, it will retain important elements of the Conservative legislation, particularly in relation to balloting. This policy was endorsed by the 1990 Labour Party Conference when it was piloted through by the Party's new Employment spokesman, Tony Blair.

The unions are not totally united on the Labour Party proposals. The 1990 Trades Union Congress passed a composite motion supporting the Party's industrial relations reforms on a show of hands. The vote also committed the TUC to supporting a variety of positive employment rights and opposing key elements in the 1990 Employment Act. However, immediately afterwards there was a card vote which led to the rejection of a radical composite motion which advocated the repeal of the Conservative industrial relations legislation by only 875,000 votes. The 3,529,000 votes for the motion included the block votes of the TGWU, Manufacturing, Science and Finance Union (MSF), NALGO, National Graphical Association (NGA) and the National Union of Mineworkers (NUM). The 4,404,000 against were cast by, among others, the AEU, GMB, NUPE, USDAW, Union of Communication Workers (UCW) and the NUT. This voting reflects the division within the TUC. The majority of unions oppose most, if not all, elements of the Conservative legislation. However, they are well aware that industrial relations legislation is one of the Labour Party's Achilles' heels. As Ron Todd, General Secretary of the TGWU, put it: 'Even those who have doubts about Labour's programme must surely see the sense of getting rid of the Tories first' (quoted in the *Guardian*, 4 September 1990, p.4). Bill Jordan, President of the AEU, was more positive when he argued:

Without a Labour Government there will be no fair laws for trade unionists; without a sensible stance by trade unions on employment law there will be no Labour Government.

(quoted in the *Guardian*, 4 September 190, p.4)

Conclusion

In this chapter we have reviewed the changing nature of relations between the Labour Party and the trade unions since 1979. Two major conclusions are clear:

1. The relationship has altered during the 1980's and in particular since the election defeats in 1983 and 1987. The Labour Party leadership has reasserted its political autonomy from the unions and this move has been actively encouraged by most union leaders.
2. In fact, this is a re-establishment of the traditional relationship between the unions and the Labour leadership. As Taylor emphasises, the unions have traditionally been a stabilising force within the Labour Party supporting the position of the PLP leadership. The developments since the mid-1980s reflect a desire by both sides to return to an earlier era of union-Party relations, which was well documented in Irvine Richter's study of the period up to 1970. In this period, unions had a limited political purpose; politics was left to the Labour Party. As we saw in Chapter 2, this pattern changed largely as a result of the incomes policy, and to a lesser extent the industrial relations policy, of the Labour governments between 1964 and 1970. If the current agreement between the unions and the party on industrial relations holds, and an incoming Labour Government doesn't resort to incomes policy, then the political role of unions within the Labour Party is likely to be a limited problem for the Party. With the benefit of hindsight, the 1970s and early 1980s look like an aberration in terms of union-party relations.

The future

The immediate future of union-party relations is likely to be more peaceful. There will be changes. Neil Kinnock is a strong advocate of one member-one vote and as such is determined to reduce the unions' role in party decision-making. In fact, two important changes which affect the unions' position are planned: the proportion of the votes allocated to the unions at the Labour Party Conference will be reduced from its current 90 per cent to 70 per cent; and the reselection of MPs will be on the basis of one member-one vote rather than the current electoral college system. Of course, this doesn't mean that the unions will have no influence on party policy; they could still potentially dominate Conference voting.

If a Labour Government is elected it seems unlikely that industrial relations legislation will be a major bone of contention. There is little organised opposition within the union movement to ballots and this is the Conservative reform to which the Labour Party remains most committed. There will be arguments about legislation on secondary action and picketing, but the party's proposals on both these issues attempt to strike a balance between the interests of unions and employers and, more importantly, are likely to be supported by the rank and file membership of the unions, a rank and file membership which is increasingly important in union decision-making given the ballot reforms and the major problems of membership recruitment and retention. In addition, the Labour Party proposals offer the unions major gains in relation to recognition and the right of individual unionists to strike; such gains might be lost if there was a major confrontation between the unions and the party over industrial relations.

If conflict does occur between a future Labour Government and the trade unions it seems much more likely to be over incomes policy than industrial relations. In the past incomes policy has always been the crucial problem for their relationship and it is likely to remain so. At present, the Labour Party is committed to allowing market forces to decide wage levels, but if the economic situation continued to deteriorate under a Labour Government, it would be tempted to return to corporatist, supply-side intervention. Such a policy would involve unions once again in policy-making but, as an almost inevitable consequence, it would also mean a return to incomes policy. In such an eventuality, it is not difficult to envisage a Labour Government faced with a re-run of the 'Winter of Discontent' as a return to incomes policy would inevitably politicise the unions.

7

The Changing Economic Context

It is frequently suggested that economic changes have played a more important role than the new industrial relations legislation in weakening the position of British trade unions in recent years (see, for example Wedderburn, 1985, p.33). This chapter examines the economic changes that have occurred which have affected union membership and organisation. The next two chapters will then assess how far such changes, and indeed the Conservatives' industrial relations legislation, has affected the unions' collective bargaining position. This chapter is divided into five sections. The first section analyses changes which have occurred in the economic structure; most significantly the increase in unemployment and the processes of restructuring and deindustrialisation. The second section then looks at one of the major consequences of these changes, the decline of union membership. The third section examines the increased use of technology, while the fourth section concentrates upon the supposed growth of flexibilisation within the British economy. Finally, I identify the changes in economic policy since 1979.

The changing economic structure

The structure of the British economy has changed significantly during the last two decades and many of these changes began before 1979. A number of these changes, together with associated developments in the social structure, have clearly affected the position of the unions, in particular: the rise in unemployment; the decline in the manufacturing sector; the changes in the class structure; and the internationalisation of production.

As Table 7.1 indicates, while unemployment fell slightly in the late 1970s it increased greatly in the period after 1979; indeed it swelled from 5.0 per cent in 1979 to a peak of 12.5 per cent in 1983. Subsequently, there was a significant fall to 8.3 per cent in 1988. Moreover, there is a distinct regional pattern in the growth in unemployment. In England the rise in unemployment has been greatest in the North, the Midlands and London and smaller in the South East and, particularly, East Anglia and the South West.

While unemployment has grown since 1979, the processes of restructuring and deindustrialisation can be traced back much further. This restructuring of the pattern of employment and production in the economy has involved a relative rise in the importance of the service sector compared with manufacturing; an increase in part-time employment and self-employment; an increase in women's employment; a decline in the number employed in the public sector; and an increase in white-collar employment.

Table 7.2 indicates that the proportion of employees employed in the manufacturing sector and in the production sector dropped by 8 per cent and 15 per cent respectively between 1979 and 1988, while the percentage employed in the service sector increased. However,

Table 7.1 *Changing economic indicators, 1979–89*

	Unemploy-ment (%)*	Inflation (%)**	Number of strikes** (thousands)	Number of workers involved in strikes** (thousands)	Number of working days lost per 1000 employees
1979	5.0	13	2080	4608	29474
1980	6.4	18	1330	834	11964
1981	9.8	12	1338	1513	4266
1982	11.3	8	1528	2103	5313
1983	12.5	5	1352	574	3754
1984	11.7	5	1206	1464	27135
1985	11.2	6	857	791	6402
1986	11.1	3	1053	720	1920
1987	10.2	2	1004	887	3546
1988	8.3	5	781	790	3694
1989	6.4	8	701	727	4128

Sources: * *Social Trends*, relevant years
** *Annual Abstract of Statistics*, relevant years

Table 7.2 (a)   *Employees in employment, 1970–78 (000s)*

Sector	1970 No.	(%)	1978 No.	(%)	% change in absolute nos employed in sector 1970–78	Change in % employed in sector 1970–78
Total employees	22471	–	22713	–	+ 1	–
Males	14002	62	13363	59	– 3	– 3
Females	8470	38	9349	41	+ 10	+ 3
Production industries	10475	47	9275	41	– 11	– 6
Manufacturing	8339	37	7309	32	– 12	– 5
Retail distribution	2676	12	2737	12	+ 2	nc
Banking finance	956	4	1150	5	+ 20	+ 1
Professional and scientific services	2897	13	3670	16	+ 27	+ 3
National government	589	3	667	3	+ 13	nc
Local government	890	4	965	4	+ 8	nc
Other services	1249	6	1516	7	+ 21	+ 1

Notes
nc = no change
Source: *Employment Gazette* (selected sectors).

Table 7.2 (b) *Employees in employment, 1979–88 (000s)*

Sector	1979 No.	1979 (%)	1988 No.	1988 (%)	Change 1979–88 (%)
Total employees	23173	–	22330	–	– 4
Males	13487	58	12330	54	– 11
Females	9686	42	10301	46	+ 6
Production industries	9213	40	5633	25	– 39
Manufacturing	7253	31	5177	23	– 29
Retail distribution	2176	9	2230	10	+ 2
Banking finance	1647	7	2601	12	+ 58
Public administration	2002	9	2012	9	nc
Education	1660	7	1714	8	+ 3
Other services	1303	6	1662	7	+ 28
Medical and other health services **	1233	5	1306	6	+ 6

Notes

nc = no change.

Source: *Employment Gazette* (selected sectors).

the table also shows that this restructuring pre-dates 1979, although the changes have been larger in the later period. Not surprisingly, as the manufacturing and production sectors have contracted, so the size of firms has decreased (McInnes, 1987, p.77).

The proportion of women employed in the work-force has grown dramatically throughout the last two decades in step with the shift of employment to the service sector. Once again, the movement has slightly accelerated in the 1980s as Table 7.2(b) confirms. There has also been a significant increase (about 6 per cent) in the number of part-time employees over the last two decades, a smaller increase in those who are self-employed (about 3 per cent) and a marginal increase in the number of temporary jobs (about 1 per cent). However, all these forms of employment are heavily concentrated in the service sector, while part-time employment is very much a gender-based phenomenon.

The decline in public sector employment is more recent and results, almost exclusively, from the Thatcher government's privatisation policy which is dealt with later. Actually, if we exclude the public corporations, the public sector's share of employment has actually grown since 1979, because of the relative decline of employment in the private sector.

These developments have led to major changes in the occupational composition of the work-force. In particular, the number of manual workers in the work-force declined from 64 per cent in 1951 to 46 per cent in 1986. It is noticeable, however, that this decline was most rapid in the 1970s and not the 1980s. Obviously, these changes are also reflected in the social class composition of the population and, more importantly, the electorate. The proportion of working-class electors has declined considerably while the percentage of routine non-manual and, particularly, the professionals (salariat) has increased significantly.

One other aspect of the process of deindustrialisation, the internationalisation of production, has accentuated since 1979 and has clearly had a major affect on unions. In the last decade particularly, larger companies have increasingly internationalised their production through the acquisition of a growing number of overseas subsidiaries and associated companies. Although this process was well developed before 1979, it was accelerated by the Conservatives' abolition of exchange controls in 1979. A Labour Research Department study (*Labour Research*, April 1983) showed that in 1981–2 overseas production accounted for 44 per cent of the output of Britain's top 50 private manufacturing companies. This compared with a figure of 36 per cent in 1979–80 and 39 per cent in 1980–81. That figure has almost certainly increased and it has been associated with the export of jobs.

Clearly, a major stimulus to the relocation of production both within Britain and abroad has been the desire to escape strong union organisation in traditional industrial areas and ensure lower labour costs. Further, as Marsh's analysis reveals, investment decisions taken by firms are increasingly influenced by labour costs, reflecting managements recognition of the greater flexibility afforded to transnational capital (Marsh, 1986).

The decline in union membership

Undeniably, such changes in the economic and social structure have had an important effect on trade unions. I shall examine how far they have affected the bargaining position of unions in the next chapter. Here I am concerned with the decline in union membership which has resulted, at least in part, from a combination of the rise in unemployment and economic restructuring.

If the rise in unemployment was the sole reason for the decline in union membership, then one would have expected union density to remain constant. As Table 2.2 indicated, however, union density has dropped markedly. If we just consider unions affiliated to the TUC then density has dropped from 54.5 per cent in 1978 to 40.8 per cent in 1987, a fall of almost 14 per cent. Historically, the unions' strength has been concentrated among male, full-time manual workers employed in large plants in the manufacturing sector in the North, the Midlands and London. This pattern has persisted. As the 1989 Labour Force Survey indicates, union density is still greatest for: those in full-time (43 per cent) rather than part-time employment (22 per cent); employees in large rather than small plants; manual (43 per cent) rather than non-manual employees (35 per cent); the middle-aged rather than the young and old; public sector employees rather than private sector employees; and in the North (52 per cent) rather than the South East (30 per cent) (see *Employment Gazette*, August 1990, pp.403–13; see also Beaumont, 1987, p.192).

Those unions who represent workers in the declining industries have experienced the largest falls in membership. As we saw in Chapter 2 union membership grew generally in the 1970s, as the Labour Government encouraged union recognition and membership, although the major expansion was in the public sector. In the 1980s, in contrast, union membership has fallen, particularly for unions whose strength was in the manufacturing sector; between 1979 and 1980 the Transport and General Workers Union (TGWU) membership declined by 39 per cent, the Amalgamated Union of Engineering Workers (AUEW) by 39 per cent and UCATT by 26 per cent (see Table 2.1).

There have also been significant changes in the regional composition of the membership of many unions (see Massey and Painter, 1989). After 1971, the growth of the AUEW was in those regions previously on the periphery of its membership at the expense of its old heartlands. Massey and Painter argue that membership of unions has become decentralised, primarily towards the less urbanised areas. The changing location of industry has unquestionably had some effect on British trade unions, although the extent of this effect is much disputed as we shall see in Chapter 8.

Not surprisingly, given the seemingly irreversible nature of many of these structural changes, the unions have become particularly conscious of the need to attract new members. However, their efforts haven't been a conspicuous success. Obviously, an area of potential recruitment for unions is among women and part-time workers. Women now constitute 46 per cent of the work-force but still make up only a third of the Trade Union Congress (TUC)-affiliated membership (*Labour Research*, March 1988). Historically, women have been more difficult to organise; they are often employed part-time in the service sector in small work-forces. In addition, the unions have been male-dominated, and many would claim male-chauvinist, organisations. In the last five years certain unions have made greater efforts to attract women members and to encourage more women to take an active role in union affairs. A *Labour Research* study of the ten unions with the largest women membership, however, found that there was no clear increase in the proportion of women members among union leaderships. Some unions had slightly increased the proportion of women executive members, while in some unions the proportion had fallen (*Labour Research*, March 1990, pp.7–8). There had been a marginal increase in the number of women on the National Executive Committees of seven of the ten unions but no increase in the number of women full-time national officers. Indeed, even a TUC report concluded:

> Whilst there had been many positive developments and a recognition amongst all unions of the need to remove barriers to women's involvement in unions, women were often still not able to play an equal role.

(Quoted in *Labour Research*, March 1988)

The unions have also had a major problem in attracting part-time workers. The proportion of part-timers among memberships varies greatly: from 1 per cent in the AUEW to 53 per cent in NUPE. While over the last five years unions have had more success in attracting part-timers, the proportion of part-timers in unions is still significantly less than the proportion in the working population (*Labour Research*, March 1989, pp.19–22). One of the major reasons for non-union membership appears to be that the majority of part-time workers who are not union members are concentrated in plants which do not recognise unions. It is evident that unions have made considerable effort to attract part-time members and have met with some success. However, the unions have not encouraged part-time members to participate in union affairs and, in most senses, they still appear to be peripheral to unions' interests, if not their finances.

The TUC has also become involved in the drive for recruits. So in 1990 the TUC organised a three-week recruitment drive at Trafford Park in Manchester. Here 14 unions combined to approach workers in 67 companies, including large retailers and hotels where they had previously made little progress. The TUC found 'widespread evidence of harassment of recruiters and intimidation of potential members' (quoted in the *Guardian*, 3 September 1990, p.19). The campaign resulted in 900 new members but at a cost of £86 per member, more than twice the £39 paid by the average TGWU member in subscriptions. In addition, it is not known how many of these new members were retained.

New technology

It is frequently argued that the increased use of new technology, and the broader but related development of the flexible firm, are changing the nature of British industrial relations and weakening the bargaining position of trade unions. In the next two sections I shall first look at the effect of the increased use of new technology on the unions and then at the development of the flexible firm.

Micro-electronic technology has been widely introduced into British industry in the 1980s, both in the office and on the shop floor. Northcott estimates that by 1985 almost 50 per cent of manufacturing establishments employing 20 or more workers were using micro-electronics in the production process. As these applications were most common in larger companies, 76 per cent of employees worked in establishments using this technology (Northcott, 1986). Similarly, the National Economic Development Office (NEDO) estimates that by 1995 30 per cent of large companies will be using integrated manufacturing systems or automated offices (NEDO, 1986).

However, as Willman argues: 'a great deal of evidence of several different types supports the view that the UK experiences some form of "innovation problem"' (Willman, 1986, p.38). The evidence that trade unions are a major obstacle to technological change is less than convincing. On the contrary, most studies suggest that this failure is the result of limited investment; a lack of knowledge about technological developments; shortages of suitably qualified staff; and, most important, a general failure to obtain efficiency (Daniel 1987a; Northcott 1986; Willman 1986). In addition, a number of studies suggest that most unions have co-operated unreservedly in the introduction of new technology (Lintner, 1987).

Certainly, Daniel's study indicated the strength and pervasiveness of support from unions and unionists for particular innovations which involved the introduction of new technology. Moreover, his analysis of the Workplace Industrial Relations Surveys (WIRS) data identified few significant differences between union attitudes in different sectors (Daniel, 1987b; see also Dodgson and Martin, 1987). This support for new technology was even strong enough to make less palatable forms of change more acceptable. Redundancies, the removal of traditional demarcations and the adoption of new patterns of work organisation, were all much more acceptable to unions and unionists when associated with the adoption of new technology.

Of course, there are a number of areas in which union opposition to the introduction of new technology has been consistent and prolonged. However, Willman confidently asserts that these are the exceptions:

> the clearest evidence of resistance – strikes in opposition to particular technological changes – has been confined in the last twenty-five years to three industries; docks, national newspapers and motor vehicles.
>
> (Willman, 1986, p.247)

Not only are they exceptions, but in each industry the resistance, while extensive and damaging, has proved ultimately unsuccessful.

There is little evidence that unions have significant influence over the introduction of new technology, although the pattern is not a simple one. Daniel found that unions and shop stewards played a role in 'the introduction of advanced technical change affecting manual workers in only 39 per cent of cases' (Daniel, 1987b, p.116). Similarly, Moore and Levie argue that, in their case studies: 'Whatever influence the trade unionists had over the shape of technological change has come by stealth' (Moore and Levie, 1985, p.513).

In contrast, Martin's analysis of responses from a sizeable sample of large corporations suggests that the companies believe they consult fairly widely. He reports that management policy in many companies was to discuss the introduction of new technology with union representatives, with the proviso that management is left free to take the final decision; this policy was reported by 77 per cent of corporate managers and 87 per cent of divisional managers (Martin, 1988, p.175). Even so, it is evident from Martin's study that the influence of unions was limited: 'Very few senior managers said ... that changes were dependent upon securing the agreement of union representatives' (ibid., pp.175–6). The introduction of new technology is clearly viewed as the prerogative of management. Not surprisingly, the amount of consultation and the union's role depend on the history of industrial relations in the firm and the economic situation (Dodgson and Martin, 1987).

The dominance of management is confirmed by studies of the introduction of New Technology Agreements (NTA), which have mostly involved white-collar unions. One survey of over 100 NTAs found that less than 10 per cent of the agreements provided for union involvement in the planning stage, but around a third assumed union involvement before implementation (Williams and Moseley, 1981).

Similarly, a Confederation of British Industry (CBI) survey of 225 NTAs found that 44 per cent of employers 'communicated' the agreement to their workers, while 42 per cent consulted with the unions, and only 9 per cent 'negotiated'. Even among larger firms, less than 20 per cent negotiated an NTA with the union. In almost all cases the NTA involved a single union and nearly 70 per cent of them provided for no compulsory redundancies (Francis, 1987, p.177). Certainly, the number of NTAs negotiated has been limited compared with the original TUC objectives and there is little doubt that they have declined in number in recent years (McIlroy, 1988, p.117).

Overall, two points seem clear. First, unions and unionists rarely oppose the introduction of new technology; the exceptions have been spectacular, as the Wapping case reveals, and ultimately unsuccessful. Second, as Clark suggests, a number of factors affect unions' influence over the introduction of new technology (Clark, 1984, 1989). The history and pattern of industrial relations in the particular company and its broad management strategy, what Jones and Rose call the 'politics of the plant' play the most important role (Jones and Rose, quoted in Eiger, 1987, p.534). However, unions usually do have certain space within which they can influence developments as long as they are cohesive, knowledgeable and pursue a coherent, co-ordinated, strategy.

There is little doubt that the introduction of new technology can have a major affect on unions and workers. Often, but by no means always, the change is associated with job loss. Certainly Daniel argues that investment in technological change is not leading to a growth in jobs. He found that, if anything, the heaviest users of new technology were more likely to have been reducing the size of their work-force (Daniel, 1987b). Not surprisingly, the jobs of less-skilled manual workers were most at risk. Similarly, Martin's responses from managers suggest that, in large firms: 'the introduction of new technology led to job loss among workers directly affected in 58 per cent of changes involving manual workers and 49 per cent of changes involving non-manual workers' (Martin, 1988, p.178). However, it appears that in most cases the number of job losses involved is small. So, Northcott calculated that by the mid-1980s the job losses resulting from technical change accounted for only 5 per cent of the overall drop in manufacturing employment (Northcott, 1986). Certainly, McIlroy seems right to conclude that other factors, particularly broad market and political factors, have a much greater effect on unemployment (McIlroy, 1988, p.107).

Some authors have also associated technological change with deskilling (see McIlroy, 1988, pp.109–12), but again the pattern is not a simple one. Certainly, some managements in both the private and the public sector have introduced new technology in an attempt to increase control over the work-force (see Wilkinson, 1983). However, this is not a novel process, it is not an unvarying one and it is not inevitably successful. Wilkinson's study indicates that management strategies are diverse and subject to constraints provided by the 'politics of plant'. On occasions, new technology forms part of a wider management initiative to increase control of the production process. In other cases new technology is introduced with the aim of deskilling and increasing management control, but fails to achieve these ends. Finally, sometimes the management pursues a dual strategy of using technology to increase control and alter wage payment systems in order to obtain the same long-term aim of increased efficiency. Certainly, it is possible to lay far too much emphasis on the capacity of new technology to increase control. Rather, new technology can produce a number of outcomes. It can increase management control. In some cases as Daniel suggests it can even produce a higher level of skill, responsibility and interest for some workers. However, even Daniel continues:

the changes appeared to have a more neutral or even slightly negative affect upon the autonomy of workers as measured by their control over how they did their jobs, the pace of their work, and the degree of supervision to which they were subject.

(Daniel, 1987b, p.276)

The introduction of new technology can, of course, also lead to considerable conflict between unions, which makes the development of a co-ordinated strategy by unions in bargaining about the introduction of new technology difficult. Indeed, as Clark argues:

rivalry and conflict between different grades or categories of staff (either belonging to the same union or organised in different unions) may play a significant role in negotiating its introduction.

(Clark, 1984, p.36)

Almost inevitably, the conflict is over how to reconcile the legitimate claims of different sections of the work-force to operate the technology. Such conflict is almost inevitably used by management to negotiate an agreement more favourable to them.

Although the pattern is complex and the outcomes often difficult to predict, McIlroy's conclusion is again sound:

> opportunities provide a degree of discretion. But new technologies are constituted not by perceptions of the needs of labour, but by perceptions of the requirements of profitability. New technology may contain the potential for a great development of human potential, undreamed of living standards, unbelievable leisure and a guaranteed income for all; but these particular technologies are being introduced for particular purposes in a particular economic and political context. Undreamed of living standards and enhanced, paid leisure are not the objectives behind their present application. *This* technology is being introduced by profit seeking employers against the background of a reversal, not a reinforcement of the post-war trends towards planning and egalitarianism, and in a situation where the distribution of power over decision making is increasingly skewed against those it will most affect. The probability is that new technology will benefit the few at the expense of the many.
>
> (McIlroy 1988, pp.103–104)

Flexibilisation

One of the current preoccupations in the industrial relations literature concerns the extent of the development of flexibilisation in the labour market and the labour process. These are two separate, if clearly related, developments and both have given rise to concepts which are widely used in the literature. Within the labour market the debate has largely revolved around arguments about the evolution of the 'flexible firm', while discussions on change in the labour process have often suggested a growing 'Japanisation'.

Atkinson's diagram depicting the 'flexible firm' must be one of the most reproduced in the field (Atkinson, 1985). In Atkinson's view the flexibility offensive by employers involves three interwoven objectives:

To increase their ability to adjust quickly and cheaply to a more uncertain, volatile and competitive market, and to an increased pace of technological change;

To continue the high rate of growth of productivity which marked the earlier years of the current recession, at a time when output and profitability are now rising; To reduce employment costs either through using cheaper sources of labour or by using forms of labour, like temporary employment, which allow quick and cheap changes in the level of employment.

(Atkinson, 1985, p.13)

According to Atkinson, management's attempt to achieve these objectives involves a fundamental restructuring of the labour force into two quite separate groups: the core and the periphery. The core consists of skilled workers and consists of groups such as managers, designers, sales staff, craftsmen and technicians. The emphasis here is upon *functional flexibility*; core workers are skilled workers able to perform a variety of tasks and work in multi-disciplinary teams. They must also be able to respond to changes in technology and work organisation. In return, such employees enjoy high wages, job security and single status. Such privileges also ensure that they are committed to, and identify with, the company. In contrast, the position of the peripheral groups is very different. In fact, Atkinson suggests there are two groups of peripheral workers. The first group consists of workers directly employed by the firm in less skilled jobs, clerical, assembly, or even supervisory. They may be employed full-time but have limited security, low wages and few prospects. The second group consists of part-time workers, temporary workers and trainees. The two groups together answer the firms' need for *numerical flexibility*. In addition, there is also a move towards the subcontracting of work outside the firm to specialist employment agencies or self-employed workers, which enables the firm to enjoy both numerical and functional flexibility.

Atkinson's analysis is empirically questionable. We have already seen that the growth in part-time and temporary working and self-employment has been limited, although not negligible. More interestingly, the growth in part-time employment has been more concentrated in large public sector organisations, not the big industrial companies which in Atkinson's terms are the putative prototypes of the flexible firm. There is also considerable debate as to the extent to which the employment rights and conditions of part-time employees are worse than those of their full-time colleagues. In addition, there has been little evidence of any dramatic increases in subcontracting, outworking and freelancing. Indeed, Marginson and Sisson reported that only 18 per cent of the establishment managers they interviewed used freelancers or outworkers (Marginson and Sisson, 1988, p.86). There was a much broader use of subcontracting and, indeed, 33 per cent of the companies in the sample reported the increased use of subcontracting (see Marginson and Sisson, 1988, Figure 4.4, p.89). However, subcontracting has always been widely used (see Pollert, 1988, p.54) and is concentrated in areas such as cleaning, maintenance, catering, transport and computer services (see Marginson and Sisson, 1988, Table 4.3, p.89). What is more, under the Conservative Government most of the major increase in subcontracting has occurred in the public sector.

If the existence of a peripheral work-force is problematic, so is that of a core. In particular, the extent of 'functional flexibility' appears limited. A NEDO study found that there was little radical job enlargement. Again, the greatest flexibility was among maintenance craftsmen; three-quarters of the company survey had achieved some overlap in this area. In contrast, there was limited flexibility (in about 30 per cent of companies) in the mechanical and electrical areas and much less (in about 15 per cent of companies) between these two areas (NEDO, 1986). This is not a surprising result as McInnes points out (McInnes, 1987, pp.119–20). Given the existence of major skill shortages, there is little pressure on skilled workers to become multi-skilled, while the slump in the commitment of companies towards training and, in particular, the collapse of the apprenticeship system, have reduced the supply of skilled labour.

Overall, there has clearly been an increase in less secure and indirect forms of employment, but the use of such forms is not novel. Indeed, Hakim argues that while the balance between the core and the periphery is changing, this labour force restructuring results largely from traditional and opportunistic responses by employers (Hakim, 1990). This restructuring has also occurred more in some sectors than others, most noticeably in the public sector. Similarly, while there is greater functional flexibility, progress in this direction has proved slow. As Pollert asserts after the best critical review of this literature:

(after) a review of the changes in the workforce and in employment practices, the 'flexible firm' model is left standing with few clothes. Where there has been most major restructuring this has been led by the state as employer. But in the private sector, sectoral continuity is far more in evidence than change, with little evidence of polarisation between an (ill-defined) 'periphery' and a privileged 'core'.

(Pollert, 1988, p.56)

Perversely, the growth of unemployment appears to have reduced rather than increased flexibility. Certainly, Jones and McKay show that as unemployment and redundancies increased, voluntary job change, clearly a crucial aspect of labour market flexibility, fell significantly. In addition, they argue that measures to promote mobility are less likely to be effective at periods of high unemployment given that the rewards of such mobility are uncertain (Jones and McKay, 1986).

In periods of employment uncertainty, job security becomes the crucial concern of employees. Indeed, the 1985 Labour Force Survey indicates that 59 per cent of men and 44 per cent of women had been in their jobs for six years or more. As McInnes argues:

It seems that high unemployment, rather than forcing labour to be more flexible, can actually encourage the opposite. It leaves many employers and workers stuck with each other.

(McInnes, 1987, p.123)

The literature on 'Japanisation' is almost as large as that on the 'flexible firm' and the 'dual labour' market. Ackroyd *et al.* identify three types of 'Japanisation'; two of which are important here (Ackroyd *et al.* 1989). 'Direct Japanisation' involves the penetration of the British economy and industry by Japanese firms and has particular significance in relation to discussions about 'greenfield' sites, non-unionism and single unionism. In contrast, 'mediated Japanisation' involves the adoption of Japanese policies and work practices by British firms.

The extent of 'direct Japanisation' is limited. Dunning calculated that, by the end of March 1984, only 4 per cent of the investment of Japanese manufacturing companies overseas was in Britain; 27 per cent was in the USA. He also suggests that by 1981 sales of Japanese subsidiaries accounted for less than 1 per cent of the sales of all foreign-owned subsidiaries in the UK (Dunning, 1986). Similarly, Morris points out that at the end of 1986 there were only 53 Japanese-owned manufacturing companies in the UK employing less than 14,000 people. This compared with the 450,000 employed in US-owned manufacturing companies. However, Morris does suggest that in the 1980s there has been a steep increase in Japanese investment areas, although he emphasises that most of this has been in North America and in the service sector, rather than the manufacturing sector (Morris, 1989).

The development of 'mediated Japanisation' is probably more important. Some British companies have sought to integrate certain Japanese practices with their own, in order to increase flexibility and efficiency. Usually, such changes have been limited and piecemeal, only rarely have they been radical. 'Mediated Japanisation' has most often involved the introduction of 'just-in-time' (JIT) working practices, although the negotiation of a single union agreement, which will be dealt with in the next chapter, is sometimes an important element. It is usual to contrast the JIT with the 'just-in-case' (JIC) system. As Sayer writes:

> the JIC system is a method of mass production based on a collection of large lot production processes separated by large buffers and feeding into a final assembly line, JIT is a system of mass production consisting of a highly integrated series of small lot production processes. Further, JIT is a learning system which generates economies by making fabrication and assembly more closely approximate a continuous flow line, by reducing the amounts of machinery, material or labour power which are at any time inactive or not contributing to the production of saleable (i.e adequate quality) outputs.
>
> (Sayer, 1986, p.56)

As such, a successful JIT system requires a co-operative, flexible, multi-skilled work-force. This involves improved communications between management and workers but can lead to confrontational industrial relations. After reviewing the available literature, Ackroyd *et al.* argue:

we would contend that the evidence for mediated Japanisation of this kind is not at all strong, and that arguments suggesting that changes in employers' practices are indicative of a trend towards a more 'Japanised' labour market in this country ...are considerably overdrawn.

(Ackroyd *et al.* 1989, p.18)

The case studies of the introduction of such production techniques in individual industries or companies point to a similar conclusion. Dickens and Savage's study of working practices in high technology companies in Berkshire, for example, concludes: 'given a broad understanding of what 'Japanisation' entails, we can find little evidence of its transfer to the new, more dynamic, sectors of the British economy' (Dickens and Savage, 1989, p.66).

Many managements have used the threat of unemployment to reform works practices but some changes, in so far as they have involved 'mediated Japanisation', have been constrained by existing practices and workers' organisation and thus have often involved a compromise between Taylorism and a more flexible model of labour deployment. The key point is that British management has often wanted both increased flexibilisation *and* increased control; two aims which, to a considerable extent, are contradictory. A brief consideration of the attempts to introduce 'mediated Japanisation' into the British motor industry amply illustrates these developments.

The 'After Japan' system (AJ) was introduced into Ford of Europe in 1979. It aimed to improve manufacturing productivity, increase motivation and involvement on the shop floor and improve communication between management and workers. In particular, this involved the establishment of quality circles. Starkey and McKinlay argue:

In the UK, AJ foundered on union resistance to quality circles. For the manufacturing unions, quality circles threatened to by-pass existing bargaining institutions by subsuming work organisation issues far beyond quality improvement.

(Starkey and McKinlay, 1988, p.96)

Faced with this opposition, Ford abandoned the notion of any broad move to Japanisation. As Starkey and McKinlay continue:

Since AJ, Ford has pursued a twin-track change strategy: on the one hand, pushing through nationalisation and efficiency measures by traditional top-down methods; on the other, pursuing a more complex, longer-term approach based on building more consensual management – labour relations.

(ibid., p.96)

However, there is a clear tension between these two aims. Flexibilisation of the process of work organisation involves trust, Taylorism emphasises control and, almost inevitably, an adversarial style of industrial relations. Lane makes the point well:

Although management is anxious to achieve working co-operation and the attainment of (increased flexibilisation), the attainment of this goal is jeopardised by the pursuit of their other goal-efficiency through increased task control.

(Lane, 1988, p.164)

This point is confirmed in Smith's analysis of the Japanisation of Rover (Smith, 1989). He points out that the position of unions was severely weakened under both the participatory management style of Sir Don Ryder (1975–7), during which the shop stewards were incorporated and emasculated, and the authoritarian style of management pursued by Michael Edwardes. Against this setting, Rover introduced three changes at Longbridge in 1986 designed to improve work-force commitment: zone briefings, zone circles and an induction foundation course. Yet, within two years there was considerable opposition to zone briefings (ibid., p.44) and zone circles were virtually redundant (ibid., p.46). Smith pinpoints the cause of these failures: zone briefings and zone circles imply either a degree of trust which does not exist in most British car factories (including Longbridge) or an etiquette for managing power relations which has little cultural support (ibid., p.49). Much of British industrial relations is based upon negotiations and bargaining between employers and unions of an adversarial nature. Unions resist control and there is no basis of trust upon which to develop more co-operative and consensual practices.

Overall, while it is clear that there have been moves towards flexibilisation, the process is by no means far-advanced. As Starkey and McKinlay argue:

However ill-defined the notions of 'flexibility' and 'Japanisation' now emerging as dominant themes of the management may be they are having a considerable impact on managerial marketing and work organisation strategies.

(Starkey and McKinlay, 1988, p.99)

Nevertheless, these moves have been limited and relatively unsuccessful.

What has been the effect of such increased flexibilisation as has occurred on the labour force and the unions? Marsden and Thompson make clear that unions don't always oppose flexibility and there has been a growth in the number of flexibility agreements (Marsden and Thompson, 1990). Clearly, flexibilisation is likely to have a negative effect on employment (Sayer, 1986, p.66). In most cases it also leads to an intensification of the work process and stress (Turnball, 1988, p.18). Certainly Marsden and Thompson suggest that most flexibility agreements have been directed at changes in work practices, in particular involving more flexible deployment of labour, but that most changes have been by agreement and have been rewarded by higher wages (Marsden and Thompson, 1990).

As far as unions are concerned, flexibilisation is sometimes associated with a move towards the negotiation of a single union agreement and, more often, by a management attempt to undermine collective bargaining involving a move towards decentralised, if not individual, bargaining. In some cases, unions are involved in 'beauty contests' competing with one another to offer a more flexible workforce. Such contests usually occur when a company, Japanese or otherwise, is opening up as a greenfield site – that is, opening a new factory in an area with little previous industrial development and no tradition of unionism. I shall deal at more length with such developments in the section in the next chapter on single union agreements.

Changes in economic and labour market policy

While changes in the economic structure and the organisation of labour process affect unions, so do changes in economic policy. Certainly, there have been major changes in economic and labour market policy since 1979. Here, I shall identify major changes in: general economic policy; wages policy; labour market policy; and privatisation. In the next chapter, I will deal in more detail with the affect of these changes on union organisation, collective bargaining and wage settlements.

General economic policy

I have dealt with the implications of the broad changes in economic policy after 1979 earlier, so it requires limited attention here. The Conservatives came to power committed to the rejection of corporatism, the pursuit of monetarism and the control of public expenditure. They appeared determined to break with the post-war consensus and, in particular, were much more concerned about the evils of inflation than those of unemployment. As we saw in Chapter 2, the move away from corporatism and towards monetarism began in 1975 when Labour were in power, although after 1979 monetarism was embraced with almost a religious fervour. Similarly, as we saw earlier, unemployment grew rapidly in the early years of the Thatcher government, although the commitment to full employment ended earlier.

We have already seen that both the increase in unemployment and the end of corporatism weakened the union movement. The increase in unemployment was associated with a decline in union membership and, potentially at least, a weakening of the bargaining position of unions. The rejection of corporatism brought to an end the era of beer and sandwiches at Downing Street and severely constrained the political involvement and influence of the TUC.

Wages policy

The Conservatives have rejected incomes policy although it is fair to say they have pursued a broad wages policy. Between 1964 and 1979 incomes policy was the norm. Sometimes the policy was statutory, but more usually it was voluntary although tight. As we saw in Chapter 3, the credibility of the Labour Party collapsed when the Callaghan government's incomes policy disintegrated in the 'Winter of Discontent'. When the Conservatives were elected, they were committed to free collective bargaining. However, there are two major qualifications to that bald statement. The government has attempted to control public sector pay by establishing and enforcing 'cash limits'. In effect, a pay guideline was set in relation to the public sector; if the public sector employer wished to offer a larger wage increase, this involved either a cut in services or the negotiation of improved productivity. In the private sector the government played an even more indirect role; essentially the government pursued a labour market policy designed, among other things, to cut wages. The abandonment of a formal incomes policy meant that industrial relations was depoliticised. If there is an incomes policy any dispute between employer and union inevitably involves the union. Without an incomes policy, the unions can be removed from politics in a way which is impossible if an incomes policy exists. Certainly, if the Conservative Government had pursued one, then more frequent, 'corporate' contracts between the government and the TUC would have been inevitable and its pursuit of industrial relations reform would have been much more difficult.

The government's pursuit of a cash-limits policy in the public sector has been much more problematic. During the 1979 Election campaign the Conservatives promised to honour the awards to public sector workers made by the Standing Commission on Pay Comparability, chaired by Professor Hugh Clegg, which had been set up by the Labour Government. The Clegg Commission awarded significant increases to restore comparability. However, subsequently the policy became much tougher. In August 1980 the government abolished the Commission, having rejected the whole notion of comparability between the private and the public sector. Even then, however, although the guideline figure in 1981–2 was 4 per cent, the most powerful public sector groups got larger settlements; the miners and waterworkers 9 per cent, firemen 10 per cent and local authority manual workers 7.5 per cent. The government successfully resisted a waterworkers' strike and two railway strikes in 1982–3, and although it was less successful in its conflict with the teachers, it abolished their collective bargaining machinery (the Burnham Committee) in 1987, when it introduced the Teachers' Pay and Conditions Act, which left central government totally in control of this field.

Certainly the government have reduced the extent of collective bargaining in the public sector. Over 5 million people work in the public sector, but now only one million have their pay settled by traditional collective bargaining. As David Metcalf puts it:

In the public sector, unlike private firms, there is a ghost at the bargaining table. Even if a direct employer like a Health Authority wants to pay more, the sponsoring Ministry lurks in the background with its cash limits. And the Health Ministry looks to the Treasury.

(*Guardian*, 23 February, 1990)

However, the government's attempt to move away from comparability was in most senses a failure. Strikes in the Civil Service led to negotiations with the Civil Service unions and to the creation of a mechanism for comparability for scientific and technical civil servants. Indeed, Brown argues:

For all their carefully chosen phrases, the current review bodies for nurses, civil servants, solicitors, judges and the like ... argue for the use of effective comparability and they warn of the danger of disrupting the loyalty and commitments of employees.

(Brown, 1986, p.167)

In addition, as we shall see in the next chapter, the cash-limits policy has had little success in controlling public sector manual workers' pay.

Labour Market Policy

In the private sector the government's wages policy has been less direct. However, there is no doubt that elements of its labour market policy have been designed to constrain, and even reduce, wages. Indeed, a number of separate developments point in that direction.

In particular, the government was anxious to eliminate laws which kept a floor under wages. In the 1980 Employment Act, the government set aside Section II of the 1975 Employment Act which permitted low-paid workers the right to government arbitration of their wage claims. In 1983 the government abolished the Fair Wage Resolution, a resolution of the House of Commons rather than a statute, which required employers with government contracts to pay wages and establish conditions in line with local industry. The apparent aim was to improve the potential profitability of contracted-out public services. The government was also keen to abolish the 27

Wages Councils, which in 1983 established legal minimum rates of pay for some 2.7 million low-paid workers, and which it regarded as a hindrance to the operation of a free labour market. Initially, the government could do little as it was bound by an International Labour Organisation contract to retain them. However, it did exercise more control over the membership of the Councils and reduced the number of inspectors who enforced their decisions by a third. Subsequently, after a White Paper issued in 1985, the Councils were retained but not permitted to set wage rates for 18 to 21-year-olds. Finally, in 1989, the government brought forward proposals to abolish the Councils.

More generally, another purpose of the government's policies on training was to reduce wage rates for young workers. As we saw in Chapter 5, allowances first replaced wages in the Work Experience Scheme of 1976 and the Youth Opportunity Programme of 1978. However, Youth Training Scheme (YTS) introduced in 1983 was a much larger programme, involving over 300,000 people per year, which again pays an allowance rather than the rate for the job. The existence of such a large number of lowly-paid trainees is clearly likely to have an effect on wage rates for younger workers.

In a similar vein, Deaton suggests that the reduction of benefits resulting from both the abolition of earnings-related supplement to unemployment benefit in 1982, and the adjustment downwards of benefits for those on strike in the 1980 Social Security Act, were designed by the government to make claimants more willing to work at lower wages (Deaton, 1985, pp.91–2).

Privatisation

Privatisation hardly featured in the 1979 Manifesto. By 1983, however, it was a major, perhaps even **the** major plank of the government's economic policy. One aim of privatisation, although it was by no means the main aim, was the reduction of public sector unions (see Marsh, 1991).

Obviously, privatisation has taken a number of forms; indeed, Young (1986) has identified seven. However, in this context two are particularly important: special asset sales, which involve either denationalisation, as was the case with British Gas (BG), British Airways and British Telecom, or the sale of public sector companies previously bought by the government – companies such as Jaguar and Rolls Royce; and 'contracting out' work previously done by direct labour in local government, the National Health Service (NHS) and the Civil Service.

The scale of privatisation is immense. In fact, Fraser calculates by early 1988 40 per cent of the public sector was transferred to the private sector; 650,000 workers had transferred sectors, of whom 90 per cent had become shareholders; 9 million people were shareholders, which represented 20 per cent of the population as compared with 7 per cent in 1979; and contracting out was well established in the NHS and the local authority sector (see Fraser, 1988, pp.14, 86–91). Similarly, Veljanovsky points out that in 1988 the nationalised sector accounted for 5.5 per cent of the UK output compared with 9 per cent in 1979. (Veljanovsky, 1987, p.xvii). Certainly, privatisation represents *the* major change in the economy brought about by this government. At the same time, it is a change which potentially had major consequences for trade unions, some of which we shall examine in the next chapter.

Conclusion

This chapter has identified major changes in the economy which have affected trade unions. Three major points emerge from this analysis:

1. The changes in the economic structure and, in particular, the process of restructuring and deindustrialisation have played a crucial role in weakening the unions' position. These changes have been associated with a major fall in union membership and have weakened the unions' bargaining position.
2. The introduction of new technology and the increased flexibilisation of production has also weakened the unions, but not as much as a cursory analysis might suggest. In particular, the extent of flexibilisation has often been exaggerated by observers.
3. Many of these changes have origins before 1979 but they have been accentuated since. The Thatcher government's changes in economic policy have clearly built upon and accentuated these developments.

The future

As far as the future is concerned, it is unlikely that any of the structural changes in the economy will be reversed. The decline of the manufacturing sector may slow down or even halt but it will not be reversed. The private service sector is likely to grow and the public sector will probably continue to contract slowly. The number of women in the work-force will increase and the South-East in general, and East Anglia in particular, are likely to be the major growth areas (see Income Data Services, 1990, pp.29–31). None of these changes will help unions, which will clearly need to adjust more quickly and effectively to them than they have to date.

Trying to predict macroeconomic trends is difficult. However, it is now generally agreed that the Thatcherite economic revolution has been less than a total success. In the late 1980s inflation began to rise again and unemployment is still high. None of this bodes well for union membership.

In contrast, government policy may change. In particular, as we saw earlier, both the European Social Charter and current Labour Party policy, advocates a right to union recognition which would be enforced where substantial support for it exists in the workplace. As Metcalf argues:

Statutory support for recognition is probably the single most helpful thing that the Labour Party could do for the unions. It could transform their dealings with employers and herald a new era of co-operation between the firm and trade unions at work-place level.

(Metcalf, 1990b, p.33)

Certainly, any move to make union recognition easier will have a major affect on union membership as it did in the 1970s when the Labour Government actively encouraged public sector unions. Willman argues it is too expensive for unions to recruit workers without employer co-operation (Willman, 1989). As such, it appears that union density will only increase if a future Labour Government introduces plans to require employers to recognise unions in certain circumstances. Otherwise most unions, at best, are involved in a damage limitation strategy as far as membership is concerned.

Of course, unions worried about membership and the future can merge; this has been a popular strategy in the 1980s and is likely to remain so. In 1979 there were 112 unions affiliated to the TUC, by 1989 that number had shrunk to 77. There have been some very large amalgamations, with more planned. In 1988 the Techcical Administrative and Supervisors Section of the AUEW (TASS) and the Association of Scientific, Technical and Managerial Staff, (ASTMS) amalgamated to form the Manufacturing, Science and Finance Union (MSF), while in 1989 the general union, the General, Muncipal, Boilermakers and Allied Trades Union (GMBATU), and the clerical union, the Association of Professional, Executive, Clerical and Computer Staff (APEX), were merged. Some of the planned mergers are even larger, notably the proposal which would amalgamate the National Association of Local Government Officers (NALGO), the National Union of Public Employees (NUPE) and the Confederation of Health Service Employees (COHSE), into a giant public sector union. The outline proposal was approved by the three unions' Conferences in 1990 and would result in a union with over 1.5 million members. It would replace the TGWU as the largest union. The general aim of mergers is to increase both the bargaining position of the unions and their services to members. However, some unions have more specific motives for amalgamating. In particular, the Civil Service unions would like to eliminate the problem of agreeing a common negotiating position with which to approach management. Overall, the merger wave is likely to continue with as many as 4 million union members involved in the period between 1990 and 1993 (see *Labour Research*, June 1990, pp.9–10). It is quite possible that by the turn of the century there will be five or six super unions who will dominate the General Council.

Economic trends are thus moving against the unions but the political trend may reverse. As such, any assessment of the future of British unions depends in part upon whether macroeconomic performance and changes in the composition of the work-force or government policy has more influence on the unions' strength and position. This question will be a key one addressed in the next two chapters which examine the extent to which shop-floor industrial relations have changed in the public and the private sector and assesses competing explanations of these changes.

8

Shop-floor Industrial Relations: The Private Sector

Given our political system, which is characterised by executive dominance and party discipline, governments have little problem passing legislation. However, legislation is not an end in itself, rather it is a means to an end. Thus, the Thatcher Government's aim in the field of industrial relations was not merely to enact legislation. Their main intention was to alter the balance between unions and management; more specifically, in their rhetoric, to reassert management's 'right to manage'. As such they hoped to encourage employers to reorganise relations with their unions and employees: to transform shop-floor industrial relations. This chapter examines the degree to which that aim and hope has been achieved. It is divided into two sections. The first section establishes the degree to which there has been a transformation in the private sector since 1979. The second section then addresses the most crucial question: To what extent have the changes which have occurred in shop-floor industrial relations resulted from the Conservative legislation rather than the processes of deindustrialisation and restructuring dealt with in the previous chapter?

Changes in shop-floor industrial relations in the private sector

Fortunately, there are a number of good studies of the changes in workplace industrial relations since 1979. Unfortunately, none of them deals with the period since 1985. In 1983 Eric Batstone undertook a small survey of large manufacturing plants: the survey was designed so as to be compared with a Warwick Industrial Relations Research Unit Study done in 1978. In 1984 the Warwick unit conducted a study of a representative sample of manufacturing

191

companies with more than 250 employees; such companies employ 60 per cent of the total manufacturing work-force. The Warwick unit also completed, in 1985, a questionnaire survey of managers at various levels in 175 establishments with more than 1000 employees in six key industrial sectors: food, drink and tobacco; mechanical engineering and vehicles; electrical engineering; textiles, clothing and footwear; retail and wholesale distribution; and banking, finance and insurance. Nevertheless, despite the useful material in these studies, the most comprehensive data are provided by the two Workplace Industrial Relations Surveys (WIRS) conducted in 1980 and 1984. They provide data on a sample of these establishments with 25 or more employees in both the private and public sector. In addition, the 1984 survey collected data upon about 200 workplaces which had been surveyed in 1980; so it is possible to identify the extent of change in those companies between 1980 and 1984.

What has changed since 1979? The picture is not simple although McInnes is in no doubt of his answer: 'there has been much less change than might have been expected' (McInnes, 1987, p. 129). This is a very bold assertion which, in part, reflects McInnes's own theoretical position. However, a disaggregated analysis suggests a conclusion rather less favourable to the unions. For this reason, the following section examines changes in: the extent of macho-management; derecognition; union density; the closed shop; collective bargaining; single unionism; the role of shop stewards; the use of ballots; strikes and picketing; and wages.

Macho-management

There are clearly a number of examples of managers attempting to change workfloor industrial relations with minimal consultation and setting out deliberately to confront the unions. However, many of these cases, for example, British Steel, British Rail and British Coal, were in the public sector where management was under direct pressure from the government to be confrontational, as we shall see in the next chapter. In the private sector, such management was generally concentrated either in industries with a poor history of industrial relations, notably printing, or those in financial trouble. This macho-management was reflected in both a willingness to use the government's industrial relations law (see Table 4.1) and a move toward derecognition of unions; the printing industry led the way in both these developments.

Batstone found that managements had made an attempt to reduce the role of the unions in only about 20 per cent of the plants surveyed (Batstone, 1984, pp. 258–260). Edwards and Marginson's (1988) analysis confirms this picture:

> The overwhelming impression was one of no change; and where there was change it was more likely to involve an increase than a decrease in the role granted to unions. Of the 103 corporate managers who could state whether or not any change had been made in ways of dealing with manual unions, 14 said that there had been some change; the figure for non-manual unions was six. A total of 20 types of change in respect of manual unions was indicated, and of these 15 involved the introduction or extension of union activities, and only five represented an elimination or reduction.
>
> (ibid p. 138; see also Edwards, 1987, pp. 146–52)

Of course, this data may give a misleading picture and merely represent a diplomatic response by directors or managers. Indeed, McKay's study of personnel managers found that they believed management was becoming tougher, stressing the increased use of the threat of unemployment (McKay,1986). Certainly, Batstone and Gourlay's (1986) analysis of shop stewards' views of changing management style presents a more complex picture. In British Telecom, 83 per cent of Post Office Engineering Union (POEU) stewards felt management was becoming tougher, compared with 38 per cent in electrical engineering, 44 per cent in printing, 50 per cent in chemicals and 60 per cent in the civil service (Batstone and Gourlay, 1986). This suggests management has become tougher, although perhaps more so in the public sector, but stewards, in contrast to managers, are likely to overestimate this change.

Marchington and Parker's conclusion seems balanced:

> despite the well-publicised examples of macho-management, employers still appear to proceed with extreme caution when seeking to make changes in their employee relations practices. Some of this has to do with a lack of desire to achieve change, considering that current relationships can provide employers with a degree of order and stability which they see little point in

jeopardising. A related issue is that employers may be rather more concerned with building employee commitment to corporate or, at least, establishment goals to be bothered with a fight with the unions, especially at a time when the latter appear more willing to co-operate with the process of change.

(Marchington and Parker, 1990, p. 257)

Overall, this development is most discernible in the public sector and in a limited number of industries with a poor history of industrial relations.

Derecognition

Millward and Stevens emphasise how rare derecognition of unions has been. Of the 181 companies the WIRS studied in both 1980 and 1984, only three withdrew union recognition, while nine granted it for the first time. Overall, they found that in their sample 68 per cent of the companies recognised unions in 1984 as compared with 66 per cent in 1980. However, there is some evidence that derecognition may have increased since 1984. Claydon identified 49 cases of derecognition in 1987–8 (Claydon, 1989). This figure is much larger than that reported by *Labour Research*, although they also found that derecognition grew from nine cases in 1986 to 15 cases in 1987. They concluded, 'the tendency towards derecognition seems to have been increasing since the GCHQ episode' (*Labour Research*, April 1988, p. 13).

Both Claydon and *Labour Research* identify the type of firms in which derecognition is more likely. The *Labour Research* study suggests that derecognition attempts have largely been restricted to companies undergoing one of the following changes: privatisation; takeover; relocation; or reorganisation. Derecognition is also most likely in firms with lower levels of union membership or in which the employer wishes to move towards a single union deal. (*Labour Research*, April 1988, p. 13).

Claydon's analysis is more interesting:

Within the private sector, two industrial groups stand out; newspaper and book publishing, where 15 or 16 cases have occurred, all but one during 1987–88, and coastal shipping, where seven companies derecognised the NUS in the wake of the P & O dispute.

(Claydon, 1989, p. 215)

This confirms a pattern we have seen before; in these two industries macho-management has been evident as has the propensity to use the Conservatives' industrial relations legislation. Claydon makes the key point:

The extent to which employers feel that it is desirable and possible to terminate collective bargaining will depend partly on their experience of trade union activity and their relations with the workforce shop stewards and full-time officials.

(Claydon, 1989, p. 219)

Overall, the conclusion of the *Labour Research* study, which confirms Millward and Stevens's findings, is probably accurate: In general, however, outside specific sectors like publishing, the unions report that de-recognition is not yet a major threat although a new and growing phenomenon' (Labour Research, April 1988, p. 13).

As always though, it is the history and current status of industrial relations in a given company which has most effect on a firm's decision to derecognise.

Union density

We have already seen that total union density dropped from 58.9 per cent in 1978 to 46.5 per cent in 1987, while the density of unions affiliated to the Trades Union Congress fell from 54.5 per cent to 38.7 per cent in the same period (see Table 2.1 and 2.2). In this way, TUC-affiliated unions suffered more than other unions and it was only in the public sector that membership density held up. However, Millward and Stevens found that union density in the companies they studied remained fairly stable. Density varied markedly from sector to sector: in 1984 union density was 21 per cent in the Hotel and Catering Sector and 95 per cent in the Post and Telecommunications Sector (Millward and Stevens, 1986, p. 54). It was also much higher in larger establishments; in establishments with 25–49 employees the average density was 26 per cent, in those with 1,000+ it was 72 per cent. Perhaps most significantly, Millward and Stevens found that union densities were highest in contracting industries and lowest in certain expanding sectors, notably the private services. (Millward and Stevens, 1986, p. 60; see also McInnes, 1987, p. 101; and Edwards and Marginson, 1988, p. 127). Bassett claims that non-unionism is now dominant in Britain. (Bassett, 1988, p. 45). This is clearly an exaggerated claim, but there is considerable evidence that the overall decline in union density reflects the restructuring of the British economy and, in particular, the decline in unionised sectors and large plants. What is more, as Kelly has argued, trade unions have tended to be poorly organised, and to make little effort, in the expanding areas (Kelly, 1987, p. 276). Of course, the level of union effort can change, and of necessity is changing, but the decline in the manufacturing sector is unlikely to be reversed, which means that union density overall is unlikely to increase.

The closed shop

The scope of the closed shop was significantly reduced between 1980 and 1984 as Millward and Stevens's evidence indicates. Since this time the closed shop has been made illegal by provisions in the 1988 and 1990 Employment Act. However, two additional points need to be made. As Dunn and Gennard show, the closed shop was in jeopardy well before the Conservative legislation came into operation (Dunn and Gennard, 1984). The growth of the pre-entry closed shop occurred almost entirely in a past era. They were not widespread and by 1979 they covered some 800 000 people, about 4 per cent of the total work-force. The two main industries in which such shops existed were printing and shipping.

In contrast, by the early 1960s, 12 per cent of the British work-force, some 3 million people, were covered by post entry closed shops, the major concentration being in the engineering and coal-mining industries. However, there was a major growth in these agreements in the late 1960s and 1970s; so that by 1979 4.5 million people were covered in a wide variety of different industries in both the private and the public sector. This growth was, to a large extent, encouraged by employers who saw the closed shop as a means by which to secure greater order on the shop floor.

As Dunn and Gennard indicate:

the growth of the closed shop had slowed and almost stopped by 1980. Without new practices to compensate for the reduction in the numbers covered in the shrinking industries like coal mining, steel, shipbuilding, clothing and footwear, vehicles and railways, where compulsory unionism was widespread, and with the rise in unemployment generally, the closed shop population began to decline fairly rapidly. By mid-1982 it had fallen by 13 per cent to approximately 4.5 million.

Despite the slowing down of the increase in unemployment, it can be safely said that this process has continued to the present because structural changes in the economy have meant continued workforce attrition in many traditional industries. These estimates assume that no substantial existing closed shops have lapsed since the late 1970s. They were made before the 1980 and 1982 Acts had any impact on established arrangements. Yet they suggest that economic trends were suitable for legal intervention that would steepen the closed shop's decline.

(Dunn and Gennard, 1984, p. 97).

In essence, this was the role legislative change played in this field between 1982 and 1988. It accelerated the closed-shop decline; a decline which was already under way, largely because of changes in the economic structure associated with technological changes and managerial opportunism.

Collective bargaining

Millward and Stevens emphasise that there has been little change in collective bargaining arrangements in either the private or the public sector (Millward and Stevens, 1986, Chapter 8; see also Ingram and Cahill, 1989, p. 281); this is hardly surprising given that there has been little attempt at derecognition. In fact, only for manual workers in private manufacturing did Millward and Stevens find that collective bargaining coverage had decreased between 1980 and 1984; it had increased for white-collar workers in private manufacturing and for all workers in private services. It is significant that while Edwards and Marginson found that there had been an increase in such coverage in the large companies they studied (Edwards and Marginson, 1988, p. 138), Ingram and Cahill report that it had fallen in establishments with less than 100 employees (Ingram and Cahill, 1989, p. 282).

This does not mean that there have been no attempts by employers to change bargaining structures, for example, *Labour Research* has charted a number of cases in the newspaper publishing industry in which employers attempted to weaken the National Union of Journalists (NUJ)'s bargaining position. It is perhaps not surprising that such a strategy had also been extensively used by management in the newly-privatised companies. So in July 1989 British Telecom moved from a negotiated pay structure to one based upon personal contracts for their 3000 most senior staff from a work-force of 40 000 (*Labour Research*, December 1989). Such developments are also occurring in the public sector as we shall see in the next chapter. Nevertheless, the coverage of collective bargaining is still extensive and not reducing significantly.

Millward and Stevens emphasise that, while collective bargaining is still the norm, fewer issues are covered by such bargaining. They suggest that collective bargaining is becoming more exclusively focused on pay. As an example, while in 1980 54 per cent of the managers interviewed reported that they negotiated with their unions over the redeployment of labour, by 1984 this figure had fallen to 29 per cent. (Millward and Stevens, 1986, p. 248). However, the pattern in this area is not totally clear. Edwards and Marginson's (1988) study of larger companies suggests that the scope of matters covered in collective bargaining has not been narrowed. Of course, the difference in these results may stem from the fact that Edwards and Marginson are only concerned with the large companies in which union representation has been historically stronger and union-management relations might, thus, be less likely to change.

As far as bargaining over pay is concerned, two developments are evident. First, management has increasingly demanded productivity or flexibility deals in return for increased wages. A 1987 Confederation of British Industry (CBI) survey, which analysed 9,000 pay settlements dating back to 1980, found that about a third involved the unions accepting changes in working practice, while 60 per cent of the employers surveyed had negotiated at least one flexibility deal between 1980 and 1987 (McIlroy, 1988, p. 206). Similarly, Millward and Stevens argue that employers have increasingly required productivity deals in negotiations on wages. Second, there has been some shift in the level at which bargaining has been carried out. Essentially, there have been two related trends: a move away from national, usually multi-employer, bargaining, and a decrease in the extent of multi-level bargaining (in which bargaining takes place first at the national level and subsequently at the local level). However, neither development should be overemphasised.

A survey of CBI members found that in the 1979–86 period there was a marked diminution in the influence of multi-employer agreements and a growth in single employer bargaining at the company level. So, by 1986, 87 per cent of the employees in these plants with collective bargaining had their basic rates negotiated at company or plant level. Multi-employer bargaining remained dominant only in certain sectors: textiles, engineering, building materials, printing and transport (Ingram and Cahill, 1989). Overall, it is evident that the UK is still neither a decentralised nor a centralised wage-bargaining economy. However, there is a move towards decentralisation.

Single unionism

There has been a considerable amount of interest in the growth of single unionism and in the negotiation of single union agreements (SUAs) by certain unions, notably, but not exclusively, the Electrical, Electronic, Telecommunication and Plumbing Union (EETPU). The archetypal SUAs negotiated by the EETPU in fact involve six elements: single unionism; no strike agreements; union acceptance of increased functional flexibility among employees; management acceptance of single status with all employees using the same facilities, car-park, dining room, toilets, etc; increased participation by the work-force in company decision-making; and binding pendulum arbitration in which the arbitrator must accept either the management offer or the union's claim and cannot compromise between them. If such single union agreements become common, they would clearly change the nature of British workplace industrial relations. In addition, of course, in the eyes of many observers single unionism is associated with the growth of New Realism in the union movement.

Single union agreements sometimes involve the derecognition of recognised unions in a multi-union plant, but this is rare. Much more frequently, when a new plant is established on a greenfield site a company will attempt to reach an agreement to recognise a single union. Most, if by no means all, of these companies are foreign-owned and often a number of unions are involved in a beauty contest; they compete with one another to obtain recognition usually by offering more co-operation with management. Such SUAs often involve a no-strike agreement, although such agreements are not legally binding. However, SUAs are not common. Bassett, who is sympathetic to the development, emphasises that there has been little move towards single status (Bassett, 1987, pp. 99–101), little interest in participation (ibid., pp. 101–9) and little increase in the use of pendulum arbitration (ibid., pp. 109–6). Similarly, in 1986 the EETPU itself only reported 30 SUA and estimated that only 20,000 employees were covered by no-strike provisions.

In the most recent and most thorough analysis, Labour Research identified only 76 SUAs in 1989. They were largely limited to four unions – Transport and General Workers' Union (TGWU) (which generally doesn't include no-strike clauses in SUAs), EETPU, Amalgmated Engineering Union (AEU) and General, Municipal, Boilermakers and Allied Trades Union (GMBATU). There were as many UK firms as Japanese or US involved but the unions generally saw the issue of SUAs as of diminishing significance as far as domestic firms were concerned. However, while the number of deals signed is small they are almost all concentrated on greenfield sites. As far as such sites are concerned, as a TGWU official emphasised:

> I can't see any greenfield site ever agreeing again to sign agreements that are not single-union deals. It's not going away and if anything its going to grow.
>
> (*Labour Research*, November 1989, p. 10).

Shop stewards

Millward and Stevens's results suggest that the shop-steward system remained largely intact; a finding which is hardly surprising given the continued coverage of union recognition and collective bargaining. In fact the WIRS survey found that the number of shop stewards increased from 317,000 in 1980 to 335,000 in 1984 (Millward and Stevens, 1986, p. 84). However, the number fell significantly in the manufacturing sector, while it rose in the private service and the public sectors. They also found that there were few changes in the way stewards organised; they were as likely in 1984 as in 1980 to be involved in multi-plant stewards' combines, but slightly less likely by 1984 to meet in joint committees in multi-union plants.

A similar pattern is reported by Edwards and Marginson who found that 60 per cent of the large manufacturing companies they analysed which recognised a manual union for bargaining purposes reported that there were meetings between shop stewards from different establishments; non-manual shop-steward committees were only slightly less common (Edwards and Marginson, 1988, p. 132). In most cases (65 per cent) these committees were recognised by management (ibid., p. 134). Obviously, such committees were most common where the most important level of bargaining was the national level (ibid., p. 135).

Overall, as Edwards argues, there have been 'few direct institutional attacks on shop stewards' (Edwards, 1987, p. 146). However, their role has changed. Managements in private sector companies have been asserting their right to manage and so there have been significant changes in working arrangements which aim to increase the efficiency of labour utilisation (see Edwards, 1987, pp. 122–7). Even so, these changes have most often been negotiated with shop stewards, not imposed upon them. As Edwards puts it:

> [Managements have asserted the right to manage] not by attacking negotiatory or consultative arrangements but by changing the way in which they are used. They have not ridden roughshod over workers interests but have tried to persuade workers of the benefits of accepting and co-operating with the logic of the market as it is interpreted by management. This inevitably means that shop stewards have a more defensive role than in the past.
>
> (Edwards, 1987, p. 147)

The use of ballots

The 1984 Act has required unions to change their rules to establish ballots before strike action. Previously, union practices on strikes varied widely. Indeed, Undy and Martin found that 78 of the 103 unions they surveyed had no specific rules for calling national industrial action. Now, union rules have to specify ballots (Undy and Martin, 1984, p. 121). However, most strike ballots are successful – more than 90 per cent since 1987. It is also interesting that, for those years where we have figures, a large number of successful ballots are not followed by strike action. As the Advisory, Conciliation and Arbitration Service (ACAS) Annual Report puts it:

it seems clear that on a number of occasions ballots have been used by trade unions to demonstrate the strength of feeling among their members in ways which some managements have found difficult to counter. At the same time, there is little doubt that there have been other occasions where members' support for officials' position has proved less forthright than had been claimed. (ACAS, 1986, p. 14)

As in other areas, the pattern then is mixed: ballots occur, they are usually won, but for unions they serve different purposes in different circumstances.

The 1984 Trade Union Act also allowed individual union members to take their case to the certification officer if they thought that the requirement that their unions hold a proper ballot for the election of its executive had not been met. Few such cases have been brought and the majority were in the first year when, presumably, the unions were less adept at operating the procedures. Once again, the legislation has led to major changes in union rules. As Undy and Martin emphasise, 44 of the 103 TUC unions they surveyed in 1981–2 (43 per cent) needed to amend their rules to comply with the requirements of the new legislation (Undy and Martin, 1984, pp. 58–60).

Of course, the government's intention by this reform was to remove unrepresentative leaderships, to give the unions back to their members. However, there is little evidence that union executives have been rejected by their members in these ballots. Indeed, a *Labour Research* study of the 32 TUC-affiliated unions with over 10 000 members who conducted a ballot for general secretary between 1988 and mid-1990 is very revealing. They found that in 18 of these unions (56 per cent) the existing general secretary was a candidate and in only one of these unions was he/she defeated. In the majority of the cases where the general secretary didn't stand, the individual concerned was usually retiring. It is also interesting that in many cases the turn out in the elections was lower than it had been when a previous, 'less-democratic', electoral system had been used (*Labour Research*, May 1990, pp. 11–12).

Strikes and picketing

There has been a significant decrease in the number of strikes since 1979, with the exception of 1984 when the figures were dominated by the miners' strike, no matter what measure is used: number of strikes; number of workers involved; number of days lost (see Table 7.1). However, the WIRS survey, which excluded the coal industry, throws doubt on the utility of the Department of Employment (DEmp) figures. Between 1980 and 1984, Millward and Stevens reported an increase in the number of strikes; strikes involved 13 per cent of the workplaces analysed in 1980 and 19 per cent in 1984. In general terms, in 1984 strikes were shorter but effected a larger proportion of workplaces than in 1980. There were also major differences between sectors; strikes in manufacturing fell by about half but rose in the public services sector. At the same time, while strikes declined among manual workers they increased among non-manual workers. The differences between the results of the DEmp and those of Millward and Stevens's results is explained by the fact that much of the action reported in the WIRS study was short, a day or less, and, as such, wouldn't be included in the DEmp. The WIRS also indicates that there has been an increased use of industrial action other than the strike: overtime bans, working-to-rule, and so on. Millward and Stevens also emphasise that in 1984, as in 1980, most industrial action was over pay, although strikes involving redundancies, and in the public sector privatisation, became more important by 1984.

Given that strikes declined in the private sector and in manufacturing, it is not surprising that picketing also fell in these sectors. However, picketing didn't increase in those sectors where strikes increased so that, overall, picketing declined by almost a half between 1980 to 1984 (Millward and Stevens, 1986, pp. 283–4). The incidence of secondary picketing was particularly affected by the legislation. The number of workplaces reporting secondary picketing halved and effective secondary picketing fell by two thirds (Millward and Stevens, 1986, pp. 290–94, Table 10.17). However, while the incidence of picketing declined, its organisation didn't change (ibid., pp. 287–8).

There is little doubt then, that the incidence of industrial action has fallen significantly. It is difficult to accept McInnes's view that, 'Thatcherism has not ushered in an era of industrial peace where there was previously strife. As with so much else, little has changed' (McInnes, 1987, p. 108). Unions still strike and they increasingly use 'cut-price' industrial action short of striking. However, they strike less, they picket more circumspectly and both these trends are most evident among manual workers in the manufacturing sector.

All is not the same, but neither is the situation transformed.

As far as the private sector is concerned, Marchington and Parker's conclusion appears most appropriate:

> The evidence from our study does not support the contention that private sector employers automatically seek to take advantage of favourable labour market conditions in order to increase direct control over employees. On the contrary, all the organisations were moving towards an investment-oriented approach, albeit at different speeds and with differing rates of success. Nor does it suggest that employers are actively pursuing strategies designed to undermine the position of the trade unions in their companies, whether by the dismissal of senior shop stewards or general restrictions on union activity; indeed, in one case, management was even attempting to bolster the position of the union. At the same time, however, it was also apparent that unions were not on the whole central to workplace employee relations, and in some cases their role was becoming more marginal. This factor did not, however, arise from any concerted management strategy directed specifically at labour relations, but was more appropriately seen as a consequence of other actions taken in pursuit of wider corporate goals – in particular, to increase employee commitment to product quality and customer service.
>
> (Marchington and Parker, 1990, p. 257).

Wages

One of the intentions of the government was to inject a 'New Realism' into wage bargaining; to ensure that higher wages were earned through higher productivity rather than conceded by weak management to strong unions. As we have seen, the Conservatives rejected incomes policy as a means of achieving wage discipline. Instead they attempted to reduce unions' disruptive bargaining power by legislative change while also setting a good example to private sector management by establishing and encouraging tighter management control in the public sector. How successful has this policy been? Have wages been constrained since 1979? In so far as they have risen, have wage rises been simply a reward for higher productivity? These are obviously crucial questions because, in an important sense, the balance of power between employers and unions is reflected in the outcome of collective bargaining. Here, I shall look at private sector wages; in the next chapter I will examine wages in the public sector. It is well documented that real wages have risen fairly consistently since 1979. As Longstreth puts it:

> In particular, the growth of real earnings, especially in the private sector, suggests that a considerable degree of bargaining power has been retained by the unions, or at least that large sections of the workforce have been insulated to a considerable degree from the pressures of a rising tide of unemployment. While the growth rate of gross earnings declined in the years of severe economic contraction from their peak level of nearly 21 per cent in 1980.
>
> Since 1984 they have continued to increase at an annual rate of around 8 to 8.5 per cent, despite the fall in inflation. Average real earnings after tax declined only in 1981 and 1982. Even here the drop was due to the effects of rising taxation. Since then the level (as opposed to changes in the level) of unemployment has had little or no discernible impact on pay determination. Net real earnings growth has crept upwards to between four and five per cent per annum, possibly the highest sustained rate ever recorded in Britain.
>
> (Longstreth, 1988, pp. 421–2; see also McInnes, 1987, pp. 80–84; McIlroy, 1988, pp. 206–10; Nickell, 1987; Brown and Wadhwani, 1990, p. 65)

There is also little evidence that the legislation has reduced the union/non-union differential; that is the premium which unionised workers enjoy over non-unionised workers in a given industrial sector. Blanchflower used pay data from the British Social Attitudes survey between 1983–9. He found that the average mark-up was around 10 per cent in every year (Blanchflower, 1990). As Brown and Wadhwani conclude:

> Our contention is simply that if there had been any weakening in the effects of unions on wages during the early 1980's ... it would have been manifested in a change in the markup and the evidence suggests that this did not occur.
>
> (Brown and Wadhwani, 1990, p. 65)

However, these authors are reporting very aggregate patterns; wage changes in the whole economy or in the manufacturing, service and public sectors. Yet, Gregory *et al.* claims that between 1979 and 1984 there was much more dispersion in the distribution of wage increases than in the previous periods, when incomes policies often operated:

> The extreme concentration which characterised periods of incomes policies has been replaced by a much more dispersed distribution. With the return to free collective bargaining, the proportion of settlements at the mode (the most common settlement) fell dramatically to 1 in 5 in each year, and to as low as 13 per cent of settlements in 1981/82 (compared with 75 per cent in 1977/78). The unique 'going rate' as understood under incomes policies has been clearly superseded by a concentration of settlements within a central zone around a much less sharply defined modal increase.

> (Gregory *et al.*, 1985, p. 345)

At the same time there were consistent winners and consistent losers over the period:

> The most striking feature here is the evidence of consistent winners and consistent losers over the period. Over the five years, no industry recorded an increase significantly above the average in any one year and below it in any other. Among the eight industrial sectors' settlement levels are significantly higher in food, drink and tobacco in four and in the chemical and paper industries in three out of the five years; conversely, mechanical engineering, with by far the highest number of settlements recorded, has a significantly lower increase than the average in every year, and metals in three out of the five years. Although the differences between industries in any one year appear small, even trivial, when maintained over several years their cumulative effect becomes important (over the five year period). Three industries, food, chemicals and paper, emerge as high settlers, and three, metals, mechanical engineering and textiles, as relatively low settlers; mechanical engineering, is 11.1 percentage points in 1979/90 pay levels.

> (Gregory *et al.*, 1985, p. 347)

Of course, such differentials between industries are not new. Haskel and Martin found that inter-industry wage structures in the manufacturing sector were very consistent over the period between 1948 and 1970. They argue:

> The relatively high wage industries in 1948, such as chemicals, metal manufacturing and vehicles, remain relatively high-wage in 1970. Similarly, the low wage industries in 1948, such as textiles and clothing and footwear, are still low wage 22 years later.
>   (Haskel and Martin, 1990, p. 3, and see table 1)

Indeed, they found that when they added more industries and extended the analysis to 1979, their conclusion was still robust (ibid., p. 3).

Interestingly, if we compare Gregory *et al.*'s results with those of Haskel and Martin, it appears clear that workers in some industries have done relatively well since, while others have done relatively poorly when compared to their past position. In particular, workers employed in the food, drink and tobacco industry, and to a lesser extent in textiles, have significantly improved their wages in relation to other workers in manufacturing. In contrast, those employed in the metal manufacturing and mechanical engineering sectors have lost ground to other workers.

Explaining the changes

Despite McInnes's conclusion that little has changed on the shop floor, there have been significant changes in industrial relations in the private sector. It is also clear both that some of these changes pre-date 1979 and that they do not result in any simple or direct way from Thatcherite policies. It is less easy to unravel the relative influence of the legislative changes, the changing composition of the work-force and the macroeconomic changes (particularly rising unemployment and inflation) on shop-floor industrial relations. Here I shall attempt to assess the relative effect of these three factors on union density, productivity, strikes and wages.

Union density

There has been a heated controversy among industrial relations specialists as to the cause of the decline in union density. Freeman and Pelletier argue that the decrease in manufacturing employment, while it may have hurt unions, cannot have been a major cause of this decline because: density declined in most sectors of the economy, not just in heavy manufacturing; it didn't decline in Ireland where the changes in the industrial mix of employment were similar; and the decrease in manufacturing employment was almost as great in the 1970s when union density rose. Similarly, they suggest that the rise in female, part-time and white-collar employment has had a limited effect on density. Their calculations indicate that the increase in female employment may explain 0.6 per cent of the decline in density, while the increase in the non-manual work-force can explain at most 1.3 per cent of this fall. They conclude:

> Our calculations imply that 3.1% points of the 1980–86 drop in density are due to changes in (structural factors) – leaving 5.5% or nearly two-thirds of the observed change attributable to other factors.
>
> (Freeman and Pelletier, 1990, p. 145)

Freeman and Pelletier are equally convinced that changes in the level of British economic performance had little influence on union density. In particular, they emphasise that the upturn in economic performance in the second half of the 1980s was not matched by an increase in density (ibid., p. 145). In addition, they cite Booth, who argues that during the 1980s a business cycle model overpredicted the level of density, such that by 1986 actual density was 7 per cent lower than the model predicted (Booth, 1989).

Freeman and Pelletier are adamant: the vast bulk of the observed 1980s decline in union density in the UK is due to the changed legal environment for industrial relations (ibid., p. 156). This conclusion is based upon an econometric analysis of levels of union density from 1945 to 1986. This revealed that density is raised by: increases in the manufacturing sector's share of employment; inflation; and unemployment. However, an index which quantified the favourableness or unfavourableness of British industrial relations laws to unions had a greater affect on density. Indeed, Freeman and Pelletier suggest a 1 point increase in the legal index, which results from a legal change in the favour of unions, induces a 1.3 per cent increase in density (ibid., p. 153).

However, these results have not gone unquestioned. In particular, Disney points out that it is difficult to separate out cause and effect (Disney, 1990, pp. 170–71). It is plausible to suggest that the government legislation is a response to the weakening of union power and union density. Certainly, I argued earlier that the Thatcher legislation built upon, rather than transformed, public opinion on unions and that it proceeded using a step-by-step approach as a response to union reaction. This would suggest that as union density fell the government became more confident and introduced more radical legislation. In fact, although Disney concedes that changes in the composition of the work-force have had little effect on density, he argues that macroeconomic factors are most important. He suggests that most critiques of business-cycle models rest upon the fact that while unemployment has decreased in the recent period density has still fallen. However, he argues that unemployment has much less impact on density than does inflation and shows that, if a business cycle model is more accurately specified to take account of the greater importance of inflation, then it has great explanatory power (ibid., pp. 168–9). He asserts:

> the explanation of the decline in trade union membership in the 1980's in Britain is straightforward: a period of rising unemployment, high real-wage growth and a Conservative Government is sufficient to explain the decline in density.
>
> (ibid., p. 168)

This debate remains unresolved. Overall, Metcalf's position is the most sound. He argues that the decline in membership was the result of a complex interaction of five factors: the macroeconomic climate; the composition of jobs and the work-force; the policy of the state; the attitudes and conduct of employers and the stance taken by the unions themselves (Metcalf, 1990a, p. 32). Certainly, all factors have played some role and it would be wrong to rely on monocausal explanations which stress either the role of the legislation or the effect of macroeconomic factors.

Productivity

There is no doubt that productivity, measured in terms of output per operative hour in manufacturing, improved significantly in the 1980s. There are, however, competing explanations of this improvement. Metcalf (1990a & b) argues strongly that it results from increased labour productivity; more efficient use of labour by employers. In contrast, the work Bennett and Smith-Garvine (1990) suggests that it is increased technological productivity, involving the installation of and the more efficient use of technology, which is crucial.

There is also a considerable debate as to the extent to which the government's legislation has contributed to this improvement. As Brown and Wadhwani (1990) suggest, if the legislation had an effect we would expect productivity to improve more in unionised, workplaces where the legislation might have removed restrictive working practices. In fact, the evidence suggests that there have been larger improvements in the more highly unionised sectors (Brown and Wadhwani, 1990, p. 65; Metcalf, 1990a).

Overall, it appears best to conclude that to the extent that labour productivity, rather than technological productivity, had increased, this owes something to the effect of the legislation. However, only Smith-Garvine and Bennett's work controls for the influence of technological productivity, and this does appear to be an important, if not the key, determinant of overall productivity.

Strikes

The decrease in the extent of striking as reflected in the DEmp figures doesn't result in any simple way from the impact of Thatcherism. The number of days lost from strikes declined throughout the world during the period between 1983–7, as compared with the previous period, 1978–82 (*DEmp Gazette*, June 1989). Most significantly, the UK ranked seventh out of 20 industrial countries in the strike table in both periods.

However, McConnell and Takla (1990), using DEmp figures, do indicate that the Conservative legislation has had an important effect on the number of strikes and the days lost through strikes, after controlling for the effect of macroeconomic variables. In contrast, it had no effect on the number of workers involved in strikes. This analysis confirms the conclusion of the WIRS study; the length of strikes has significantly reduced. The legislation then appears to have played a role in reducing the length of strikes but has not necessarily reduced all forms of industrial conflict, given that, as we saw earlier, unions are increasingly resorting to 'cut-price' forms of industrial action.

Wages

We saw earlier that wages have significantly increased in the private sector since 1979. This conclusion is confirmed by Marsh *et al.* who reported a disaggregated time-series analysis of wage changes in 14 different industrial groupings, 12 of them covering the private sector, between 1963 and 1987 (Marsh *et al.*, 1991). Indeed, they found that in 11 of the 12 sectors (agriculture was the only exception), only two variables, inflation and a Thatcher dummy variable, had a significant effect on wage change. As expected, as inflation rises so do wages. At the same time, wages are higher during the period of Thatcher Government than they were previously, even when we control for the levels of unemployment, inflation and trade union membership and the number of strikes and days lost through strikes. What is more, the Thatcher dummy is the most powerful explanatory variable for 6 of the 12 groupings.

Of course, the 'Thatcher effect' may be a spurious one. Perhaps the relationship results from the rise of productivity in Britain since 1979 (see Maynard, 1989, p. 156), or from the increase in company profitability over the same period (see Daniel, 1984; Gregory *et al.*, 1985, especially pp. 350–51; Gregory *et al.*, 1987, p. 146). However, Marsh *et al.*'s data doesn't support such an interpretation. Marsh *et al.* found that sectoral profitability only has a significant, positive effect on wages in three sectors: paper, printing and publishing; construction; and engineering. Similarly, sectoral productivity has a significant, positive effect in two sectors: timber and furnishing; and construction. In no case did the addition of either variable add much to the explanatory power of the model.

However, Marsh *et al.* do conclude that the 'Thatcher effect' is spurious. When they included a dummy variable to reflect the presence or absence of incomes policy, the Thatcher dummy ceased to be significant variable in all but one sector: paper and printing. It seems that wages have gone up under Mrs Thatcher more than one would have expected given the rate of inflation and increased in profitability and productivity because of the removal of incomes policy.

Of course, Marsh *et al.*'s data are only disaggregated to the sectoral level. Yet it is clear that wages in companies are at best partially effected by the government macro- economic policy, or by sector-wide levels of business performance. Only data on individual firms can really come to grips with the question involved.

Marsh *et al.*'s results certainly suggest that there is a 'Thatcher effect' if we analyse sectoral-level data. However, we are no closer to explaining this relationship. In fact, we clearly need data on individual firms to come to grips with the relationship. A number of studies have used this approach to examine the relationship between wages and various 'insider' and 'outsider' factors; 'insider' factors refer to characteristics (profitability, productivity and so on) of a specific firm, 'outsider' factors are the characteristics of the broader economic environment (level of employment, level of inflation).

Gregory *et al.* uses the CBI Databank which has questionnaire material on 1,200 manufacturing establishments. Their material reports firms' perceptions of the relative importance of various factors influencing pay negotiations and is particularly interesting. They found that the two key factors seen as exerting *upward* pressure on the level of pay settlements were inflation (stressed by 60 per cent of respondents in 1979–80 and 40 per cent in 1983–4) and the level of establishment/company profits (11 per cent in 1979–80, 21 per cent in 1983–4). Three factors were seen as exerting *downward* pressure on pay settlements, the level of establishment company profits (45 per cent in both years), the level of profitability (38 per cent in 1979–80 and 51 per cent in 1983–4), and the risk of redundancy (20 per cent in 1979–80 and 21 per cent in 1983–4). Generally, 'insider' factors rather than 'outsider' factors had more influence on wage settlements (see Gregory *et al.*, 1985, pp. 350–52, and also Gregory, *et al.*, 1987).

Nickell and Wadhwani use data based upon the published accounts of 219 UK quoted manufacturing companies over the period 1972–82. They found that 'insider' forces, particularly the firms own prices and productivity levels, had a major effect on the level of wages. The top 20 per cent of companies raised the real wages of their employees by some 18 per cent more than the bottom 20 per cent 'solely because of their superior average revenue product growth and financial performance'. (Nickell and Wadhwani, 1990, p. 507).

It has also been pointed out that wage rises have been higher in the more recent period in large rather than small companies (Daniel, 1984, p. 83 and Table 1, p. 86). They have also been higher for skilled workers and particularly for sections of management (Mc-Innes, 1987, pp. 80–84). All this means that any analysis conducted at the sectoral level is still aggregated; what we need is an analysis which can distinguish both between individual companies and between different levels of the companies' work-force.

Overall, the firm-based findings we have are fairly convincing and support the analysis throughout this book. It is the state of industrial relations and the specific economic circumstances within individual companies which effect the level of wages and strikes. Of course, government can have little direct influence on these factors. 'Outsider' factors are not unimportant but they appear less important. At the same time, what we need is a longer-run time series data set, of the type used by Nickell and Wadhwani, which would allow us to discover if the 'Thatcher effect' holds when firm-level data, on profitability and productivity particularly, is used. Nevertheless, the major conclusion must be that there is little evidence that in the private sector wages have been significantly constrained as a result of Thatcherism. It might be argued that the government has established a climate in which there is greater emphasis upon productivity and profitability, or that the government legislation has restricted the unions' ability to take industrial action in pursuit of higher wages, but there is limited evidence here to support a strong version of this argument.

Conclusion

This chapter has examined the extent and cause of changes in shop-floor industrial relations in the private sector since 1979. Three key conclusions emerge:

1. Unfortunately, we still await the third WIRS study which will give us a fuller picture of what has changed since 1984. Nevertheless, the current empirical material suggests that there has been less change in shop-floor industrial relations in the private sector than the Conservative Government wanted and than many journalists and social scientists have claimed. How-

ever, there have been significant changes and it is misguided to suggest, as McIlroy does, that little has changed. There is no doubt that unions at the national and the shop-floor level play a more defensive role than they did prior to 1979.

2. The change has been most marked in industries and companies in which there has been a long history of poor industrial relations. In particular, it is in the printing and shipping industries that the government legislation has been most used, macho-management is most evident and derecognition of unions is most widespread.

3. It is difficult to assess whether the changes which have occurred are more the result of economic changes or government legislation. Clearly both have played an important role. However, the wide variation in employers reactions to, and use of, the government legislation suggest that it is the history and climate of industrial relations in, and the economic circumstances of, the individual company which are crucial in determining the precise balance between capital and labour in that company. Governments can only have an indirect effect on those relations.

The future

As far as the future is concerned the current trends appear likely to continue unless a Labour Government is elected. There will be a continued, slow move towards derecognition and individual rather than collective bargaining for management and some skilled workers. However, change will continue to be greatest in industries which have always had poor industrial relations. In addition, a new style of industrial relations, characterised by single union deals, is only likely to make substantial headway on greenfield sites. In contrast, there would be significant changes if a Labour Government was elected which encouraged union recognition and thus a more harmonious relationship between unions and management. In such circumstances, union density, recognition and the coverage of collective bargaining would increase.

9

Shop-floor Industrial Relations: The Public Sector

Governments have little direct control over industrial relations in the private sector. Of course, they can introduce and operate statutory incomes policies which fundamentally constrain collective bargaining. However, this was never an option for the Conservative Government. Otherwise, a government can only alter the legal framework within which shop-floor industrial relations operate. This legal framework may have a significant effect on relations between employers and unions but the extent of this effect depends most upon strategic decisions taken by employers. In the public sector, in contrast, government has the potential for greater direct control over industrial relations. It can attempt to force management to take a firmer line with unions by cutting back grants, establishing cash limits, establishing profit targets and encouraging the import of private sector management methods. As such, government can exercise a more direct influence over the context within which public sector industrial relations takes place. However, it cannot determine those outcomes which still depend on the history and current state of the relations between management and unions within the particular section of the public sector.

This chapter assesses how much change there has been in industrial relations in the public sector since 1979. It is divided into four sections. The first section looks at the aggregate pattern reported by Millward and Stevens. The second section examines in more detail industrial relations in three particular branches of the public sector: the nationalised industries; local government; and the Civil Service. The third section deals with the effect which privatisation has had on the public sector unions. The final section assesses how far the changes which have occurred in public sector industrial

215

relations have resulted from the policies of the Thatcher governments.

The aggregate pattern

Unfortunately we have few studies of shop-floor industrial relations in the public sector. The Workplace Industrial Relations Study (WIRS) study which, it must be remembered, deals only with the situation up to 1984, is the last to present an overall picture and, unlike the private sector, there have been few more detailed studies which update this analysis.

The WIRS study distinguishes two public sector groupings: the nationalised industries, although excluding the coal industry; and the public services, that is local authorities, the National Health Service (NHS) and central government. The findings are fairly clear, although there are notable differences between the two groupings. Union membership remained more common in the public sector and indeed increased between 1980 and 1984 in the workplaces analysed. All the nationalised industry workplaces had non-manual and manual union members in both 1980 and 1984. In contrast, 80 per cent of the public service workplaces had manual union members in 1980 but this had increased to 94 per cent in 1984. However, the equivalent figures for non-manual workers were higher in both years; 98 per cent in 1980 and 100 per cent in 1984 (Millward and Stevens, 1986, p. 51, Table 3.1).

Union density was also higher in the public sector than elsewhere, although here the data Millward and Stevens report uses different categories. In 1984, union density for those employed in public administration was 78 per cent: 73 per cent for manual workers and 80 per cent for non-manual workers. In education, where 90 per cent of employment was in the public sector, there was 69 per cent unionisation: 57 per cent for manual workers and 75 per cent for non-manual workers. This compared with an average density in all service establishments of 58 per cent: 63 per cent among manual workers and 55 per cent among non-manual workers (ibid., p. 56, Table 3.3). As such, density was higher in the public sector than in the private services or the manufacturing industry (see ibid., p. 55 Table 3.2). In addition, within the public sector, in contrast to the other sectors, it was higher among non-manual workers.

Union recognition in the public sector also increased after 1980 and remained higher in that sector than elsewhere. Unions were recognised for collective bargaining purposes for manual workers in 76 per cent of the public sector workplaces studied in 1980; by 1984 this had increased to 91 per cent. As far as non-manual workers were concerned, unions were recognised in 91 per cent of the cases in 1980 compared with 98 per cent in 1984 (ibid., p. 63, Table 3.6); the comparable figures for all establishments were much lower. In addition, multi-unionism remains more common in the public sector, although Millward and Stevens's figures suggest that it is becoming less common. More unions are recognised and have bargaining rights for both manual workers and, particularly, non-manual workers in the public sector as compared with the private sector (ibid., p. 72, Table 3.7 and p. 784, Table 3.8). However, until its recent abolition, the closed shop remained most common in the nationalised industries; indeed, in 1984 68 per cent of the nationalised industries in the WIRS study operated a complete closed shop for manual workers, compared with only 17 per cent of the total sample (ibid., p. 98–9 Table 4.1, and see also ibid., p. 102, Table 4.3).

The WIRS survey also suggests that the number of shop stewards in the public sector increased between 1980 and 1984 (ibid., p. 84, Table 3.13), but that increase occurred among non-manual workers; there was a decline for manual public sector unions (ibid., p. 80, Table 3.13). However, while the number of joint shop steward committees increased in the nationalised industries for manual workers, they fell for non-manual workers in the same sector.

The results analysed so far suggest that the position of unions in the public sector has been less changed since 1979 than those in the private sector. Density is still high and recognition now almost universal. However, there is evidence from Millward and Stevens and elsewhere that unions are under pressure. In particular, as we saw in Chapter 7, there has been a move away from traditional collective bargaining. In addition, the scope of negotiations in the public sector is contracting and industrial conflict, particularly involving 'cut-price' industrial action, has increased. There was much less negotiation with manual unions over *non-pay* issues in both nationalised industries and public services in 1984 as compared with 1980. In particular, while in 1980 there were negotiations over redundancy in 99 per cent of the nationalised industry and 90 per cent of the public service workplaces studied, by 1984 these figures had fallen to 37 per cent and 48 per cent respectively (ibid., p. 248, Table 9.19). Millward and Stevens also report a significant increase in strike activity in the public sector between 1980 and 1984 (ibid., p. 266, Table 10.2). Of course, much of that action involved limited rather than extended stoppages, but the most interesting finding is the extent to which such action was national, rather than local, among non-manual workers. The figures indicate a tendency for such workers to engage in short but widespread action (ibid., p. 275, Table 10.6).

Overall, the WIRS report suggests that the basic *institutional structures* involved in industrial relations in the public sector have changed less than they have in the private sector. In addition, there remain more joint consultative committees between management and the unions in the public sector than elsewhere, indeed they increased between 1980 and 1984 (ibid., p. 139, Table 6.1), and a greater stress on other forms of communication between management and employees (see ibid., p. 152, Table 6.6).

Industrial relations in particular sections of the public sector

The nationalised industries

The government has attempted to force managements in the public sector to take a firmer line with their unions; to break what the Conservatives saw as the cosy relationship between public sector managements and unions, particularly in the nationalised industries. The Conservative Government has attempted to expose the nationalised industries to market forces, particularly since 1983, in two main ways. First, it has cut back on government grants to the industries; although the extent and pattern of those cuts vary from industry to industry. Second, it has attempted to establish profit targets as a guide to management activity. These changes have significantly affected industrial relations in the nationalised industries.

Batstone *et al.*'s study of the Post Office (Batstone *et al.*, 1984), Ferner's study of British Rail (Ferner 1985 and 1988) and Edwards and Heery's study of the National Coal Board (NCB) (Edwards and Heery, 1989b) all confirm this pattern, although with significant variations. All these studies suggest that, because managers in state-owned industries are usually dependent upon government for a substantial section of the industries' income and are directly account-able to ministers, they are subject to recurrent political control. This 'political contingency' renders the task of management much more difficult.

If we take British Rail (BR) as our example, government grants grew in cash terms up to 1983 but subsequently declined (see Pendleton, 1989, p. 283). In 1982 British Rail was also reorganised into separate business sectors. Each sector was given profit targets and time limits within which to achieve profitability. Overall, BR has concentrated on reducing manpower and increasing labour productivity. There was a drop of 42,000 (23 per cent) in the numbers employed by BR between 1979 and 1987 (see Ferner, 1985, p. 71, and Pendleton, 1989, p. 285), which resulted mainly from a number of schemes to improve staff productivity, particularly the flexible rostering of train crews introduced in 1982, and the intro-duction of single manning of locomotives in 1986. As Pendleton argues:

> The dynamics of the process can be simply stated: the creation of profit targets and reductions in financial support have forced BR managers to break out of the hitherto cosy-relationships with the rail unions and, to vigorously tackle restrictive practices.
>
> (Pendleton, 1989, p. 287)

Of course, there is nothing new in a government interfering in nationalised industries to forward its economic policy and political interests. However, the argument of both Ferner and Pendleton is that in the 1960s and 1970s, and indeed up until 1983, BR and the rail unions response to government interference, and the uncertainty it caused, was to attempt 'to insulate the industry from politics by forming what can be termed a tacit alliance' (Pendleton, 1989, p. 289 and, for evidence to support this view, see p. 290). In the 1980s, however, Pendleton argues that the stable industrial relations system in the railways began to break up because of the changed nature of government intervention in the industry. Initially, the tacit alliance strengthened as both BR and the unions sought to defend the industry against the hostility of the Thatcher Government. However, in 1981 and 1982, the British Railway Board came under greater pressure from government to escalate the process of reform. As Ferner indicates, during 1982 the government decided that it was more important to defeat the Associated Society of Locomotive Engineers and Firemen (ASLEF) than to achieve a negotiated settlement of the flexible rostering dispute (Ferner, 1988, p. 114–16). Faced with this new political contingency involving a government anxious to subject public sector unions to market forces, BR managers had little choice but to break the tacit alliance and confront the unions. As Pendleton points out:

> The key difference is that up until 1981 the 'political contingency' to use Ferner's words, favoured a management-union alliance, whilst now it supports the exclusion of worker organisations.
>
> (Pendleton, 1989, p. 294)

A similar pattern emerges in Edwards and Heery's study of the coal industry. Certainly, they strongly support the argument that the conduct of industrial relations in nationalised industries has always been constrained by the operation of political contingency. However, while both Batstone *et al* (1984) and Ferner argue that in the 1970s, and particularly in the 1980s, a new 'commercial paradigm' disrupted existing, and largely co-operative, industrial relations in the state industries, Edwards and Heery take issue with this view as far as coal is concerned. They argue that, 'developments in coal have not been driven by the displacement of service with more "commercial" objectives at the industry's centre' (Edwards and Heery, 1989b, p. 249). The coal industry has never operated as a service industry; rather it has always been subject to commercial discipline, but this has been tempered by two other objectives:

> the provision of well paid employment in mining areas and secondly the maintenance of a large, domestic coal industry as an economic buffer against fluctuations in the price and supply of oil.
>
> (Edwards and Heery, 1989b, p. 249)

In Edwards and Heery's view, these two other objectives were dropped after 1979, partly for commercial reasons but mainly for industrial relations ones. The Conservative Government's abandoning of earlier objectives for the industry, for instance:

was motivated in the first instance by a desire to cut the NCB's mounting financial losses. We also believe, however, that this policy was motivated by explicitly industrial relations considerations. The pursuit of the two objectives described above had the effect of strengthening the National Union of Mineworkers and of increasing national dependence on what had proved to be a powerful and militant group of workers. Under the Conservatives an alternative strategic calculation has influenced policy towards the industry. There has been a rejection of the argument that coal should be protected from market forces because this has the effect of increasing the economy's vulnerability to a national miners' strike. The movement to tighter commercial discipline in mining, therefore, and the abandoning of earlier objectives, has been motivated by a desire to escape dependence on the NUM.

(ibid., p. 250)

It is likely that Edwards and Heery overestimate the coherence of Conservative policy, although certainly, given Heath's experiences in 1974, the Conservatives were clearly worried about the NUM's power. In addition, they perhaps give too much emphasis to the change that occurred in 1979; the pressure toward commercialism was occurring in the 1970s. Certainly, Batstone *et al.* (1984) emphasise that both 'political contingency' and commercialism were key pressures in the Post Office before 1979, although commercial pressures on Posts grew subsequently while Telecommunications, of course, was privatised.

All these studies concentrate more on relations between management and government rather than on shop-floor industrial relations. At the local level, while the institutions remain largely intact, practice appears to have changed more. Certainly Edwards and Heery's study of Freightliners (1989a) found that the operation of the local institutions of industrial relations were more or less unchanged, although the management style was more aggressive and some changes in working practices had occurred. A similar picture emerges from Pendleton's work on British Rail. He argued that many of the basic structural features of workplace industrial relations in British Rail are more or less unchanged although in some respects the approach of some local management had changed. (Pendleton, 1991). In particular, there was less consultation and less adherence by management to agreements. In consequence, he found that of the train drivers' representatives he surveyed in 1989 only 30 per cent believed that local industrial relations were good, while 28 per cent believed they were bad; in contrast, in 1980 70 per cent of respondents in a similar survey responded positively and only 6 per cent negatively (ibid., p. 212).

Local authorities

As Rhodes says, pay negotiation in local government is 'essentially voluntary, complex, highly centralised and based on collective bargaining' (Rhodes, 1986, p. 157). There were 2,377,000 local authority employees in 1987–8 which represented 11 per cent of the total work-force and 44 per cent of the public sector work-force. In addition, local authority employees constituted about 20 per cent of total trade union membership. Local authorities are not bound to belong to the system of collective bargaining; they can, if they so wish, set their own wages and conditions of employment. Rhodes emphasises that the system is also voluntary in that the agreements entered into by the national negotiating bodies, except in the case of teachers, before 1987, and police officers' pay levels, are not binding upon individual local authorities. However, few local authorities retained independence as regards negotiation and, as Rhodes points out, 'the authority of the machinery depends upon authorities standing by national level agreements' (ibid., p. 158).

In fact, there are 40 national negotiating bodies which differ widely in the number of employers for whom they are responsible, the number of occupations and fields they cover and in their constitutions, structures and procedures. Rhodes again makes the point clear: 'In short, the system is complex. It is also centralised' ibid., p. 158).

Despite its complexity the present arrangements are based upon the Whitley Council system which was introduced into local government in 1946, when several National Joint Councils (NJCs) were created, the most important of which were the NJCs for manual workers and for local authority administrative, professional, technical and clerical staff. At the same time, the teachers had the Burnham Committees, which operated in a similar way to the Whitley Councils, until the Teachers Pay and Conditions Act

1987 abolished them. In both the Whitley Councils and the Burnham Committees, pay and major conditions of service were negotiated nationally between the national representatives of the local authorities and union representatives. The close links at the national level were replicated at the regional level in 27 provincial councils also composed of union and local authority employers representatives. Rhodes calculates that the employee side of the national negotiating bodies and the provincial councils include representatives from some 80 trade unions and staff associations (ibid., p. 161). However, five major unions dominate representation. Laffin calculates that 65 per cent of local government manual workers belong to three unions; National Union of Public Employees (NUPE) (38 per cent), GMBATU (16 per cent) and the Transport and General Worker's Union (TGWU) (11 per cent). Unlike manual workers, white-collar staff are concentrated into a single union, National Association of Local Government Officers (NALGO), which has 72 per cent of local authority non-manual workers in membership. There is a similar level of unionisation among teachers, with half of those unionised belonging to the National Union of Teachers (NUT) (Laffin, 1989, pp. 45–6).

Rhodes's study of pay negotiations in the local authority sector certainly makes it clear that, throughout the 1970s and 1980s, the local government faced five broad problems in its relationship with central government:

inadequate consultation, inconsistent settlements elsewhere in the non-trading public sector and in the private sector; interference in actual negotiations and the imposition of enquiries; control of manpower numbers; and cash limits.

(Rhodes, 1986, p. 164)

These pressures existed before 1979. The Labour Government consistently attempted to persuade or pressure local authorities to keep down wages and the Local Authorities Conditions of Service Advisory Board (LACSAB) acquiesced in the first three stages of the Labour Government's incomes policy. This government also instituted a 'manpower watch' in the 1975–6 rate support grant settlement with the local authorities which pressured them to hold manpower levels (Rhodes, 1986, pp. 167–9). Subsequently, in the

April 1976 Budget, the Chancellor, Dennis Healey, introduced a cash-limits system. Finally, during the 'Winter of Discontent' the government's intervention in local authority pay bargaining became 'more intense than ever' (ibid., p. 182).

However, Rhodes also argues that the control exercised by the Conservative Government has been significantly greater than previously. The government had no incomes policy, but the cash-limits policy fulfilled that role in the public sector. As Rhodes emphasises:

> They have avoided detailed interference in pay bargaining but they have used cash limits most vigorously. Indeed, the two are directly related – the Government has no need to intervene in detailed bargaining because cash limits so rigidly set the limits to bargaining'.
>
> (ibid., p. 190)

Rhodes also suggests that:

> while the 1979–83 Conservative Government may have employed indirect controls over the level of pay settlements it pursued a more direct approach in its efforts to restrain, and indeed to cut, local authority manpower.
>
> (ibid., p. 193)

In fact, the government transformed the 'manpower watch' scheme introduced by Labour into an attempt to effect manpower cuts in individual local authorities by requiring manpower figures from individual local authorities.

If Rhodes's study gives an insight into how the national picture of local authority pay negotiation has changed since 1979, Laffin's more detailed study of industrial relations in two unnamed boroughs confirms the view that the changes which have occurred have been significant. Laffin suggests that the formal institutions of industrial relations at the local level have not changed. Labour and many Conservative councillors still attached considerable value to being 'model employers' and so prefer to find savings through negotiations within the existing industrial relations machinery (Laffin, 1989, p. 128).

Similarly, consultation wasn't abandoned. Significantly, despite their sceptical view of the consultative machinery and procedures, the Conborough Conservatives continued to regard any violation of these procedures as a major risk (ibid., p. 125). However, while the institutions remained much the same, the decision-making situation had changed. Local authorities were faced with the cash-limits policy and by changes in the system of local government financing which attempted to reduce local authority financial autonomy. In Laffin's study, Conborough Conservatives were committed to retrenchment and 'financial discipline', while Labton's Labour councillors attempted to resist government financial stringency and take a major new policy initiative. However, in the end the Labour authority had little choice but to retrench and, as such, confront the unions. For this reason, as Laffin argues:

> Industrial relations has become increasingly adversary across British local government. The growing pressures of financial stringency and a more intensely ideological form of politics have compounded the problems of policy change through negotiation.
>
> (ibid., p. 119)

Laffin's conclusion is less circumspect than Rhodes's and he may overestimate the extent of change and allocate too much responsibility to Thatcherism for that change. Nevertheless, it is clear that there have been important changes since 1979. Government has intervened more significantly, if rarely directly, in local authority industrial relations and, for this reason, industrial relations in this sector have become more adversarial.

At the same time, the role of local bargaining has increased significantly. Kessler suggests:

> This was partly a consequence of attempts to introduce more flexible payment systems for selective groups, but more generally in response to the pressures for the change in employment practice and conditions generated by financial constraints and the drive for greater 'efficiency and effectiveness'.
>
> (Kessler, 1989, p. 188)

Nevertheless, few authorities have moved outside national agreements. As Kessler says: 'The essential point remains that the pressures generated since 1979 have largely continued to be handled within the framework of national terms and conditions' (Kessler, 1989, p. 190).

Kessler, again, makes the key point:

> In the changed bargaining context of the post-1979 period, local authority employers and trade unions at both the national and local levels have been forced to review the manner in which they conduct industrial relations. Both sides have modified and developed their objectives and strategies in response to the limited financial resources available and to a statutory framework which forces the testing of the 'value' provided by services in the market place.
>
> (Kessler, 1989, p. 194)

Civil Service

Under the Whitley Council system introduced in 1919, the Civil Service attempted to set an example as a good employer. The Whitley Council system provided a framework for consultation and joint decision-making over 'all matters which affect the conditions and service of the staff' (Reed and Ellis, 1987, p. 176). The National Council was complemented by a system of local Whitley Councils which together 'provided a comprehensive framework for management-union consultation' In addition, the civil service staff handbook stressed the contribution unions made and urged civil servants to become active trade unionists.

If the Whitley Councils provided the main institutional setting in which consultation and negotiation took place, it was the issue of comparability with private sector pay, within the context of government attempts to reduce the Public Sector Borrowing Requirement (PSBR) and cut civil service manpower, which led to most conflict between unions and government after 1979. In 1957 the Priestly Commission established the principle of fair comparability between wages in public and private sectors. At the time, interest rates, inflation and unemployment were low and the Civil Service had difficulty in attracting sufficient recruits. In that context, a system which linked civil servants' pay to private sector rates had considerable appeal. By the 1970s the situation was different. Inflation, interest rates and unemployment were much higher, the Civil Service was bigger, and financial pressures were growing, which made cuts in public expenditure an increasingly important aspect of successive governments' policy. Indeed, although major changes have occurred since 1979, the first large rise in the price of oil in the early 1970s and the resulting recession, led a number of governments, notably those of the United States, Canada and Australia as well as Britain, to react similarly and attempt to overturn or change existing arrangements for determining public sector pay.

Of course, in Britain the Labour Government relied on a combination of incomes policy and cash limits to control public sector pay, while the Conservatives rejected incomes policy and instead instituted a broader battery of measures. Nevertheless, it must be recognised that the changes since 1979 do not represent a reversal of the 1970s situation, but rather a very significant extension of previous developments (see Blackwell and Lloyd, 1989, pp. 68–73); nor are they unique in a world context.

The Conservatives immediately acted to alter the industrial relations climate in the Civil Service when they came to power, although the pace of change was substantially increased after the 1981 Civil Service pay dispute which lasted 21 weeks. In fact, the Conservative Government's policy towards the Civil Service has had four aims: to cut manpower and reduce expenditure; to assert greater ministerial and managerial control; to transfer work to the private sector; and to import private sector management methods.

The first two aims which have had most effect on industrial relations are examined here; the next section will deal with the effect of privatisation. There has been a manpower reduction of over 20 per cent in the Civil Service since 1979, mainly brought about by the imposition of manpower ceilings and cash limits by the government. Indeed, the Treasury's own figures indicate that this manpower reduction has been achieved more by streamlining, privatisation and curtailing public sector functions, than by increased efficiency (see Reed and Ellis, 1987, p. 170). The government has been particularly concerned to decrease consultation with unions and staff and assert managerial prerogatives; indeed, it could be argued that macho-management is more evident in the public sector than the private sector. Certainly, the government took a number of steps to assert control: in 1979 it announced a recruitment freeze with no consultation; subsequently the government refused to discuss redundancies within the collective bargaining framework; in

1980 it unilaterally repudiated the pay agreement based upon comparability which had been established in 1956 after the Report of the Priestley Commission; and although in 1982 it accepted arbitration as part of the settlement to the 1981 strike, in all other cases, the government refused to accept arbitration, although under the 1925 Civil Service Arbitration Agreement both sides had the right unilaterally to appeal to an independent arbitration tribunal (Reed and Ellis, 1987, pp. 179–80).

The government was also anxious to remove what it regarded as the privileged position of public sector workers generally and civil servants particularly. As such it established two inquiries: the Scott Committee to examine the value of public sector pensions and the Megaw Committee which investigated pay determination in the non-industrial Civil Service. The Scott Committee, in fact, recommended that the pensions remained inflation-proofed, which was not what Mrs Thatcher had hoped for or expected (Hennessey, 1989, p. 678). However, the Megaw Committee's proposals were much more to the government's liking. It recommended an end to the system of comparability and its replacement by a system which allowed for regional differences, productivity incentives and rewards related to performance (Gretton and Harrison, 1987, Chap. 7).

The government had already disbanded the Civil Service Department (CSD) before establishing the Megaw Committee. This move, in part, resulted from the belief in government that the CSD had acted as gamekeeper turned poacher in the 1981 pay negotiations (Tyson, 1987, p. 63, see also Blackwell and Lloyd, 1989, pp. 81–2). As such, the responsibility for Civil Service industrial relations, pay, grading and manpower-control issues was transferred to the Treasury. As Tyson emphasises: 'With control of pay and related issues in the hands of the Treasury, the Government could expect economic objectives to remain permanent' (Tyson, 1987, p. 63).

On the basis of the Megaw Committee's Report, the government also abolished the Pay Research Unit which had been responsible for assessing and establishing comparability with the private sector. Once more the aim was to subject wage bargaining to market forces and this strategy was again reflected in the imposition in 1985 of a performance-based scheme for senior civil servants up to Under-Secretary level.

Despite all these changes, it was the government's decision to proscribe unions in Government Communication Headquarters (GCHQ) in 1984 which had the most political resonance in this area. Employees at GCHQ were involved in seven industrial disputes between February 1979 and April 1981 which led to government claims that such action posed a threat to national security. In addition, in the light of a spy case involving a GCHQ employee Geoffrey Prime, the government wished to introduce the polygraph (lie-detector) for the security vetting of GCHQ staff. The staff and the unions resisted this move. On 22 December 1983 Mrs Thatcher used the powers she possessed to revise the terms of service of GCHQ staff so as to proscribe membership of any trade union. The staff had a choice; they could resign their union membership, receive £1,000 compensation and continue working at GCHQ, or they could apply for a transfer elsewhere in the Civil Service. The government refused to accept the unions' offer of a no strike deal and, despite support from other public sector unions, nearly a year after the original prohibition a majority of employees at GCHQ voted in favour of a new staff association whose constitution forbids industrial action. This has not set a precedent for derecognition in the public sector, but it did severely damage industrial relations within the Civil Service.

The government's attitude towards industrial relations and the shift in management style was reinforced by changes in management methods (see Blackwell and Lloyd, 1989, pp. 86–95). Initially, the government appointed Sir Derek Rayner with a brief to increase efficiency in the civil service. Subsequently, in 1983 the Cassell's Committee undertook a review of personnel management in the Civil Service. However, it was the Financial Management Initiative which had most lasting effect. It was designed to establish a clear management structure and line of responsibility within departments. The aim was to increase efficiency and decrease costs.

Most of these new developments were opposed by the nine unions representing civil servants. Only the Association of First Division Civil Servants, the association representing top civil servants, and the Institution of Professional Civil Servants (IPCS), which represents scientific and technical civil servants, gave the Megaw Committee's report a cautious welcome. Indeed, a survey undertaken by the Council of Civil Service Unions in 1984 found that 83 per cent of the respondents felt that industrial relations had deteriorated since

1979. The unions reported that consultations had dramatically reduced, so that only 27 per cent of the respondents said that they were consulted on most matters affecting staff conditions of service before management took a decision (Reed and Ellis, p. 178).

There have clearly been major changes in both the structures and the management style affecting Civil Service industrial relations. However, the government has not been able to persuade, or force, the large Civil Service unions, the Civil and Public Servants Association and the Society of Civil and Public Servants, to accept the new order suggested by the Megaw Committee. Indeed, by the end of 1987, Sir Robert Armstrong, the Cabinet Secretary, reported that only 80 000 civil servants, less than a sixth of the Civil Service, were covered by the new arrangements (Hennessey, 1989, p. 679). At the same time, the government's attempts to prevent comparability with the private sector were not totally successful. By March 1987, recruitment to the scientific and technological grades had become so difficult that the government agreed a deal with the IPCS giving these grades an average increase of more than 10 per cent above the rate of inflation, while establishing a new system of pay determination based on comparability with similar private sector jobs.

Despite these qualifications however, Civil Service industrial relations have changed significantly since 1979. As Blackwell and Lloyd emphasise:

> There has been little scope for national collective bargaining (that is joint regulation of employment) and other forms of rule-making, notably joint consultation, but including unilateral government-employer regulation and statutory regulations have become more important. Indeed, the unions have complained that the scope and significance of joint consultation has been reduced, with the opportunities for discussion of options early in the decision making process being largely replaced by consultation on the details of implementation after final decisions have been taken.
>
> (Blackwell and Lloyd, 1989, pp. 105–6)

Overall, the studies of individual branches of the public sector suggests that more has changed than the WIRS study indicated.

Privatisation

As we saw in Chapter 7, one of the aims of privatisation, although by no means the most important was to reduce the power of the public sector unions (see Marsh, 1991). Two aspects of privatisation were particularly important given this aim: the asset sales and the move towards contracting out of public sector services. How far have public sector unions been influenced by these two processes?

Contracting out

Brittan argues that even the threat of privatisation has led to a reduction in overmanning and increased productivity (Brittan, 1985, p. 120). Similarly, Milne's study indicates that the introduction of competitive tendering in the NHS has led to compulsory redundancies, although not on a large scale (Milne, 1987, pp. 154–60). Indeed, Milne's conclusion is confirmed by the broader analysis of Ascher who calculates, for example, that when local authority cleaning was put out for tendering there was a 38 per cent job loss (Ascher, 1987, p. 104, Table 4.1), but also argues that the number of redundancies 'does not adequately portray the dynamics of the job loss process' (ibid., p. 105). In particular, Ascher emphasises that as:

> between 60 per cent and 80 per cent of an in-house cleaning force will generally apply to continue working under the contractor, there is overwhelming evidence that contractors select only the youngest and strongest applicants from the former in-house staff and that any shortages in staffing totals are generally filled by the recruitment of outsiders.
>
> (ibid., p. 106)

The tendering process also affects the pay and conditions of workers. As far as pay is concerned, the government's decision to rescind the Fair Wages Resolution in 1983 also had a significant influence. Ascher quotes one Department of Health and Social Security (DHSS) administrator: 'the government wants to keep pay as an issue between the contractor and his staff, related to local conditions; it should not be determined by nationally negotiated public sector wage settlements' (ibid., p. 107).

Competitive tendering has affected pay in two major ways. It has led to major changes in the bonus schemes. As Ascher argues:

> The impact of revised work schedules and bonus schemes upon employees is straightforward: less pay for the same work or more work for the same pay.
>
> (ibid., p. 108)

At the same time, it has led to a reorientation of the hours worked by individual employees; more specifically, a reduction in holiday and overtime and increased use of part-time workers.

As Ascher concludes: 'the tendering process means a deterioration in the workers' financial position, regardless of which side is awarded the contract' (ibid., p. 110).

Certainly, reductions in employment and pay occur even if the final contract is awarded in-house, because the in-house tender has to attempt to compete on equal terms with the private sector. In contrast, changes in workers' conditions of service only occur when the contract is awarded externally; but they are often very significant. Holiday entitlements, sick leave provisions, and pension rights are much worse after privatisation. (Ascher, 1987, p. 110). As Jeremy Corbyn noted in the House of Commons, competitive tendering thus inevitably has a negative effect upon trade union members (ibid., p. 111).

However, we should be wary about emphasising the deleterious efforts of privatisation on public sector unions. Overall, while the membership of public sector unions has declined, there is no clear pattern in that decline; unions affected by contracting out like NALGO and NUPE have stable memberships, while in public sector industries largely unaffected by privatisation (the coal industry and the railways) and the Civil Service, union membership fell most dramatically. Even so, it is contracting out which has had the greatest effect on union members. In other areas of the privatisation process, notably asset sales, the picture is more complex and there is less agreement among observers.

Asset sales

Curwen examined the industrial relations systems in those companies privatised before June 1984. He found that only two attempts had been made to change the bargaining systems and concluded:

> The picture presented is, on the whole, quite favourable to the unions with jobs being created as well as being lost. That privatisation should bring both gains and losses is hardly unexpected, but the government must be somewhat disappointed and the Unions pleasantly surprised, at the way in which the balance between the two has worked out in practice.
>
> (Curwen, 1986, pp. 168–9)

However, this conclusion may be misguided. Certainly the Trades Union Congress (TUC)'s publication, *Bargaining in Privatised Companies*, presents a different picture. They argue that virtually all the privatised companies have had major redundancies and that, while management salaries have risen significantly after privatisation, unions have only been able to achieve an improvement in non-management real wages in return for important concessions on conditions or large-scale redundancies. In addition, the TUC specifies a number of detailed complaints against the industrial relations practices of the management of most of the privatised companies (TUC, 1987).

In fact, it appears that there is no consistent pattern. Certainly developments within British Telecommunications (BT) and British Gas (BG) after privatisation have been very different. Privatisation led to rapid and major changes in BT's bargaining structure but not in BG's, while unions claim a marked reduction in areas for negotiation and consultation in BT in contrast to BG. In both companies, there were perceptible changes towards a more assertive management style, but this was much more noticeable in BT. In BT, privatisation was followed by a major managerial initiative to change key elements in the terms and conditions of employees; indeed in 1986–7 there was a major industrial dispute over BT's efforts to link pay increases to changes in work organisation and other efficiency measures. (see IRS Employment Trends, 1989, pp. 12–14).

There seems little doubt that the situation for unions has worsened in many privatised companies, but there is doubt both as to how much it has worsened and how far this change results from privatisation. If a company passes into the private sector it doesn't inevitably lead to fundamental changes in the industrial relations system. Industrial relations in many of the industries privatised, and particularly in most of the first ones sold, were good prior to the change in ownership, which may explain Curwen's results. There is little doubt that here, as elsewhere, the changes in industrial relations practice have been greatest in companies in which there was a poor history of industrial relations. At the same time, other factors appear to be more important than ownership in affecting industrial relations practice and bargaining.

As Abromeit suggests: 'one look at the capacity-reduction policies of the British Steel Corporation or [British Coal] makes the union's contention that privatisation would increase unemployment sound slightly ridiculous' (Abromeit, 1988, p. 73).

Vickers and Yarrow's conclusion is even more interesting:

> privatisation may do little by itself to reduce union power. It does not diminish the cost and damage that strikes could inflict, and if monopoly power persists, the company's purse is likely to remain effectively bottomless. Indeed, it can be argued that Government can resist union pressure, and, by virtue of its involvement with numerous groups of public sector workers, the Government has reputation reasons for not wanting to concede an unduly generous settlement to any one group. Both these effects were at work in the year-long coal strike in 1984–1985. The Government was content to incur massive financial losses to secure victory, and its resolve to defeat the National Union of Mineworkers was inspired in large part by demonstration (or signalling) effect on other wage bargains in the economy – a factor that would not have entered the calculations of private sector negotiators.
>
> (Vickers and Yarrow, 1988, p. 159)

Overall, it seems fair to conclude that the change in ownership involved in privatisation has had a major effect on trade unions in one or two cases, notably BT, but a more limited effect elsewhere.

Explaining the changes

It is clear that there have been significant changes in public sector industrial relations since 1979, perhaps more than have occurred in the private sector. While many of the institutions of industrial relations in the public sector remain the same, as the WIRS study suggests, in the three sections of the private sector we have examined, there have been major alterations in relations between management and unions. To what extent do these changes result from Thatcherite polices?

In some senses it is not easy to answer this question in relation to the public sector as we have no econometric studies of changes in productivity, wages or strikes in the public sector, and Freeman and Pelletier's (1990) analysis of union density doesn't differentiate between public and private sector union levels. However, the analysis of the changes since 1979 presented in this chapter does point to a clear conclusion. Many of the changes in public sector industrial relations we have identified had origins before 1979. However, the Conservative Government's economic and industrial relations policies significantly changed the economic and political situation within which public sector managements operated. Management became more constrained by political contingencies. The result is less consultation and negotiation between unions and management and more direction by management, with the government looking on closely. Of course, as Rhodes in particular is at pains to point out, such direction doesn't necessarily achieve the ends which management, or government, seek.

There is particular evidence of the way in which public sector unions have been affected by government policy on the wagefront. It is clear that there have been lower pay increases in the public sector since 1979 than in the private sector. As we saw earlier, only 20 per cent of public service workers now have their pay settled by traditional collective bargaining. As such, it is perhaps not surprising that public sector workers have done badly, relative to private sector workers, in the period since 1979. Certainly, Daniel presents data taken from a national survey of the economically active in 1983 ($n = 1,394$) which indicates both that 'public service employees received substantially less than people in other sectors' (see Daniel, 1984, p. 79, and also Tables 1 and 2, pp. 86, and 87) and that there was 'a profound and pervasive sense of grievance in the public services' (ibid., p. 79).

The New Earnings Survey data throw some light upon this conclusion [New Earnings Survey, 1989] Generally, private sector non-manual workers have done best during the Thatcher years. This is particularly the case as far as women workers are concerned. However, both manual and non-manual workers in the private sector did better during the second term of Conservative Government than during the first term. Certainly, Mrs Thatcher's indirect attempts to control public sector wages seems to have had some effect, at least if we compare the movement in public sector as compared to private sector wages. It is also noticeable that it is in the sector over which the government has most direct control, workers employed by central government, where wage rises, especially for manual workers, have been lowest. Once again we have evidence that the Thatcherite project in relation to trade unions, and here wages, has had more effect in the public sector than the private sector.

Conclusion

The chapter has examined the extent and causes of changes in industrial relations in the public sector. Key conclusions are evident:

1. There have been changes in industrial relations in the public sector. In particular, the government has placed many more constraints on the autonomy of management through its control of the purse strings and its ability directly to change the rules of the game within which public sector managers are operating. As such, there is little doubt from the analysis of particular branches presented here that the consultation and agreement which often marked public sector industrial relations has been replaced by a more adversarial style.

2. Even so, there have been relatively few alterations in the institutions of industrial relations in the public sector. So, there has been no real move towards derecognition and no significant decline in collective bargaining.

3. While institutions have not changed, it appears clear that there

have been a significant number of changes in work practices, although those changes have usually been agreed with shop stewards rather than imposed on them. Nevertheless, public sector unions at the national and the local level clearly occupy a much more defensive role than before 1979.

4. It is difficult to assess the relative effect of government policy and economic changes on public sector industrial relations given the question has received little attention in the literature. However, the government has more direct influence on management in the public sector and it seems clear that its influence is consequently greater.

The future

As far as the future is concerned, again no significant change is likely unless a Labour Government is elected. Any Conservative Government is likely to continue to attempt to squeeze the public sector and encourage a more adversarial management style, even if with limited effect. However, a Labour Government would almost certainly encourage union membership in the public sector and greater consultation between unions and management.

10

Thatcherism and Industrial Relations

As Rod Rhodes and I have argued elsewhere, Thatcherism is a diffuse phenomenon (Marsh and Rhodes, 1990; Marsh and Rhodes, 1991). In fact, we identified five broad dimensions of Thatcherism in the literature: an economic dimension; an electoral dimension; an ideological dimension; a policy style dimension; and a policy agenda/outcome dimension. This is not the place to rehearse these distinctions. However, it is clear from our analysis that relatively little attention has been given to the question of policy change.

Some authors clearly agree with Marquand's cavalier assertion that the policies are 'small beer' and share his view that the paradoxes of policy and the limited degree of change in some policy areas is 'not very surprising or very interesting' (Marquand, 1988, pp.159–60). This seems a dubious argument. The Thatcher Government set out to change policies and outcomes. In addition, it is the policies, and in particular the administration of those policies, not the rhetoric, which effect people. Policies matter and an assessment of the extent to which policies have changed since 1979 is an essential starting point for any analysis of Thatcherism and its effect on British politics.

Industrial relations is a particularly important policy area in this context. Many argue that it is one of the fields in which the Thatcher Government has had most success. In fact, Savage and Robins, in a volume which attempts to assess the influence of the Conservatives on public policy, identify industrial relations as one of four areas (the others are privatisation, local government and housing provision) which have undergone serious and even radical transformation during the Thatcher years (Savage and Robins, 1990, p.245).

As is evident from the analysis presented in this book, I am wary about such a claim. What is more, this case study suggests both why many assessments overestimate the change in policy outcomes since 1979 and, to an extent, why there have been less changes than the government wished and intended. The government, and a number of political scientists who have superficially assessed its influence on policy, have been operating with a top-down view of policy making which implies that government is omnipotent and omnicompetent. In fact, the Thatcher Government, like its predecessors, was neither.

This conclusion briefly examines both these themes. The first section assesses the influence of the Thatcher Government on industrial relations. The second section then draws upon this case study to suggest that the Thatcher Government has had limited influence in transforming policies, in large part because it has tried to impose policies without consultation, negotiation or co-operation.

Thatcherism and industrial relations

In this section I return to the three questions which have provided the focus of this book: How much has changed? Why has it changed? What is the future for unions?

How much has changed?

In the introduction I outlined four aims which the Conservative Government had when it was elected in 1979: to reduce the unions' role in the policy-making process; to assert its authority, and therefore its image of governing competence; to stimulate greater 'realism' among unions and unionists; and to alter the balance on the shop floor in favour of management. To what extent has it achieved these aims?

The political role of unions

The political role of unions has virtually disappeared. The election of the Thatcher Government saw the rejection of corporatism, an antipathy towards consultation and a reassertion of strong government. Certainly, meaningful consultation between the unions and government has almost ceased since 1979, as we saw in Chapter 4.

Indeed, the unions had virtually no influence on any of the Conservative legislation; the only exception being their success in preventing the inclusion of a provision to require unionists to contract into a union's political fund from the 1984 Trade Union Act. Elsewhere, as is clear from the consideration of youth unemployment policy in Chapter 4, the unions' role in policy-making was significantly reduced after 1979. In retrospect, Richter's analysis appears correct (Richter, 1973); generally unions have had a limited political role in Britain. They had a limited political role before 1966 and virtually no such role since 1979. It is the period between 1966 and 1979 which provided the exception, not the period since 1979.

Asserting the governments' authority

There is no doubt that the Conservative Government has successfully reasserted the authority of government in relation to trade unions. Not only have unions had little effect on policy but, in addition, the legislation once passed has been, to a large extent, complied with by the unions. The problem of compliance, which turned the 1971 Industrial Relations Act into a virtual dead letter by the time it was repealed, has not proved crucial, despite the fact that the Conservative legislation is very radical. At the same time, the government's commitment to strong decisive action was also reflected in their attitude to a series of strikes in the public sector which culminated in the 'defeat' of the National Union of Mineworkers (NUM) in 1984–5. In both cases the government's stance clearly reinforced an image of governing competence (see Bulpitt, 1986) which Crewe argues has been the key cause of the Conservatives' electoral successes (Crewe, 1988).

The development of New Realism

New Realism is a catch-all concept. Bassett (1987, Chap.4) and McIlroy (1988, pp.54–6) see New Realism in terms of the changed attitudes and strategies of the TUC and individual unions after the 1983 election defeat. The argument put forward by Len Murray, then Trades Union Congress (TUC) General Secretary, and others was that unions had to be prepared to take a conciliatory, rather than confrontational, approach and talk to Mrs Thatcher. However, this initiative quickly received two body blows. In January 1984 the government banned trade unions in Government Communications Headquarters and then the miner's strike further damaged relations between the unions and the government. Subsequently, as we saw in Chapter 6, the TUC has been most concerned to present a united front with the Labour Party and their contacts with the Conservative government have not improved.

Of course, a number of observers identify New Realism with a new system of industrial relations associated with the Electrical, Electronic, Telecommunications and Plumbing Union (EETPU) and characterised by single union agreements and strike-free deals (see Bassett, 1987, esp. Chap.5). However, as we saw in Chapter 8, these new industrial relations are hardly an important feature of contemporary arrangements. Single unions agreements and strike-free deals are almost exclusively confined to greenfield sites.

In fact, it is difficult to see New Realism as a key aspect of industrial relations except in a very minimalist sense of the term. Of course, there is more 'realism' in unions' attitudes to government, and in their relations with employers, because they are faced with a harsher economic, political and legal climate. However, three points need emphasising. First, unions have always been more realistic in hard times. Second, as we shall see in the next section, the institutions and many of the practices of shop-floor industrial relations remain the same despite this increased 'realism'. Third, if the situation changes, then so will the strategies and tactics adopted by unions.

Changing the balance between management and unions

There is little doubt that the relations between government and unions have changed significantly since 1979. Relations between unions and employers have changed much less. In particular, the institutions of shop-floor industrial relations remain largely intact in both the public and the private sector. There has been no major move to derecognise unions or restrict collective bargaining. In addition, few employers use the industrial relations legislation. Nevertheless, it is misleading to claim that little has changed. The coverage of collective bargaining may have remained fairly constant but its content and scope have changed. Similarly, while industrial conflict is still not a thing of the past, the number, and especially the duration, of strikes has significantly reduced.

Overall, it is impossible to generalise about the strength of unions

242 The New Politics of British Trade Unionism

on the shop floor. In particular, as was always the case, it is the informal industrial relations practices which have developed over time in an industry, or more significantly a company, and the economic situation with which the company is faced, which have most influence on shop-floor industrial relations. For that reason, it is not surprising that in the private sector it is in the printing and the shipping industries, industries marked by a history of poor industrial relations, that most has changed. In those industries employers are most assiduous in their use of the legislation (see Chapter 4) and they have also been most anxious to derecognise unions and move away from collective bargaining (see Chapter 8). Similarly, in the public sector, as we saw in Chapter 9, while the government has attempted to exercise more direct control over management, the relationship between management and unions is still strongly influenced by tradition, precedent and previous practice.

Why have things changed?

The changes in the position of unions in recent years owe something to the politics pursued by Mrs Thatcher, but only something. The unions have been particularly weakened by the deindustrialisation of heavy manufacturing industry, where the level of unionisation and the strength of union organisation was high. The restructuring which has taken place in Britain has led to: a growth in the importance of the service sector; an increase in part-time working and female employment, and the development of a distinction between a core and a peripheral work-force; a fall in the size of plants; a movement of manufacturing industry away from the large conurbations; and, perhaps most important, a relocation of production abroad by British transnational companies. As we saw in Chapter 7, some authors overemphasise such changes. Certainly, the increase in flexibilisation or 'Japanisation' is much less than many assert. Nevertheless, there have been important changes. What is more, those changes clearly pre-date 1979, although they have been exacerbated by the policies pursued by the Conservative Government.

All of these factors have weakened the position of the unions and have contributed to a 25 per cent decline of union membership since 1979; a decline which is unlikely to be reversed. The level of unionisation is clearly important and the sustained fall has reduced both the resources available to unions and their legitimacy in the eyes of both employers and government. Both factors limit the unions' effectiveness.

The last decade has also seen major technological changes. Many authors have suggested that new technology inevitably involves de-skilling and increased control by management over the work process. However, as we saw in Chapter 7, new technology has been introduced into Britain in a very uneven way. Certainly, some managements, notably in the printing industry, have used the political and economic climate to weaken unions which exercised control over the work process. Elsewhere, however, change has been negotiated and unions have gained pay increases, and what McIlroy calls 'responsible autonomy', as the price of co-operating with the introduction of new technology. This is an area where no simple conclusion can be drawn and in which the issue of control of the work process is crucial.

The termination of the political role for unions, and the legislative assault on them, resulted from the election of a Conservative Government committed to the end of cosy consultation and the curbing of union power. Certainly, it is difficult to imagine a Labour Government, or even a Conservative Government led by someone such as Jim Prior, restricting the unions' political role or their legal immunities in the way that occurred between 1979 and 1990. Nevertheless, the government's ability to assert its authority and, in particular, the virtual absence of the problem of compliance, owed something to the fact that the unions' position had already been weakened by economic changes and rising unemployment.

It is more difficult to assess whether government legislation or macroeconomic developments have had more influence on shop-floor industrial relations. The econometric material dealing with union density, strikes and productivity is inconclusive. However, it is clear that there has been greater change in those industries marked by a history of poor industrial relations. This evidence, together with the fact that company-level studies suggest that wages are strongly affected by the levels of profitability and productivity in individual companies, indicates that it is the history and current state of relations between capital and labour within a given company, which at root is an economic relationship, which has most effect on the institutions and outcomes of industrial relations in that company. In the private sector at least, the government can only influence the legal framework and the ideological context within which industrial relations occurs; this is an important influence but it is an indirect one. Even in the public sector, while government can change its relationship to management, this change is not simply reflected in a concomitant change in the relationship between management and labour.

The future

Speculating about the future is never easy, but the analysis of the past and the present in this book does point towards certain conclusions. Here I shall concentrate upon the future of the unions' political role and of patterns of shop-floor industrial relations.

The unions' political role

The political future of the trade unions is clearly linked to the electoral chances of the Labour Party. Of course, another Conservative administration might put through more legislation, perhaps to restrict strikes in the public sector, but it is difficult to imagine them reinvolving the unions in policy-making. This is not the place to speculate on the Labour Party's electoral future, although it looks brighter now (winter 1990) than it did after the 1987 election. However, it is important to assess what would be likely to happen if Labour did come to power.

There is little doubt that if the Labour Party were elected the unions would be consulted more on policy. However, the unions and the Labour Party are unlikely to return to the type of relationship which characterised the Social Contract period. Much more likely is that the traditional role of the trade unions within the Labour Party would be reasserted. The unions will be a stabilising force supporting the Parliamentary Labour Party (PLP) leadership and opposing the Left. In effect, the unions will regain a limited political role.

A Labour Government would also significantly change the legal framework within which unions operate, but it would retain many of the elements of the Conservative legislation. At present the Labour Party proposes to: create a new legal framework; allow certain secondary action; establish a right to strike; and make injunctions harder to obtain. However, it is also committed to retaining pre-strike ballots and ballots for the election of union leaders and not to restore the closed shop. So, even if a Labour Government is re-elected, the legal position of unions will be significantly different than it was in 1979 as a result of the legislation passed by the Thatcher Government. Here, there will be a Thatcher legacy.

Of course, the position of British trade unions may be increasingly affected by policies made in Europe. However, as we saw in Chapter 5, the Social Charter, which contains a variety of provisions on employment rights, is not binding on the British Government, nor is it likely to be so. No Conservative Government appears likely to adopt the Charter, but the Labour Party is strongly committed to it and would be likely to adopt the Charter's provisions if it were elected.

Overall, it is evident that the fate of the unions depends to a large extent on the election of a Labour Government.

Shop-floor industrial relations

It seems unlikely that shop-floor industrial relations will change fundamentally. There will be more single union agreements in green-field sites. There will be a move away from collective bargaining for non-manual, particularly managerial, workers. The move towards company-level bargaining will continue. Unions in many declining companies will remain on the defensive unless or until the company's fortunes pick up. In the public sector, the government's policy will have more direct effect than in the private sector, both through its control of resources and its efforts to undermine collective bargaining. However, governments can only have an indirect influence on private sector industrial relations, and the relationship between unions and employers in a particular company will depend more on the history of industrial relations in, and the economic situation of, the company. The major change is likely to occur if a Labour Government is re-elected which encourages recognition, and therefore union membership, and co-operation between employers and unions.

Thatcherism and the top-down view of policy-making

Many of the assertions concerning the influence of the Conservative Government on policy are implicitly underpinned by a top-down view of the policy-making process. What is more this was clearly the view which the Government held. In Mrs Thatcher's words: 'It must be a conviction government. As Prime Minister I could not waste time having any internal arguments' (*Observer*, 25 February 1979). And as Ivor Crewe persuasively argues, Mrs Thatcher has a 'warrior style – setting objectives, leading from the front, confronting problems, holding her position...' (Crewe, 1988, p.45).

The government's intention was to establish centrally determined policy objectives, stick to them and ensure they were carried out. Certainly, the government rejected negotiation as its preferred strategy by which either to make or to implement policy.

The top-down view assumes that government: knows what it wants to do; has the required resources available; is able to marshal and control these resources to achieve the desired end; and is able to communicate what it wants to, and control the performance of, those who implement the policy (adapted from Barrett and Fudge, 1981): 'A policy without the requisite rationale, resources, organisation or controls is unlikely to achieve its objectives' (see also Hogwood and Gunn, 1984, Chap.11; Hood, 1976).

This is an inaccurate view of policy-making. Any government which operates with such a view finds that slippages can occur throughout the process. In a few narrow areas the Thatcher Government achieved its policy objectives. This was most often because the objective was simple, the policy tools were clear and there were minimal problems of compliance. The classic example of such a policy during the period of the Thatcher Government is the sale of council houses. The Conservatives assumed office in 1979 with strong commitment to promote a growth in home ownership and, in particular, to give council tenants a statutory right to buy their house or flat at significantly below its market price. Sitting tenants were given the right to buy in the 1980 Housing Act. The legislation required councils to sell and the initial limited resistance of some councils was quickly dealt with by the courts. Not surprisingly, council tenants were anxious to buy. By 1987 more than one million council houses had been sold, two-thirds of them to sitting tenants. In addition, a further 1.5 million households had become home-owners for the first time (Kemp, 1992).

Few policies have proved so easy to implement. Indeed, even in the housing field, another of the Conservatives objectives, to expand the private rented sector, has been a conspicuous failure (Kemp,

1992). In a larger number of areas government has achieved some of its aims, often only partially, but failed to achieve others. At the same time, its actions have sometimes produced unintended consequences which run counter to its aims or undermine policy in another area. The industrial relations area is one in which a number of aims have been achieved but where its main objective has to a large extent not been realised. At the same time, the government's pursuit of its policy objectives have had some unintended consequences.

As we saw earlier, the government has excluded the unions from the policy-making process and established its authority in relation to the unions. At the same time the unions have, for the most part, complied with the implementation of the legislation. Certainly, compliance is not the problem that the government feared, given the experiences with the 1971 Industrial Relations Act. To this extent, industrial relations policy can be counted a government 'success'. They introduced their reforms gradually rather than in one act and, partly as a consequence, the unions' response was muted rather than combative. In addition, the Conservatives stood firm against a series of public sector strikes. Two objectives were thus clearly achieved, although even here the government was aided by the fact that the unions had been weakened by growing unemployment and economic restructuring.

However, their main aim, which was linked to their general economic strategy, was to change significantly the balance between employers and unions. Yet, much on the shop floor remains the same. In this policy area the government passed its legislation virtually unamended, the courts interpreted the legislation in a rigorous way, and the unions largely complied with the courts' decisions. So implementation was not a major problem. In fact, the major problem was that changing the legal framework within which industrial relations operated did not inevitably change the informal processes of industrial relations. As Otto Kahn-Feund put it forty years ago:

> British industrial relations have, in the main, developed by way of industrial autonomy. This notion of autonomy is fundamental and ...it means that employers and employees have formulated their own codes of conduct and devised their own machinery for enforcing them.
>
> (Cited in Coates, 1989, pp.44–5)

The government legislation clearly significantly reduced the unions' autonomy and affected these informal codes of conduct. However, it didn't reduce management's autonomy and it is still the employer who decides whether to use the Conservative's legislation, not the government. It is the economic situation of, and the history and 'informal' system of industrial relations in, a company which continues to shape developments on the shop floor, more than the government's legislation. In a number of policy areas the Conservatives passed legislation but couldn't ensure its implementation because those affected by the legislation refused to comply with its implementation. The failures of the attempts to control local government finance amply illustrates this problem (Rhodes, 1991). In this case the problem was that the government had limited control of the environment within which shop-floor industrial relations operated. Employers' strategic decisions were affected by a variety of factors over which the Government had limited, if any, influence.

It is also worth emphasising that employers, like unions, were not consulted before the government introduced its legislation. Certainly, the Confederation of British Industry (CBI) has been as excluded from the policy-making process as the TUC. This may have helped the government establish its authority *vis-à-vis* particular interests. However, as we have seen, it is the employers who are charged with using the legislation and transforming industrial relations. Broader consultation might have produced a government more informed about shop-floor industrial relations and with a better idea about how their objectives could be achieved.

The Conservatives' industrial relations legislation has also produced a number of unintended consequences. Most, but not all, of these consequences have been political. First, relations between the Labour Party and the TUC have improved as the unions have become increasingly conscious that only a change of government can arrest, and perhaps reverse, their declining membership and bargaining position. Second, communications within unions have improved as a result of the requirement that unions conduct ballots. Now, union leaderships are able to proselytise among their membership much more effectively than previously because unions have national membership lists; such a campaign was very effective in relation to the political fund ballots. Third, the requirement for ballots before strikes means that, if the membership support the leadership in that ballot, and as we saw in Chapter 8 they usually do, then the union leadership can claim greater legitimacy in the pursuit of its claim. This can strengthen their bargaining position, particularly if the action also has broad public support as was the case during the rail strike in 1989. As far as shop-floor industrial relations is concerned, one unintended consequence is particularly worthy of note. A main theme of the government's legislation was to weaken the position of the union leadership in relation to their members. The Government's argument was that union leaderships were radical and the member-ships, if consulted, would modify that radicalism. In fact, the union memberships have normally endorsed industrial action in ballots. However, more importantly, while official extended strikes have reduced in the 1980s, shorter, often unofficial, actions have remained common. Of course, the authority of union leaders in relation to such local actions had been undermined by the Conservative legislation. An increase in such actions was not what the government intended and, as a result, the main provision of the 1990 Employment Act made union leaderships responsible for unofficial strikes unless they specifically denounced it. It is too soon to see what effect this legislation will have, but its passage indicates a problem with the previous policy.

Overall, it is too easy to view governments as omnipotent and omnicompetent, particularly when they themselves attempt to project this image. The Conservatives have had some success in achieving their aims in the industrial relations field, but it has been limited by the realities of industrial relations on the shop floor.

Bibliography

Abromeit, H.(1988) 'British privatisation policy', *Parliamentary Affairs*, pp. 68–85.

Ackroyd, S., *et al.*(1989) 'The Japanisation of British industry', *Industrial Relations Journal*, pp. 11–29.

Adeney, M. and Lloyd, J. (1986) *Loss Without Limit: The Miners' Strike of 1984–5* (London: Routledge & Keegan Paul).

Advisory Conciliation and Arbitration Service (1986) *Annual Report* (London: ACAS).

Ashby, P. (1990) 'Training and enterprise councils: assessing the gamble', *Policy Studies*, pp. 31–40.

Ascher, K.(1987) *The Politics of Privatisation: Contracting Out Public Services* (London: Macmillan).

Atkinson, J.(1985) 'The changing corporation', in D.Clutterbuck (ed.), *New Patterns of Work* (London: Gower).

Auerbach, S.(1987) 'Legal restraint of picketing: new trends; new tensions', *Industrial Law Journal*, pp. 227–44.

Baldwin, P.(1985) *The Politics of Youth Unemployment Policy*, MPhil., Kingston Polytechnic.

Barnes, D. and Reid, C (1980) *Government and Trade Unions* (London: Heinemann).

Barrett, S. and Fudge, C. (1981) 'Examining the policy action relationship', in S.Barrett and C.Fudge (eds) *Policy and Action* (London: Methuen), pp. 3–32.

Bassett, P. (1987) *Strike Free: New Industrial Relations in Britain*, (Basingstoke: Macmillan).

Bassett, P. (1988) 'Non-unionism's growing ranks', *Personnel Management*, March, pp. 44 7.

Batstone, E. (1984) *Working Order* (Oxford: Blackwell).

Batstone, E. (1988) *The Reform of Workplace Industrial Relations* (Oxford: Oxford University Press).

Batstone, E., Ferner, A. and Terry, M. (1984) *Consent and Efficiency: Labour Relations and Management Strategy in the State Enterprise* (Oxford: Blackwell).

250

Batstone, E. and Gourlay, S. (1986) *Unions, Employment and Innovation* (Oxford: Blackwell).

Beaumont, P.(1987) *The Decline of Trade Union Organisation* (London: Croom Helm).

Benedictus, R. (1985) 'The use of the law of tort in the Miners' Dispute', *Industrial Law Journal*, 14, pp. 176–90.

Bennett, A. and Smith-Garvine, S. (1990) *The Index of Percentage Utilisation of Labour* Bulletin No. 55 University of Aston Business Scheme.

Biddiss, M.(1987) 'Thatcherism: concept and interpretation', in K.Minogue and M.Biddiss (eds) *Thatcherism: Personality and Politics* (London Macmillan) pp. 1–20

Blackwell, R. and Lloyd, P. (1989) 'New managerialism in the Civil service: Industrial relations under the Thatcher administrations, 1979–86', in R.Mailley *et al.* (eds) *Industrial Relations in the Public Services* (London: Routledge).

Blanchflower, D. (1990) *Fear, Unemployment and Pay Flexibility*, NBER Working Paper 3365.

Booth, A. (1989) 'The bargaining structure of British Establishments', *British Journal of Industrial Relations*, 27, pp. 225–34.

Brittan, S. (1985) 'The politics and economics of privatisation', *The Political Quarterly*, pp. 109–27.

Brown, W.(1986) 'The changing role of trade unions in the management of labour', *British Journal of Industrial Relations*, 24, pp. 161–8.

Brown, W. and Wadhwani, S. (1990) 'The economic effects of industrial relations legislation since 1979', *National Institute Economic Review,* pp. 57–70.

Bulpitt, J. (1986) 'The discipline of the new democracy: MrsThatcher's domestic statecraft', *Political Studies*, pp. 19–39.

Burns, A. *et al.* (1985) 'The restructuring of the British coal industry', *Cambridge Journal of Economics*, 9, pp. 93–110.

Burton, J. (1979) *Trade Unions and Inflation* (London: Macmillan).

Cassels, J. (1989) 'Reflections on tripartism', *Policy Studies*, 3, pp. 31–40.

Clark, J. (1984) 'Industrial relations, new technology and divisions within the workforce', *Industrial Relations Journal*, pp. 36–44.

Clark, J. (1985) The juridification of industrial relations: a review article', *Industrial Law Journal*, pp. 69–90.

Clark, J. (1989) New technology and industrial relations', *New Technology, Work and Employment*, pp. 5–17.

Claydon, T. (1989) 'Union deregulation in the 1980s', *British Journal of Industrial Relations*, 27, pp. 214–24.

Coates, D. (1980) *Labour in Power* (London: Longman).

Coates, D. (1983) 'The question of trade union power', in D.Coates and G.Johnston (eds) *Socialist Arguments* (Oxford: Martin Robertson) pp. 55–82.

Coates, D. (1989) *The Crisis of Labour* (Oxford: Philip Allan).

Crewe, I. (1988) 'Has the electorate become more Thatcherite?' in R. Skidelsky (ed.) *Thatcherism* (London: Chatto & Windus) pp. 25–50.

Crewe, I. (1990) 'The decline of labour and the decline of Labour: social and electoral trends in post-war Britain', *Essex Papers in Politics and Government*, no.65.

Cronin, J. (1979) *Industrial Conflict in Modern Britain* (London: Croom Helm).

Crouch, C. (1977) *Class Conflict and the Industrial Relations Crisis* (London: Heinemann).

Crouch, C. (1986) 'Conservative industrial relations policy: towards Labour exclusion', O. Jacob *et al.* (ed), *Economic Crisis, Trade Unions and The State* (London: Croom Helm) pp. 131–58.

Curwen, P. (1986) *Public Enterprise: A Modern Approach* (Brighton: Wheatsheaf).

Daniel, W. (1984) 'Who didn't get a pay increase last year?', *Policy Studies*, pp. 78–89.

Daniel, W. (1987a) 'New technology – a lubricant for the reform of industrial working practices', *Policy Studies*, pp. 19–28.

Daniel, W. (1987b) *Workplace Industrial Relations and Technical Change* (London: Frances Pinter/PSI).

Dawson, P. and Webb, J. (1989) 'New production arrangements: the totally flexible cage?', *Work, Employment and Society*, pp. 221–8.

De Friend, R. and Rubin, G. (1985) 'Civil law and the 1984–5 coal dispute', *Journal of Law and Society*, pp. 321–54.

Deaton, D. (1985) 'The labour market and industrial relations policy of the Thatcher Government' in D.Bell (ed) *The Conservative Government, 1979–84* (London: Croom Helm).

Dickens, P. and Savage, M. (1989) 'The Japanisation of British industry? Instances from a High Growth Area', *Industrial Relations Journal*, pp. 60–75.

Disney, R. (1990) 'Explanation of the decline in trade union density in Britain: an appraisal', *British Journal of Industrial Relations*, 28, pp. 165–78.

Dodgson, M. and Martin, R. (1987) 'Trade union policies on new technology: facing the challenge of the 1980s', *New Technology, Work and Employment*, pp. 9–18.

Dorfman, G. (1979) *Government versus Trade Unions in British Politics since 1968* (London: Macmillan).

Dorfman, G. (1983) *British Trade Unionism against the TUC* (London: Macmillan).

Dunn, S. and Gennard, J. (1984) *The Closed Shop in British Industry*, (London: Macmillan).

Dunning, J. (1986) *Japanese Participation in British Industry* (London: Croom Helm).

East, R. *et al.* (1985) 'The death of mass picketing', *Journal of Law and Society*, 12, pp. 305–9.

Edwards, C. and Heery, E. (1989a) 'Recession in the public sector industrial relations in freightliner 1981–1985', *British Journal of Industrial Relations*, pp. 57–71.

Edwards, C. and Heery, E. (1989b) *Management Control and Union Power:*

A Study of Labour Relations in Coal-Mining (Oxford: Clarendon).

Edwards, P. K. (1987) *Managing the Factory* (Oxford: Blackwell).

Edwards, P. and Marginson, P. (1988) 'Trade unions, pay, bargaining and industrial action', in P. Marginson *et al.*, *Beyond the Workplace* (Oxford: Blackwell), pp. 123–64.

Eiger, T. (1987) 'Flexible futures? New technology and the contemporary transformation of work', *Work, Employment and Society*, pp. 528–40.

Elias, P. and Ewing, K. (1982) 'Economic torts and labour law', *Cambridge Law Journal*, 41, pp. 321–58.

Ellis, J. and Johnson, R.W. (1970) *Members from the Unions* (London: Fabian Research Series, 316).

Evans, S. (1985) 'The use of injunctions in industrial disputes', *British Journal of Industrial Relations*, 23, pp. 131–7.

Evans, S. (1988) 'The use of injunctions in industrial disputes 1984–April 1987', *British Journal of Industrial Relations*, 26, pp. 419–35.

Eversley, J. (1980) 'Trade union responses to the MSC', in C.Benn and J.Fairley (eds), *Challenging the MSC on Jobs, Education and Training: Enquiry into a National Disaster* (London: Pluto Press) pp. 200–26.

Ewing, K.D. (1985) 'The strike, the courts and the rule books', *Industrial Law Journal*, pp. 160–75.

Ewing, K.D. and Napier, B.W. (1986) 'The Wapping dispute and labour law', *Cambridge Law Journal*, pp. 285–304.

Fatchett, D. (1987) *Trade Unions and Politics in the 1980s: The 1984 Act and Political Fund Ballots* (London: Croom Helm).

Ferner, A. (1985) 'Political constraints and management strategies: the case of working practices in British Rail', *British Journal of Industrial Relations*, 23, pp. 47–70.

Ferner, A. (1988) *Governments, Managers and Industrial Relations: Public Enterprises and their Political Environment* (Oxford: Blackwell).

Finer, S. (1974) 'The political power of organised labour', *Government and Opposition*, pp. 391–406.

Finer, S. (1987) 'Thatcherism and British Political History', in K. Minogue and M. Biddiss (eds). *Thatcherism: Personality and Politics* (London: Macmillan) pp. 127–40.

Fosh, P. (1981) *The Active Trade Unionist* (Cambridge: Cambridge University Press).

Fosh, P. and Littler, C. (eds) (1985) *Industrial Relations and the Law in the 1980s: Issues and Future Trends* (London: Gower).

Francis, A. (1987) *New Technology at Work* (Oxford: Clarendon).

Fraser, R. (ed.) (1988) *Privatisation: The UK Experience and International Trends* (London: Longman).

Freeman, R. and Pelletier, J. (1990) 'The impact of industrial relations legislation on British union density', *British Journal of Industrial Relations*, 28.

Gamble, A. (1988) *The Free Economy and the Strong State* (London: Macmillan).

Gennard, J. (1984) 'The implications of the Messenger Newspaper Group dispute', *Industrial Relations Journal*, pp. 7–20.

Gibbon, P. (1988) 'Analysing the British miners' strike of 1984–5', *Economy and Society*, pp. 139–96.

Gibbon, P. and Bromley, S. (1990) 'From an institution to a business? Changes in the British coal industry, 1985–9', *Economy and Society*, pp. 56–94.

Grant, D. (1987) 'Unions and the political fund ballots', *Parliamentary Affairs*, pp. 57–72.

Grant, W. and Marsh, D. (1977) *The CBI* (London: Hodder & Stoughton).

Gregory, M. *et al.* (1985) 'Wage settlements in manufacturing 1979 84: evidence from the CBI pay databank', *British Journal of Industrial Relations*, 23, pp. 339–57.

Gregory, M. *et al.* (1987) 'Pay settlements in manufacturing industry, 1979 84', *Oxford Bulletin of Economics and Statistics*, 49, pp. 129–50.

Gretton, J. and Harrison, A. (1987) *Reshaping Central Government* (Hermitage, Berks: Policy Journals).

Griffiths, J. (1985) *The Politics of the Judiciary* (London: Fontana).

Hakim, C. (1990) 'Core and periphery in employers' workforce strategies: evidence from the 1987 ELUS survey', *Work, Employment and Society*, pp. 137–88.

Haskel, J. and Martin, C. (1990) 'The inter-industry wage structure: evidence from Britain', mimeo (London Business School).

Hennessey, P. (1989) *Whitehall* (London: Secker and Warburg).

Hogwood, B. and Gunn, L. (1984) *Policy Analysis for the Real World* (Oxford: Oxford University Press).

Holmes, M. (1985) *The First Thatcher Government, 1979–83* (Brighton: Wheatsheaf).

Hood, C. (1976) *The Limits of Administration* (London: Wiley).

Incomes Data Services. Employment Trends (1989) 'Industrial relations after privatisation', *IDS Employment Trends*, 439, pp. 12–14.

Ingram, P. and Cahill, J. (1989) 'Pay determination in private manufacturing', *Employment Gazette*, June, pp. 281–5.

Jenkins, P. (1970) *The Battle of Downing Street* (London: Charles Knight).

Jones, D. and McKay, R. (1986) 'Labour adjustments and the limits to voluntary choice', mimeo (Institute of Economic Research, University of North Wales, Bangor).

Kavanagh, D. (1987) *Thatcherism and British Politics* (Oxford: Oxford University Press).

Kavanagh, D. and Seldon, A. (1989) *The Thatcher Effect* (Oxford: Clarendon Press).

Keep, E. (1986) 'Designing the stable door: a study of how the Youth Training Scheme was planned', *Warwick Papers in Industrial Relations*, 8.

Kelly, J. (1987) *Labour and the Unions* (London: Verso).

Kemp, P. (1992) 'Housing the two nations? The implementation of housing policy under the Conservative Governments of Mrs Thatcher', in D.Marsh and R. Rhodes (eds) *Implementing Thatcherism* (Milton Keynes: Open University Press, forthcoming).

Kessler, I. (1989) 'Bargaining strategies in local government', in R.

Mailly *et al.* (eds), *Industrial Relations in the Public Services* (London: Routledge) pp. 156–97,

King, A. (1975) 'Overload: problems of governing in the 1970s', *Political Studies*, XXII, pp. 289–96.

King, A. (1988) 'Mrs Thatcher as a political leader', in R.Skidelsky (ed.) *Thatcherism* (London: Chatto & Windus) pp. 51–64.

Laffin, M. (1989) *Managing Under Pressure: Industrial Relations in Local Government* (London: Macmillan).

Lane, C. (1982) 'The unions: caught on the ebb tide', *Marxism Today*, September, pp. 6–13.

Lane, C. (1988) 'Industrial change in Europe: The pursuit of flexible specialisation in Britain and West Germany', *Work, Employment and Society*, pp. 141–68.

Lewis, R. and Simpson, B. (1981) *Striking a Balance* (Oxford: Martin Robertson).

Lintner, V. (1987) 'Trade unions and technological change in the UK mechanical engineering industry', *British Journal of Industrial Relations*, 25, pp. 11–29.

Longstreet, S. (1984) *Dissension in the Labour Party 1974–9*, PhD thesis, University of Essex.

Longstreth F. (1988) 'From corporatism to dualism? Thatcherism and the climacteric of British trade unions in the 1980s', *Political Studies,* pp. 413–32.

McConnell, S. and Takla, L. (1990) 'Mrs Thatcher's trade union legislation: has it reduced strikes', *Centre for Labour Economics,* London School of Economics, Discussion Paper 374, January.

McIlroy, J. (1988) *Trade Unions in Britain Today* (Manchester: Manchester University Press).

McInnes, J. (1987) *Thatcherism at Work: industrial relations and economic change* (Milton Keynes: Open University Press).

McKay, L. (1986) 'The macho manager: it's no myth', *Personnel Management*, January, pp. 24–8.

Manpower Services Commission, (1982) *Youth Task Group Report: New Training Initiative* (London: MSC).

Marchington, M. and Parker, P. (1990) *Changing Patterns of Employee Relations* (London: Harvester).

Marginson, P. *et al*, (1988) *Beyond the Workplace: Managing Industrial Relations in the Multi-establishment Enterprise* (Oxford: Blackwell).

Marginson, P. and Sisson, K. (1988) 'The management of employees', in P. Marginson *et al.* (eds) *Beyond the Workplace* (Oxford: Blackwell) pp. 80–122.

Marquand, D. (1988) 'The paradoxes of Thatcherism', in R. Skidelsky (ed.) *Thatcherism* (London: Chatto & Windus).

Marsden, D. and Thompson, M. (1990) 'Flexibility agreement and their significance in the increase in productivity in British manufacturing since 1980', *Work, Employment and Society,* pp. 83–104.

Marsh, D. (1986) 'The politics of private investment', in A. Blais (ed.) *Industrial Policy* (Toronto: University of Toronto Press) pp. 83–118.

Marsh, D. (1990) 'Public opinion, trade unions and Mrs Thatcher', *British Journal of Industrial Relations*, 28, pp. 57–65.

Marsh, D. (1991) 'Privatisation in Britain: A review article', *Public Administration*, forthcoming.

Marsh, D. (1992) 'Youth employment policy 1970–1990: Towards the exclusion of the trade unions', in D. Marsh and R. Rhodes (eds), *Policy Networks in British Politics* (Oxford: Oxford University Press).

Marsh, D. and Locksley, G. (1983) 'Labour: The dominant force in British politics', in D. Marsh (ed.), *Pressure Politics* (London: Junction Books) pp. 53–82.

Marsh, D. and Rhodes, R. (1990) 'Implementing "Thatcherism": a policy perspective', *Essex Papers in Politics and Government*, No.62.

Marsh, D. and Rhodes, R. (1991) 'Implementing Thatcherite Policies', *Parliamentary Affairs*, forthcoming.

Marsh, D. and Rhodes, R. (eds.) (1992) *Implementing Thatcherism* (Milton Keynes: Open University Press).

Marsh, D. *et al.* (1991) 'The Thatcher effect – explanations of wage change, 1963–1987', mimeo (University of Essex, Department of Government).

Martin, R. (1985) 'Ballots and trade union democracy: the role of government', in P.Fosh and C.Littler (eds), *Industrial Relations and the Law in the 1980s: Issues and Future Trends* (London: Gower).

Martin, R. (1988) 'The management of industrial relations and new technology', in P. Marginson *et al.*, *Beyond the Workplace* (Oxford: Blackwell), pp. 165–82.

Massey, D. and Painter, J. (1989) 'The changing geography of trade unions', in J.Mohan (ed.) *The Political Geography of Contemporary Britain* (London: Macmillan).

May, T. (1975) *Trade Unions and Pressure Group Politics* (London: Saxon House).

Maynard, G. (1989) *The Economy under Mrs Thatcher* (Oxford: Blackwell).

Metcalf, D. (1989) 'Water notes dry up', *British Journal of Industrial Relations*, 27, pp. 1–31.

Metcalf, D. (1990a) 'Union presence and labour productivity in British manufacturing industry: a reply to Nolan and Marginson', *British Journal of Industrial Relations*, 28, pp. 249–66.

Metcalf, D. (1990b) 'Movement in motion', *Marxism Today*, September, pp. 32–5.

Metcalf, D. (1991) 'Labour legislation 1980–1990, philosophy and impact', Working Paper 12,London School of Economics, Industrial Relations Dept.

Middlemas, K. (1979) *Politics in Industrial Society* (London: Dent).

Milligan, S. (1976) *The New Barons: Union Power in the 1970* (London: Temple Smith).

Millward, N. and Stevens, M. (1986) *British Workplace Industrial Relations, 1980–1984* (Aldershot: Gower).

Milne, R. (1987) 'Competitive tendering in the NHS: an economic analysis of the early implementation of HC (83) 18', *Public Administration*, pp. 154–60.

Minford, P. (1988) 'Mrs Thatcher's economic reform programme', in R. Skidelsky (ed.), *Thatcherism* (London: Chatto & Windus) pp. 93–106.

Minkin, L. (1975) *The Labour Party Conference* (London: Allen Lane).

Minkin, L. (1978) *The Labour Party Conference London* (London: Allen Lane).

Minkin, L. (1986) 'Against the tide: trade unions, political communication and the 1983 General Election', in I. Crewe and M. Harrup (eds), *Political Communications: The General Election Campaign of 1983* (Cambridge: Cambridge University Press) pp. 190– 206.

Minkin, L. (1989) 'Mobilisation and distance: the role of trade unions in the 1987 election campaign', in I.Crewe and M.Harrop (eds.) *Political Communications: The General Election Campaign of 1987* (Cambridge: Cambridge University Press) pp. 261–74.

Mitchell, N. (1987) 'Changing pressure group politics: the case of the TUC, 1976 1984', *British Journal of Political Science*, 17, pp. 509–17.

Moore, P. and Levie, H. (1985) 'New technology and the unions', in T. Forester (ed.), *The Information Technology Revolution* (Oxford: Blackwell).

Moran, M. (1974) *The Union of Post Office Workers: A Study in Political Sociology* (London: Macmillan).

Moran, M. (1977) *The Politics of Industrial Relations* (London: Macmillan).

Moran, M. (1979) 'The Conservative Party and the trade unions since 1974' *Political Studies*, XXVII, pp. 38–53.

Morris, J. (1989) 'The who, why and where of Japanese manufacturing investment in the UK', *Industrial Relations Journal*, pp. 31–40.

Muller, W. (1977) *The Kept Men: The First Century of Trade Union Sponsored MPs in the British House of Commons 1874 1975* (Brighton: Harvester).

National Economic Development Council (1986) *IT Futures Surveyed* (London: NEDO).

Nickell, S. (1987) 'Why is wage inflation in Britain so high?', *Oxford Bulletin of Economics and Statistics*, pp. 109–27.

Nickell, S. and Wadhwani, S. (1990) 'Insider forces and wage determination', *Economic Journal*, pp. 469–509.

Nolan, P. and Marginson, P. (1990) 'Skating on thin ice? David Metcalf on trade unions and productivity', *British Journal of Industrial Relations*, 28, pp. 227–47.

Northcott, J. (1986) *Micro Electronics in Industry: Promise and Performance* (London: Policy Studies Institute).

Northcott, J. *et al.* (1985) *Chips and Jobs: Acceptance of New Technology at Work* (London: Policy Studies Institute).

Norton, P. (1980) *Dissension in the House of Commons* (Oxford: Clarendon Press).

Pendleton, A. (1989) 'Markets or politics? The determinants of labour relations in a nationalised industry', *Public Administration*, pp. 279–96.

Pendleton, A. (1991) 'Workplace industrial relations in British Rail: Change and Continuity in the Workplace', *Industrial Relations Journal*, 29, forthcoming.

Percy-Smith, J. and Hillyard, P. (1985) 'Miners in the arms of the law: A statistical analysis', *Journal of Law and Society*, 12, pp. 345–54.

Pinto - Duschinski, M. (1989) 'Financing the General Election of 1987' in I. Crewe and M. Harrop (eds), *Political Communications: The General Election Campaign of 1987* (Cambridge: Cambridge University Press) pp. 15–28.

Pollert, A. (1988) 'Dismantling flexibility', *Capital and Class*, pp. 42–75.

Prior, J. (1986) *A Balance of Power* (London: Hamish Hamilton).

Reed, D. and Ellis, V. (1987) 'A union assessment' in J. Gretton and A. Harrison (eds), *Reshaping Central Government* (Hermitage, Berks: Policy Journals) pp. 165–91.

Rhodes, R. (1986) *The National World of Local Government* (London: Allen & Unwin).

Rhodes, R. (1991) 'Now nobody understands the system: the changing face of Local Government' in P.Norton (ed.) *New Directions in British Politics* (Aldershot: Edward Elgar).

Richter, I. (1973) *Political Purpose in Trade Unions* (London: Allen & Unwin).

Riddell, P. (1983) *The Thatcher Government* (Oxford: Martin Robertson).

Roberts, B. (1989) 'Trade unions', in D. Kavanagh and A. Seldon (eds.) *The Thatcher Effect*, (Oxford: Clarendon Press).

Rodgers, W. (1984) 'Government under stress: Britain's Winter of Discontent 1979', *The Political Quarterly*, pp. 171–9.

Rogers, S.H. and Fodder, D. (1987) *Industrial Action: Rights and Remedies* (London: Longman).

Sarlvik, B. and Crewe, I. (1983) *Decade of Dealignment* (Cambridge: Cambridge University Press).

Savage, S. and Robins, L. (eds) (1990) *Public policy under Thatcher* (London: Macmillan).

Sayer, A. (1986) 'New developments in manufacturing: the just in time system', *Capital and Class*, pp. 43–72.

Seifert, R. (1988) 'Industrial relations in the school sector', in R. Mailly *et al.*, *Industrial Relations in the Public Services* (London: Routledge) pp. 199–258.

Shaw, E. (1989) 'The policy review and Labour's policy making system', paper presented at the Annual Conference of The Political Studies Association, Warwick University, April.

Shrubsall, V. (1984) 'Industrial action and the interlocutory injunction: the Mercury and Dimbleby cases', *Industrial Relations Journal*, pp. 91–4.

Smith, D. (1989) 'The Japanese example in South West Birmingham', *Industrial Relations Journal*, pp. 41–50.

Starkey, K. and McKinlay, A. (1988) 'Beyond Fordism? Strategic choice and labour relations in Ford UK', *Industrial Relations Journal*, pp. 93–109.

Steel, M.,Gennard, J. and Miller, K. (1987) 'The Trade Union Act 1984: political fund ballots', *British Journal of Industrial Relations*, pp. 443–68.

Stevens, M. and Wareing, A. (1990) 'Union density and workforce composition', *Employment Gazette*, August, pp. 403–13.

Strinati, D. (1982) *Capitalism, the State and Industrial Relations* (London: Croom Helm).

Stringer, J. and Richardson, J. (1984) 'Policy stability and policy change: industrial training 1964–1982', *Public Administration Bulletin*, pp. 22–39.

Tant, A. (1987) *Freedom of Information: A Challenge to the British Political Tradition*, PhD, Essex University.

Taylor, A. (1986) 'The trade unions as a source of stability in the British Labour Party', paper delivered to the Political Studies Association Conference, University of Nottingham.

Taylor, A. (1987) *Trade Unions and the Labour Party* (London: Croom Helm).

Taylor, A. (1989) 'When dinosaurs ruled the earth: the Labour Party's policy review and the role of the unions', paper delivered at the Political Science Association Conference, Warwick University.

Taylor, G. (1991) *The Miners' Strike: The Final Chapter in The Plan for Coal*, PhD, University of Essex.

Teague, P. (1989a) 'Constitution or regime? The social dimension to the 1992 project', *British Journal of Industrial Relations*, pp. 310–29.

Teague, P. (1989b) 'The British TUC and the European Community', *Millennium*, pp. 29–46.

Tebbit, N. (1988) *Upwardly Mobile* (London: Weidenfeld & Nicolson).

Times, The (1987) *Guide to the House of Commons, June 1987* (Lava: Times Books).

Trades Union Congress (1987) *Bargaining in Privatised Companies* (London: TUC).

Turnball, P. (1988) 'The limits to "Japanisation" – just-in-time, labour relations and the UK automotive industry', *New Technology, Work and Employment*, pp. 8–20.

Tyson, S. (1987) 'Personnel management', in J.Gretton and A. Harrison (eds), *Reshaping Central Government* (Hermitage, Berks: Policy Journals) pp. 57–76.

Undy, R. and Martin, R. (1984) *Ballots and Trade Union Democracy* (Oxford: Blackwell).

Undy, R. *et al.* (1981) Changes in Trade Unions (London: Hutchinson).

Veljanovsky, C. (1987) *Selling the State: Privatisation in Britain* (London: Weidenfeld & Nicolson).

Vickers, J. and Yarrow, G. (1988) *Privatisation: An Economic Analysis* (London: MIT Press).

Wallington, P. (1985) 'Policing the miners' strike', *Industrial Law Journal*, pp. 145–59.

Webb, P. (1987) 'Union, party and class in Britain: the changing electoral relationship, 1964–83', *Politics*, pp. 15–21.

Wedderburn, K.W. (1965) *The Worker and the Law, London* (Harmondsworth: Penguin).

Wedderburn, K.W. (1972) 'Labour law and labour relations in Britain', *British Journal of Industrial Relations*, 11.

Wedderburn, Lord (1985) 'The new policies in industrial relations law', in

P.Fosh and C. Littler (eds), *Industrial Relations and the Law in the 1980s: Issues and Future Trends* (London: Gower).

Weekes, B. *et al.* (1975) *Industrial Relations and the Limits of the Law* (Oxford: Blackwell).

Wigham, E. (1976) *Strikes and the Government 1873–1974* (London: Macmillan).

Wilkinson, B. (1983) *The Shopfloor Politics of New Technology* (London: Heinemann).

Williams, R. and Moseley, R. (1981) 'Trade unions and new technology: an overview of technology agreements', mimeo, University of Aston Technology Policy Unit.

Willman, P. (1986) *Technological Change, Collective Bargaining and Industrial Efficiency* (Oxford: Clarendon).

Willman, P. (1989) 'The logic of "market-share" trade unionism: is membership decline inevitable?', *Industrial Relations Journal*, pp. 260–79.

Willman, P. and Morris, T. (1988) *The Finances of British Trade Unions, 1975–1985*, Research Paper No.62, Department of Employment, London.

Young, H. (1989) *One of Us* (London: Macmillan).

Young, H. and Sloman, A. (1986) *The Thatcher Phenomenon* (London: British Broadcasting Corporation).

Young, S. (1986) 'The Nature of privatisation in Britain, 1979–85', *West European Politics*, 9, pp. 235–52.

Index